Judging Juveniles

Judging Juveniles

*Prosecuting Adolescents in
Adult and Juvenile Courts*

Aaron Kupchik

NEW YORK UNIVERSITY PRESS
New York and London

NEW YORK UNIVERSITY PRESS
New York and London
www.nyupress.org

Library of Congress Cataloging-in-Publication Data
Kupchik, Aaron.
Judging juveniles : prosecuting adolescents in adult and juvenile
courts / Aaron Kupchik.
p. cm. — (New perspectives in crime, deviance, and law series)
Includes bibliographical references and index.
ISBN-13: 978-0-8147-4794-0 (cloth : alk. paper)
ISBN-10: 0-8147-4794-9 (cloth : alk. paper)
ISBN-13: 978-0-8147-4774-2 (pbk. : alk. paper)
ISBN-10: 0-8147-4774-4 (pbk. : alk. paper)
1. Juvenile justice, Administration of—United States. 2. Criminal
justice, Administration of—United States. 3. Juvenile delinquents
—United States. I. Title.
HV9104.K87   2006
364.360973—dc22   2006018396

Manufactured in the United States of America
c 10 9 8 7 6 5 4 3 2 1
p 10 9 8 7 6 5 4 3 2 1

To Elena and Sarah

Contents

Acknowledgments

I first want to thank my parents, Herb and Leona Kupchik. They have been wonderful models for my work, my life, and my new role as a parent. My brother, Philip, has also done his job as a big brother well: to teach me, while antagonizing me just enough to want to succeed.

While at New York University, I was extremely fortunate to work with several amazing scholars. I am very grateful to Jo Dixon for her tireless efforts to steer me in the right direction, and to David Garland and David Greenberg for their inexhaustible patience and superb guidance. The mentorship of Jeffrey Fagan, as well, has made this book possible by providing access to data, advice, lessons on successful research from beginning to end, and phenomenal exposure to established scholars who share my interests. Friends and colleagues at NYU have also contributed in countless ways to this work, particularly my reading group of Vanessa Barker, Joseph De Angelis, and Karen Snedker, as well as Brian Gifford.

A number of friends and colleagues at Arizona State University have helped this project advance, and have made the School of Justice and Social Inquiry at ASU a warm, supportive, and intellectually stimulating place to be an assistant professor. I owe thanks to Madelaine Adelman, David Altheide, Thomas Catlaw, Gray Cavender, Suzanne Fallender, Marie Griffin, John Hepburn, Pat Lauderdale, Cecilia Menjivar, Laura Peck, Marie Provine, Brad Snyder, and Marjorie Zatz for their friendship and for helping my work to develop. Nancy Jurik and Torin Monahan were especially generous with their time and effort in offering advice on this manuscript. Several ASU students, as well, contributed to this project, for which I am grateful: Francisco Alatorre, Gregory Broberg, Angela Harvey, William Parkin, and Sheruni Ratnabalasuriar.

Within the academic community at large, a number of other individuals have helped this project move forward as they have watched it with interest. I appreciate the conversations I have had about my work with

Donna Bishop, Barry Feld, Mona Lynch, Ben Fleury-Steiner, Alexes Harris, Joachim Savelsberg, Simon Singer, Geoff Ward, and Franklin Zimring. Additionally, Akiva Liberman has worked with me patiently over the past several years and has had a substantial influence on the research process as well as my interpretation of what I found.

I am indebted to all of the participants of my research, most of whom could not have been more inviting. These anonymous judges, prosecutors, defense attorneys, probation officers, security guards, court liaisons, and clerks allowed me to study what I wished while making each site a pleasant place to visit. Furthermore, this research was supported in part by funding from the National Institute of Justice (2001-IJ-CX-0005) and the National Science Foundation (SES-0004334); all opinions and errors are mine alone and do not represent either funding agency.

I would also like to thank my editors, Ilene Kalish and Salwa Jabado at NYU Press, as well as John Hagan, especially for their confidence in my work and in me. It delights me to know that they saw promise in my manuscript, and I appreciate their help in the book's development. The comments of Richard Redding and Laurie Schaffner, as well as those of two anonymous reviewers, facilitated this development by sharpening the point of the book.

Finally, I want to acknowledge the endless love and support from my proofreader, consultant, counselor, accountant, guide, and wife: Elena. I am very lucky to be able to spend this much time on something without sacrificing other areas of life—thank you.

1

Introduction
Growing Up Quickly

Just over a century ago, the juvenile court was created in Cook County, Illinois. Although scholars might disagree about the motives of the court's founders, most would agree that the creation of a juvenile court was a natural result of shifting social consciousness about youth. Throughout the seventeenth, eighteenth, and nineteenth centuries, childhood developed as a social category,[1] as the Enlightenment ushered in new ideas about children as incompetents in need of care. A new ideal of children as dependent, lacking the mental and physical capacities of adults, and in need of guidance arose and was universally accepted. This modern conception of youthfulness necessitated separate court systems for juveniles and adult offenders.

Over the past few decades, however, increasing numbers of adolescents have been denied the protections of the juvenile court in favor of prosecution and punishment in criminal, adult court. Since the mid-1970s, nearly every U.S. state has revised its laws to facilitate the transfer of adolescents from juvenile to criminal court (these laws are thus referred to as "transfer laws").[2] Some states have lowered the age at which an adolescent is eligible to be transferred by a judge to criminal court; some states have allowed prosecutors to directly file adolescents' cases in criminal court, prior to any hearing in the juvenile court; and some states created laws that automatically exclude certain adolescents (based on their ages and charged offenses) from juvenile court. The specifics of states' transfer laws vary considerably, but the end result is that more and more youth under age eighteen are now prosecuted in criminal court rather than juvenile court.

What happened to the idea that adolescents are less mature, and therefore less culpable, or blameworthy, for their offenses than adults? Slogans like "old enough to do the crime, old enough to do the time" offer a new logic to compete with the modern conception of reduced culpability for youths relative to adults by suggesting that youth who commit severe crimes should be treated as adults rather than as juveniles. Policy makers who create transfer laws and academics who study them focus on the worthiness and potential effects of transfer policies while accepting at face value the assumption that reduced culpability for youth ends at the transfer hearing. In contrast, this book argues that prosecuting adolescents in criminal court creates an awkward ambivalence for courtroom decision makers who must apply adult laws to adolescent defendants. This results in a hybrid form of justice in the criminal court, what I call a *sequential model of justice*, that borrows from both a criminal justice model and a juvenile justice model.

This finding, in conjunction with evidence from prior research showing that the transfer of large numbers of youth to criminal court is counterproductive and might actually increase crime, strongly suggests the need to limit the number of youth who are prosecuted as adults. By introducing "get tough on crime" measures that are popular with the general public, policy makers have instituted a set of practices that not only have the potential to put the public at greater danger, but are also "filtered" by court actors in ways that reintroduce the very elements of juvenile justice these policies are intended to avoid. Though this reintroduction of juvenile justice may be positive in that it adds some sensibility to a counterintuitive policy, it does not sufficiently mitigate the counterproductiveness of policies that result in large numbers of juveniles being transferred to criminal court.

The well-publicized recent case of Lionel Tate illustrates the ambivalence that arises when adolescents are prosecuted as if they were adults. On July 28, 1999, in Florida, twelve-year-old Lionel Tate was playing with six-year-old Tiffany, whom his mother was babysitting as a favor to the girl's mother. Lionel assaulted Tiffany by repeatedly imitating professional wrestling moves, thereby killing her. Since Florida law allows prosecutors to bypass the juvenile court for children younger than fourteen and seek indictment by a grand jury, Lionel was prosecuted in criminal rather than juvenile court. He was indicted by a grand jury, convicted in criminal court, and, by the time he was fourteen years old, sentenced to life in prison for killing Tiffany. On March 3, 2000, he became the youngest American ever sentenced to life in prison.[3] This sentence, however, was later voided; a Florida Appeals Court reversed Lionel's conviction and granted him a new trial. Rather than holding a new trial, Lionel accepted a plea bargain in January 2004, the same bargain that he had refused during his initial trial: three years of incarceration, a year of house arrest, ten years of probation, and a thousand hours of community service. Having already served his three years in prison, Lionel was released (and subsequently re-incarcerated on a probation violation in 2006).

The apparent absence of age as a determining factor in Lionel's trial illustrates my point. Lionel's age did not alter the results of his trial; in the end, the evidence against him was the most important factor. According to the trial judge: "The evidence of Lionel Tate's guilt is clear, obvious and indisputable."[4] The defense argued that Lionel was not mature enough to comprehend that professional wrestling is staged, and therefore that Tiffany's death was accidental. However, rather than being swayed by this argument hinging on Lionel's immaturity and lack of comprehension, jurors focused on the level of violence inflicted upon Tiffany. The jury agreed with prosecutors that the number and severity of Tiffany's injuries indicated intentional cruelty rather than an immature mistake of a child who did not comprehend the consequences of his actions. Tiffany suffered as many as thirty-five injuries before her death, including a fractured skull, brain contusions, multiple bruises, a rib fracture, injuries to her kidneys and pancreas, and the detachment of part of her liver.[5] According to a juror, "The injuries were so extensive we all felt that wasn't an accident. We had to abide by the law and the law spelled it out. It wasn't just wrestling."[6] Thus, the physical evidence against Lionel led to conviction; once convicted of first-degree homicide, Florida law left no option but life in prison without parole. Lionel's age at the time of the offense—twelve—was neither a determining factor in the jury's decision, nor a consideration during sentencing.

Yet upon further inspection, we see that age *was* a paramount factor in Lionel's case. The prosecutor had offered Lionel a plea bargain (which was eventually accepted after the successful appeal) of three years in prison, due to his youthfulness. Lionel's mother, a Florida highway patrol trooper, denied his guilt and told him to refuse the deal. She stated: "How do you accept a plea for second-degree murder when your child is playing? How do you send him to prison when you know that he was playing?"[7] After the trial, the prosecutor criticized a life sentence as inappropriately harsh for Lionel, and stated his intention to appeal to Governor Jeb Bush for clemency for Lionel. For his part, the judge blamed the life sentence on the defense and prosecutor, and defended his inability to depart from the life sentence mandated by law.

More importantly, the success of Lionel's appeal hinged on his immaturity. The Florida Appeals Court voided Lionel's conviction because he was not given a competency evaluation during his trial. As a result, the court could not be sure that Lionel was competent to stand trial, and questioned if he had the ability to appreciate the charges against him, understand the potential penalties he could face, relate to his attorney and assist in his defense, challenge the testimony of witnesses for the prosecution, testify relevantly, and, most importantly, understand the plea bargain he was offered. This decision may have been surprising to some, since Lionel's competency was discussed during his trial, even if it was not officially evaluated. The defense alleged that his I.Q. was ninety or ninety-one, and thus at the twenty-fifth percentile for his age—this gave him "an age equivalent of nine or ten years old," according to a neuropsychologist testifying during the trial.[8] Though Lionel was given a competency assessment by a state witness, the Appeals Court ruled that this assessment was insufficient and not court ordered. Thus Lionel received a new trial.

Multiple psychological professionals assessed Lionel, and his competency was discussed during his trial. His I.Q. was undisputed in court and by the Appeals Court. Lionel was diagnosed as immature and below average in intelligence, but not mentally unstable nor handicapped. He was nowhere near the seventy I.Q. level normally used by courts to indicate mental retardation.[9] Yet the fact that he was so young persuaded the Appeals Court of the necessity for an official, thorough competency evaluation:

> The question we resolve, here, is whether, due to his extremely young age and lack of previous exposure to the judicial system, a competency evaluation was constitutionally mandated to determine whether Tate had sufficient present ability to consult with his lawyer with a reasonable degree of rational understanding and whether he had a rational, as well as factual, understanding of the proceedings against him. We conclude that it was.

The inconsistency here between logics of the legislature and the Appeals Court embodies the difficulty of prosecuting adolescents as adults. The Florida legislature has created a system in which prosecutors can indict juveniles directly in criminal court, based only on their charged offenses. As the Appeals Court judges wrote:

The legislature, however, has supplanted the common law defense of 'infancy' with a statutory scheme, which includes section 985.225, specifying when a juvenile is capable of committing a crime under which he or she should be treated as an adult. See State v. D.H., 340 So. 2d 1163, 1165 (Fla. 1976) (holding that the common law presumption of incapacity of a minor between the ages of seven and fourteen years to commit a crime no longer applies).

The law referred to by the judges, Florida Statute §985.225, states that "a child of any age who is charged with violation of state law punishable by death or by life imprisonment" is subject to criminal rather than juvenile court if indicted, and "must be tried and handled in every respect as an adult." In fact, this last phrase (about being handled "in every respect as an adult") is repeated throughout the legislature's wording of this statute. Thus, in Florida a child's offense can be more important for judging culpability than age; in fact, by statute age is entirely irrelevant for youth who commit certain offenses.

The Appeals Court judges note in this passage that with this statute the legislature overrules a legal tradition of presuming incapacity among youth younger than fourteen. This doctrine holds that youth younger than seven are not to be held responsible for their crimes, since they do not have a sufficient understanding of right and wrong to make punishment efficacious; for youth between the ages of seven and fourteen, courts should assume that they are not mature enough to comprehend right from wrong, to understand court proceedings, or to help in their own defenses, but with an opportunity for the state to rebut this presumption. By requiring that offense-based criteria determine whether children from seven to fourteen can be held fully responsible for their offenses in criminal court as if they were adults, the Florida legislature rebuts this longstanding presumption. Yet the Appeals Court judges seem to disagree, as they reversed Lionel's conviction based only on his age and lack of experience with the judicial system, not on any signs of mental deficiencies (other than the natural deficiency of immaturity).

I begin with a discussion of this case because it illustrates a central theme of this book: that the prosecution of adolescents in criminal court fails to resonate with culturally inscribed understandings of youthfulness. Prosecuting youth in criminal courts is a rejection of widely held principles about the immaturity of adolescents.[10] It creates tension for courtroom decision makers and forces them to creatively filter court proceedings in a way that reintroduces the modern principles that gave rise to the juvenile court: that adolescents are less mature than adults, and therefore less culpable for crimes than adults. However, the reintroduction of juvenile justice principles is incomplete, as Lionel Tate's initial sentence shows us; the current state of jurisdictional transfer laws results in harsh punishments for adolescents in criminal courts, often regardless of whether court decision makers recognize a reduced level of culpability for youth.

This ambivalence is not present only in cases with extremely young defendants like Lionel. The case of Lee Boyd Malvo, one of the snipers that terrorized the Washington, D.C., metropolitan area during the fall of 2002, illustrates an ambivalence between full and reduced culpability as well. By his own admission, the seventeen-year-old Lee was the triggerman—working with a father figure and mentor, John Allen Muhammad —in many of the sniper shootings that killed ten and injured three others. He was a serial killer who struck seemingly random targets, and was less than a year from the bright line of eighteen that marks legal adulthood in most arenas. Because the sniper killings occurred throughout the D.C. area, the defendants were eligible for prosecution in counties in both Virginia and Maryland. U.S. Attorney General John Ashcroft had the case prosecuted in Virginia, since at the time, Virginia's laws allowed for the execution of offenders who commit crimes before age eighteen.[11]

If only offense severity matters in determining punishment, then it is likely that both Lee and Muhammad would have received the death penalty, or perhaps only Lee (as the triggerman). Yet Muhammad was sentenced to death, while Lee was spared the death penalty and sentenced to life in prison. Most likely, Lee's life was spared because of the defense's strategy during the trial; the defense made a case for Lee's reduced culpability due to his immaturity and childish attachment to Muhammad. Lee doted on Muhammad and called him his father. He absorbed Muhammad's violent teachings and listened to Muhammad's wishes to rebel against the government. At one point before the killing spree, Lee followed an extreme diet set by Muhammad consisting of crackers and water.[12] The defense portrayed Lee as an immature and misled adolescent who followed his father-figure down the wrong path, and was thus less culpable for his serial murders than Muhammad.[13] As a result, the likely triggerman received a lesser penalty than his mentor.

Of course, Lee did not receive a mild slap on the wrist, nor was he treated as if he lacked culpability. Rather, he was sentenced to life in prison. Yet when we consider the severity of his offenses—he is a serial murderer at least partially responsible for ten deaths—and his age, his case is a far cry from that of a twelve-year-old who killed a playmate by mimicking professional wrestling moves. Nonetheless, his immaturity appeared to play a significant role in the jury's decision making and helped to spare him from execution. Though less visible in this case than in Lionel Tate's, we again see that the cultural belief in reduced culpability for juveniles has some role in their prosecution as adults. This seems to be true even in one of the most horrible cases imaginable for an adolescent, one who was very close in age to legal adulthood.

Of course, these two cases are unusually violent and sensational cases and do not represent the population of adolescent offenders. Yet they highlight the tensions involved in prosecuting youth in criminal courts, and the lessons learned from these cases apply to other less sensational cases as well. In this book I explain how and why adolescents are prosecuted as if they are adults, then are judged with their youthfulness in mind. To best understand what happens when adolescents are transferred from juvenile to criminal courts, I compare the criminal court prosecution of adolescents to its alternative: the prosecution of adolescents in juvenile courts.

Models of Justice

The reason why Lionel Tate, Lee Boyd Malvo, and other adolescents are prosecuted in criminal court is because policy makers assume that criminal courts act differently than juvenile courts. This assumption is based on the theoretical models of justice that best describe each court type. Traditionally, the juvenile court and the criminal court have relied on very different models of justice regarding case processing, evaluating offenders, and punishing them. The criminal court is often characterized by reference to a criminal justice model, and the juvenile court by reference to a juvenile justice model. Relative to a juvenile justice model, a criminal justice model suggests that case processing is formal, evaluation of offenders is centered on offense-relevant criteria rather than offender-relevant criteria, and the primary goals of sentencing are to punish and deter rather than to rehabilitate. Conversely, relative to a criminal justice model, a juvenile justice model suggests that case processing is informal, evaluation of offenders focuses on offender-relevant criteria rather than offense-relevant criteria, and the primary goal of sentencing is to rehabilitate rather than to punish. Thus, these two models of justice vary from each other along three major dimensions: (1) formality of case processing, (2) evaluation of defendants, and (3) sanctioning goals and punishment severity. These models of justice describe case processing and due process, normative associations about culpability and responsibility, as well as informal communications and modes of interaction among courtroom workgroup members. A model of justice incorporates the shared understandings that informally, but forcefully, guide both juvenile and criminal courts in addition to court rules and procedures.

The differences between these two models offer a very helpful theoretical guide for predicting how juvenile and criminal courts differ from each other, or at least how they should vary if transfer laws act as promised by policy makers by subjecting adolescents to a different model of justice in criminal court than they would receive in juvenile court. Hence, I use these models of justice as ideal types to guide my comparisons of juvenile and criminal courts as I seek to understand what happens when adolescents are prosecuted as adults.

Criminal Justice Model

According to a criminal justice model, criminal court case processing is an adversarial contest between defense and prosecution, with interaction proceeding according to formal due process rules. Prosecutors and defense attorneys argue about evidence, present different characterizations of the defendant's conduct, and compete with one another for victory. Judges oversee this process and ensure that the prosecutors and police follow procedural mandates such as a defendant's right to confront his or her accusers and the exclusion of evidence that has been obtained improperly.

Certainly, over the past few decades scholars have portrayed criminal courtroom workgroups[14] as cooperative rather than adversarial, especially during plea bargaining.[15] An array of sociological studies of courts has used an organizational perspective to demonstrate the complex patterns of interactions that allow court actors to pursue case processing efficiency in ways that often limit their adversarial battles. For example, the legal scholar Herbert L. Packer identifies two models of the criminal justice process: a crime control model and a due process model.[16] Of these two models, the due process model better resembles the criminal justice model that I describe because it consists of adversarial proceedings and protections for defendants. In contrast, the crime control model dispenses with formalities to pursue efficient and speedy disposition of cases. Yet even the crime control model partially reflects a criminal justice model because it is based on an "assembly line" process composed of "routinized operations";[17] the routine operation of a crime control model is antithetical to the idiosyncratic nature of informal case processing that the original juvenile court was designed to produce. Moreover, Packer's description of a crime control model in the criminal court has elements that establish it as a more formal style of case processing—even with few cases proceeding to trial—than many scholars argue is found in juvenile court.

Criminal courts allow jury trials,[18] courtrooms are open to the public and thus vulnerable to external scrutiny, and courtroom workgroups traditionally are limited to prosecutors, defense attorneys, and judges (especially in the crime control model). In contrast, most juvenile courts do not allow jury trials, most courtrooms are closed to the public and thus shielded from external scrutiny, and juvenile courtroom workgroups traditionally include many external participants such as treatment program providers, social workers, and clinicians. Furthermore, defendants are more likely to receive legal representation in criminal courts than in juvenile courts.[19]

Additionally, according to this criminal justice model, evaluations of defendants are guided by offense-oriented factors such as quality of the evidence, legal severity of the offense, and prior record of the offender. Characteristics of individual offenders or their future welfare are considered unimportant or secondary, as all defendants are presumed equally culpable under the law. Decision making in this model is intended to be proportional to the severity of offenses. Hence, many researchers find that extralegal factors related to individual attributes do not significantly affect prosecution and sentencing decisions once legal factors are held constant.[20] Recent policy trends such as fixed sentencing guidelines demonstrate policy makers' intentions that offense-oriented factors ought to guide criminal court evaluations.

Relative to the juvenile court, the criminal court pursues a more punitive punishment framework. This includes a goal of retribution rather than rehabilitation, and sentences of greater severity than those in the juvenile court. Emphasis on this theme of punishment in the criminal court has grown over the past three decades as U.S. criminal courts have relied increasingly on incarceration as a solution to the problem of crime.[21] One of the first to recognize such a trend was the criminologist Francis A.

Allen, whose claim of *The Decline of the Rehabilitative Ideal* announced a shift in sentencing goals away from rehabilitation and toward incapacitation.[22] More recently, legal scholars Malcolm Feeley and Jonathan Simon have popularized the notion of the "new penology."[23] They use this term to describe an actuarial style of justice that prescribes punishments based on risk assessment rather than assessment of needs, and that warehouses criminals rather than treats offenders. Though some scholars dispute in part the claims of Feeley and Simon by arguing that actuarial justice is a continuation of modern criminal justice rather than the invention of a new postmodern penality,[24] each of these accounts agrees that contemporary criminal courts sentence offenders with a primary goal of punishment for past offenses, rather than rehabilitation or harm reduction.

There is reason to expect that each of these dimensions of the criminal justice model may guide the prosecution and punishment of adolescents in criminal court. Policy makers who create jurisdictional transfer policies explicitly state the primary goals of increased severity of punishment for adolescents and greater proportionality in evaluating defendants.[25] Transfer laws are intended to subject youth to a more offense-based, formal, and punitive treatment in the criminal court than they might receive in the juvenile court.[26] The popular phrase I cite above, "Old enough to do the crime, old enough to do the time," connotes a need to prescribe increased punishment for youth; but it also suggests that adolescents transferred to the criminal court should be subjected to a punishment framework that is proportional to the offenses committed, rather than one that recognizes immaturity. For example, according to the National District Attorneys Association, transfer to the criminal court is necessary because "the traditional role of the juvenile justice system in seeking to place rehabilitation and the interests of the child first should no longer be applicable in the case of serious, violent, or habitual offenders."[27] This association argues that transferring youth to the criminal court will subject what they call "a new breed of delinquents" to a more severe sentencing framework relative to what could be found in the juvenile court.[28]

Juvenile Justice Model

Certainly, the initial juvenile courts, formed just over a century ago by Progressive-era reformers, were intended by their creators to have a greater focus on rehabilitation than criminal courts. Faced with the modern realization that children are different than adults and would benefit from intervention strategies, treatments, and punishments different from those for adults, the juvenile court's founders created a new court system for juveniles that encouraged age-graded decision-making standards and treatments.[29]

Although juveniles had previously been punished in separate institutions, the advent of a distinct juvenile justice system marked the genesis of a new era. This movement was shaped by the growing belief that juveniles required unique court procedures and facilities in addition to separate institutions. Founders of the juvenile justice system believed that juveniles who misbehaved were products of pathological environments rather than intrinsically evil. The target of the juvenile justice system was the deprivation, not the depravation, of delinquent youth. The court's mission was to resocialize youth and provide them with the necessary tools for adopting a moral lifestyle. The juvenile justice system thus adopted a *parens patriae* ethic, whereby the State assumed the role of surrogate parent in fostering the proper growth and development of juveniles whose environments the State considered substandard.

In an effort to normalize delinquent juveniles through rehabilitation, the initial juvenile courts attempted to provide whatever treatment was necessary to resocialize the individual juvenile. Eclipsed by this concern for the individual needs of the juvenile, the particulars of the offense as well as concerns about retribution tended to become unimportant. In order to ensure that these reforms were instituted, great discretion was allocated to juvenile court judges. Juvenile courts were designed to be informal environments where juveniles' needs would not be superseded by procedural or formal legal concerns. The founders of the juvenile court imagined a judge and probation officer, assisted by medical and psychological treatment professionals, diagnosing and remedying a youth's problems without the need to constrict due process rules.[30]

Of course, this rosy description of the juvenile court is not one that is shared by every writer. Most famously, in *The Child Savers*, Anthony M. Platt, a social historian and professor of social work, argues that turn-of-the-century middle-class reformers and industrialists shaped the initial juvenile court into a class-based disciplining institution.[31] He contends that the juvenile court initially served a class control function—it trained a pool of young laborers with the skills necessary (especially obedience to class-based authority) for factory labor. Yet even in Platt's version of events, the juvenile court instituted a novel system of justice that sought to alter future behavior rather than simply to punish for past offenses; such a system facilitated the social control he describes. Thus, even the harshest critics of the initial juvenile court describe a jurisdiction with a relatively greater focus on rehabilitation and shaping future behavior than on punishment and incapacitation.

Several studies of more modern juvenile courts find evidence to support this idea of an individualized, therapeutic model of justice. For example, according to criminologist Franklin Zimring, "The high value placed on the future life opportunities of the delinquent is a defining aspect of the juvenile court that sets it apart from the open-ended punishment portfolio of the criminal court."[32] And, according to philosopher Jacques Donzelot, "Juvenile court does not really pronounce judgment on crimes; it examines individuals."[33]

Ideal Types and Practical Distinctions

Of course, these models of juvenile justice and criminal justice are ideal types that are unlikely to exist in pure form in the empirical world of actual institutions. Rather, most if not all courts incorporate some elements of both models of justice. Mitigating circumstances such as an offender's background or disadvantage often are important considerations in the criminal court, as are due process concerns and offense characteristics in the juvenile court. Fixed sentencing schemes, an attempt to institute a neoclassical rationality in the criminal court, have also appeared in the juvenile court recently. Sentencing in the juvenile court can sometimes be retributive, rather than rehabilitative, and sentencing in the criminal court can incorporate rehabilitation. Moreover, both juvenile and criminal courts seek to protect the public from offenders deemed to have high risk of recidivism—yet as the above ideal typical models illustrate, they do so in different ways, using somewhat different logics and procedures.

Furthermore, an important and growing body of sociological research on courts demonstrates how local legal culture and organizational features of courts can lead to substantial differences among courts in different areas. Such regional disparities can cause substantial variation of practices within the categories of juvenile court and criminal court; not all juvenile courts will be alike, nor will all criminal courts. One good example of this body of research is a series of books by political scientists James Eisenstein, Roy Flemming, and Peter Nardulli that studies courtroom workgroups and "courts as communities."[34] This perspective demonstrates that the patterns of interaction among court actors and the structure of work schedules—routine aspects of court organization such as the assignment of judges, frequency and nature of communication between different agencies (prosecution, defense, judge, and probation), modes of training and supervising court staff in each agency, size of jurisdiction, the court's caseload, or local political environment—can influence court actors' goal-oriented behaviors, strategies for working together, and informal norms for processing cases. In other words, the organizational context of court decision making in both criminal courts and juvenile courts[35] can vary sharply among courts or regions and needs to be considered when we try to understand how courts go about the business of prosecuting and punishing offenders. Because of these varying norms and practices across court communities, individual criminal and juvenile courts will adhere to a criminal justice model or juvenile justice model in different ways and to varying extents.

Despite the fact that no court reflects either model of justice equally or perfectly, there are important practical differences between the two types of jurisdictions that one would expect to be consistent across different areas. Additionally, in creating and promoting transfer laws, policy makers very clearly pronounce the distinctions between juvenile justice and criminal justice that I describe.[36] Though the actual distinctions between juvenile and criminal courts in practice may not be as great as the differences between these two models of justice predict, these models conform to policy makers' rhetoric and suggest significant differences between these two jurisdictions.

Though it considers very different court systems, there is one prior piece of comparative research that supports such a distinction between the two court types. In his book *Children and Justice*, criminologist Stewart Asquith compares the manner in which adolescents are prosecuted in England's juvenile courts and Scotland's children's hearings.[37] Both of these forums are products of a reform movement in the 1960s to introduce a welfare philosophy—one that sought to emphasize the needs of adolescents rather than their criminal behaviors, and treatment rather than punishment as a response to their behaviors—into the State's system of dealing with delinquency. England's reform strategy was to modify its juvenile courts by emphasizing treatment, community sanctions, and participatory proceedings while retaining a traditional juvenile court. Scotland's reform strategy was much more radical in that it disbanded its juvenile court and created an administrative tribunal called a children's hearing, which was less procedurally formal and was presided over by laypeople, not magistrates.

Asquith's study is relevant to this book because it looks for distinctions in the prosecution and punishment of youth in two systems, one of which is designed to be more formal and more punitive than the other. This comparison is a parallel to my own juvenile/criminal court distinction. Asquith finds several organizational, structural, and administrative differences between England's juvenile courts and Scotland's children's hearings due to their different models; these differences lead to disparate court processes and outcomes by structuring the manner in which decisions are made. For example, the Scottish laypeople who serve as panel members are more likely to think in terms of the needs and welfare of the child because they do not have legal backgrounds or training, and they spend time interacting with the defendants informally instead of through prescribed legal procedures. He finds that the type of information considered, the manner in which decisions are made, the structure of interaction within the hearing, and the training and ideological background of decision makers are shaped by organizational and administrative differences; these differences in turn lead to different methods and outcomes of delinquency hearings.

Consistent with Asquith's results and with the distinction between a juvenile justice model and a criminal justice model, one would expect that the prosecution and punishment of adolescents in each court would be very different in each of the three dimensions I discuss above (formality, evaluation, and punishment). Yet no prior research has addressed whether or not the actual practices of these two court types resemble these two models of justice. We do not know whether institutional practice bears out the assumptions and expectations that are conventionally projected onto it. More importantly, we know very little about what actually happens as a result of transfer policies, which put adolescents into jurisdictions designed for adults.

As I allude to in the discussion of the Lionel Tate case, criminal courts reintroduce some elements of juvenile justice. They do so because of the ambivalence and tensions produced by prosecuting youth in criminal court. Transfer policies written by state legislatures do not automatically trump culturally inscribed beliefs about youthfulness. Rather, the mismatch between an adolescent's immaturity and a criminal court environment causes tensions and practical difficulties that must be resolved by criminal court personnel processing youthful defendants. Court decision makers are unable to ignore adolescents' immaturity, or to hold adolescent defendants fully culpable for their actions as suggested by a criminal justice model.

To understand how criminal courts reintroduce elements of juvenile justice, I turn to prior research that describes the idea of "courts as communities." In addition to demonstrating how courts vary according to local legal culture and organizational features, this body of work also shows that courts are complex institutions whose contextual features and patterns of interaction dictate how court actors interpret and follow legal rules.[38] From this literature, I take the understanding that court actors "filter" laws to match their cultural beliefs, structural surroundings, and immediate contexts. Sociologist Joachim Savelsberg describes the application of this filtering process with the use of sentencing guidelines in the U.S. federal courts and in Minnesota; Savelsberg demonstrates that broad structural and cultural forces impede efforts to formalize sentencing through neoclassical sentencing guidelines. The formal rational sentencing guidelines do not "fit society" because they clash with the substantively rational norms guiding courtroom workgroups' decision making and with the organizational characteristics of courts, and thus court actors reinterpret how to apply the guidelines.[39] Savelsberg's statements (and the organizational view on which they are based) offer a helpful theoretical template for making sense of what happens when adolescents are prosecuted in criminal courts. Indeed, I find that when criminal court actors face adolescent defendants, they filter the law to accommodate the culturally inscribed belief that youth are less culpable for their crimes than adults. Thus, our contemporary transfer laws do not "fit society."

Understanding the Scope of the Problem

Jurisdictional transfer is hardly an innovation. Since the creation of the juvenile court, judges have been able to designate certain serious offenders who require punishments beyond that which the juvenile court can give, and to transfer these youth to criminal court.[40] However, the methods by which states transfer youth to criminal courts and the numbers of youth transferred have recently shifted significantly. Each state sets its own boundaries that define what ages and/or offenses make a child eligible for transfer, and each state has its own combination of mechanisms for transfer. Over the past few decades, legislatures have broadened these eligibility criteria in many states, with this pace increasing over the past fifteen years. Between 1992 and 1997, forty-four states revised their laws to expand their abilities to transfer youth to criminal court;[41] between 1998 and 2002, eighteen states expanded their transfer laws in some way.[42]

Three primary methods are used in transferring youth to criminal court. First a judge can select the most serious juvenile court cases for transfer. These cases usually involve the most severe offenses or chronic offenders. This method is usually called *judicial transfer*, or *judicial waiver*. Although judicial transfer has in the past been the most common transfer method, in recent years other methods have replaced many judicial transfer laws.

A second transfer method is *legislative transfer*, or *statutory exclusion*. This method represents attempts by state legislatures to take control over transfer decision making by defining age and offense categories whose members are automatically prosecuted in criminal rather than juvenile court. In New York, for example, thirteen-year-olds charged with homicide, and fourteen- and fifteen-year-olds charged with any of seventeen felony offenses, are automatically sent to criminal court. Though it is an attempt to limit court decision makers' discretion, in practice legislative transfer simply shifts discretion from judge to prosecutor, since the prosecutor sets charges against the defendant and thereby earns some youth the entry to criminal court. This method of transfer has become more popular recently, with several states defining increasing numbers of offense and age categories as automatic transfer categories.[43]

The third primary method by which youth are transferred is *direct file*, or *prosecutorial transfer*. With direct file, prosecutors have the ability to file cases in either juvenile or criminal court, based on defined eligibility criteria. This method gives prosecutors substantial authority without any oversight or judicial supervision. Direct file policies have grown at a fast pace in recent years, with states shifting decision-making power from judges to prosecutors.

Recent juvenile justice reforms have lowered the threshold for transfer to criminal court, often with laws that combine these three different transfer methods. California's recent Proposition 21, the Gang Crime and Juvenile Crime Prevention Act, enacted by voter referendum in March 2000, is a good example. Before then, transfer in California was limited to judicial transfer for small numbers of youth, mostly those over age fifteen. Proposition 21 altered this by removing most discretion from judges and shifting it to prosecutors, who can now directly file youth as young as fourteen in criminal court. Proponents of Proposition 21 argued that it was necessary to stem a wave of rising juvenile crime, despite six years of historic declines in rates of juvenile violence nationwide.[44]

Adding to the effect of transfer laws, many offenders younger than eighteen are excluded from juvenile court due to their states' ages of majority. In New York, for example, the age of majority is sixteen for the criminal justice system. This means that *all* sixteen- and seventeen-year-olds in New York are prosecuted as adults, regardless of offense; once any resident of New York becomes sixteen, he or she is forever barred from prosecution in juvenile court, even for petty offenses. Connecticut and North Carolina join New York with the nation's lowest age of criminal majority (sixteen), and ten other states set the age of majority at seventeen (for the remaining thirty-eight, including Washington, D.C., the age is eighteen). Though we have no data on how many youth under age eighteen are excluded from juvenile court by states' ages of majority, the fact that these lines exist for all youth of those ages in each state leaves the potential for low ages of majority to exclude more youth from juvenile court than all transfer provisions combined.[45]

Transfer laws are popular legal reforms. Proponents of transferring youth to the criminal court claim that transfer laws are necessary to reform an outdated juvenile justice system initially created to deal with truants, not violent predators.[46] They argue that the need to protect the community from violent youth and the moral requirement for retribution in response to violence necessitate more severe punishments than are available in the juvenile court's punishment portfolio. These proponents—often prosecutors and policy makers—argue that the need to prescribe punishment proportional to serious offenses outweighs the desire to consider adolescents as less culpable than adults. In other words, serious offenses and chronic offenders require a more punitive response than the traditional, relatively lenient juvenile court is able to prescribe. These demands for increased accountability for youth show no signs of receding, even as juvenile crime rates have dipped at a record-setting pace since the mid-1990s. Rather, the popularity of transfer laws among legislators seems to occur at a time when the juvenile court—to the extent that we judge the court's success based on decreasing crime rates—seems to be at its most effective, ever.

According to most public opinion polls, the public supports legislatures' efforts to prosecute youth in criminal court. In analyzing data from the National Opinion Survey of Crime and Justice, criminologist Daniel P. Mears found that 70 percent of respondents support adult sanctions for youth if charged with selling illegal drugs, 64 percent support adult sanctions for youth charged with property crimes, and 87 percent for youth charged with violent crime.[47] The reasons for such high support for transfer—as much as 87 percent of the public—are complex and may be based on racial bias of those who view juvenile crime as chiefly a problem of African American youth.[48] Yet it also appears to be based on general ideas rather than particular circumstances or types of cases, since rates of public approval for adult punishments for adolescents drop considerably when survey questions add contextual information, such as hypothetical offenders' backgrounds or available rehabilitative treatment options.[49] Thus, the general public is very supportive of transfer overall, though this support may not apply equally to all cases of youth who come before the court.

We can also understand the popularity of transfer laws as part of a broader trend in punishing criminal offenders. The rise of transfer policies corresponds with a broader shift in penal practices whereby increased punishment for criminal offenders (relative to thirty years ago) has become an accepted norm. Increases in the number of youth prosecuted in the criminal court have come at the same time as the increases in sentencing practices that have led to the emergence of mass imprisonment in the United States. A number of scholars address the causes of this increasing use of punishment. Most notably, sociologist and legal scholar David Garland's recent book, *The Culture of Control*, discusses the broad structural and cultural shifts in society that have sparked and shaped this punitive turn.[50] Given that an important part of this shift toward punitiveness is the apparent decline of the rehabilitative ideal that defined correctional goals during the Progressive era,[51] one would think that transfer would be particularly prominent within this recent broad policy shift, and it is.[52]

Despite its popularity, transferring large numbers of youth is counterproductive and, from an instrumental point of view, bad policy. Research examining the general deterrent effect of transfer laws finds either no general deterrent effect, or possible increases in juvenile crime overall after the passage of transfer laws.[53] Moreover, research comparing recidivism among individuals prosecuted in juvenile and criminal courts finds that adolescents transferred to criminal court tend to be rearrested at either similar or greater rates than those retained in juvenile court.[54] The majority of research suggests that prosecuting adolescents in criminal court tends to stigmatize them and possibly increases levels of crime rather than deter future offending among either individuals or the general population. What is most compelling about this research is the convergence of a wide variety of studies that use different methodologies. This consistently bad news for transfer laws' efficacy offers strong evidence that, if anything, prosecuting large numbers of youth in criminal court increases, rather than decreases, crime. Transfer laws may serve symbolic or solidarity enhancing functions,[55] and they may be important retributive devices, but they do not seem to prevent crime.

Furthermore, transfer laws reveal a lack of understanding of children's cognitive development. Research by developmental psychologists demonstrates that, relative to adults, adolescents are less likely to foresee the consequences of their actions, more influenced by peer pressure, more likely to act rashly and without thought about their behavior, and less likely to comprehend the law and their legal rights.[56] One of the guiding notions of the initial juvenile court was that juveniles are more likely to commit crimes than adults because of their relative immaturity and incomplete development. If this is true—and modern science gives us every reason to believe that it is—then wouldn't the least mature offenders commit some of the worst offenses? Holding juvenile offenders to an adult standard seems to directly refute the idea that youth are less culpable for their offenses than adults.

In addition to being counterproductive and counterintuitive, recent transfer laws that give greater discretion to prosecutors and legislatures (while stripping discretion from juvenile court judges) remove necessary protections from the transfer process. Despite the Supreme Court's 1966 *Kent v. U.S.* decision, in which the Court requires that all youth transferred to criminal court receive a formal hearing prior to transfer, direct file and legislative transfer create a shortcut to the transfer process by transferring youth without a hearing and therefore no judicial oversight. Though these transfer laws are a conceptual rejection of the Supreme Court's logic, they have withstood legal challenges; their proponents have successfully argued that since the juvenile court is a legislative creation rather than a right granted to all juveniles, its protections can be denied at will, so long as it is done fairly.

Finally, one can challenge recent reforms that lead to greater numbers of youth in criminal courts because of their implications for racial/ethnic disproportionality. Research on transfer to criminal court generally finds that African American and Latino/a youth are more likely to be transferred to criminal court than white youth, even when controlling for offense severity and prior record. Yet even these apparently objective indicators, offense severity and prior record, may not be racially neutral. This would be true if racial/ethnic minorities are more likely to be targeted by law enforcement and build prior records, or if their offenses are unintentionally interpreted as more severe than those of whites; some evidence suggests that both of these conditions exist.[57] Thus, opponents of transfer may argue that transfer to criminal court adds to the hazard faced by African American and Latino/a youth, and exposes them to even more disproportionately severe punishment than they would face in juvenile court.

Of course, my criticisms of transfer laws are not based on an absolute distinction but a relative one. Like other opponents of new laws that increase the number of transferred youth, I would still support a limited use of transfer. Transferring small numbers of youth to criminal court is a necessary safety valve for the juvenile court. That is, by removing the most serious offenders from juvenile court, the vast majority of juvenile cases can be dealt with more effectively, without as much criticism from the public (for coddling serious criminals), and without diverting resources to offenders who may not benefit from them.[58] Moreover, the most serious juvenile offenders are indeed beyond the court's capacity to punish, and society is best served if these exceptional cases are dealt with more severely in the adult justice system. The debate is therefore one of degree. It makes sense to select the most serious and appropriate cases for transfer and to punish these juveniles as adults, but to expand the numbers of youth sent to criminal court with new transfer policies—a policy reform we have seen across the United States—is counterproductive, counterintuitive, aggravates existing racial/ethnic disparities, and erodes necessary protections for juveniles.

Outline of the Argument

In this book I offer a description of what actually happens when adolescents are prosecuted in criminal court, and how some aspects of juvenile justice muddy the waters of criminal court prosecution. The conceptual contradiction of prosecuting adolescents as if they were adults is an important piece in the case against transferring large numbers of youth, yet one that is largely neglected by prior research. That is, in addition to being counterproductive from a policy perspective, transferring large numbers of youth leads to the sticky, counterintuitive situation in which court actors are asked to punish youth in ways that contradict their culturally inscribed understanding of youthfulness. In response, criminal court actors reintroduce elements of juvenile justice. Such actions result in an inefficient policy since cases of adolescents are processed by criminal court actors, who become innovative in an attempt to reinterpret the law and to filter case processing, rather than juvenile court actors, who are better trained and have greater resources for implementing a juvenile justice model. Not only does this mean that adolescents are prosecuted and punished by court decision makers who do not have the appropriate expertise or treatment and punishment options, but it also means that these cases consume greater financial and time resources than if they were processed in a system designed to process these cases in large numbers. A return to a restrained, case-by-case determination by juvenile court judges who decide which cases are beyond the capacity of the juvenile court would limit these problems and create a more sensible and efficient system of jurisdictional transfer. With this more limited use of transfer, criminal court judges would be better able to apply a criminal justice model to these youth whose offenses or offending histories are severe enough to make them less appealing candidates for "child saving."

This book thus addresses a void in the juvenile justice literature about the practical differences between prosecution in juvenile court and in criminal court. Policy makers and academics seem to assume that as a result of jurisdictional transfer, criminal courts subject youth to a very different model of justice than juvenile courts, yet this hypothesis remains entirely untested. In the following chapters I illustrate how the degree of similarity between juvenile and criminal courts depends on the stage of case processing. During the early stages of case processing, prior to conviction, juvenile and criminal courts do indeed look very different regarding level of formality and evaluative criteria. Yet during sentencing, these differences narrow as criminal courts reintroduce elements of juvenile justice. Punishments in criminal court are still much more severe than in juvenile court, but the ways that the court reaches these punishments are surprisingly similar. Thus, as I show in the following chapters, the criminal court follows what I call a *sequential model of justice*; it adheres to a criminal justice model during the initial phases of case processing, but moves toward a juvenile justice model during sentencing. In contrast, the juvenile court follows a juvenile justice model throughout.

I also relate the prosecution of adolescents to cultural scripts about youthfulness and immaturity. This conversation about cultural understandings of what it means to be a juvenile is sorely missing from discussions about transfer to criminal court. It seems to have been set aside in favor of outcome evaluations such as conviction, incarceration, and recidivism rates among youth prosecuted as adults.[59] These are extremely important topics, but it is unfortunate that they seem to have eclipsed work that seeks to understand what it means conceptually to prosecute youth as if they are adults. I find that ideas about youthfulness are not eradicated by transfer laws and left behind at the juvenile court/criminal court boundary. Rather, they appear in various, often hidden ways within the criminal court. The case of Lionel Tate illustrates this, as does the case of Lee Malvo, even if one has to look harder to find it.

To illustrate my argument, I compare cases of like-aged adolescents facing similar charges in two adjacent states with very different boundaries between juvenile and criminal courts: New York and New Jersey. I describe my research sites in chapter 2, focusing on the legal and contextual differences of each jurisdiction I study, and how they offer a suitable contrast. Rather than offering a detailed methodology about my research, I focus my discussion on how the statutes differ across New York and New Jersey. I also present detailed contextual information that is necessary for understanding and comparing case processing in each jurisdiction, such as the physical settings, organization of court work, and stability of professional membership within them. Readers can find details about my research methods in the Appendix.

The following three chapters present the evidence for my claims about the durability of a modern conception of youthfulness. I compare juvenile and criminal courts along each dimension on which they *should* differ if they conform to a juvenile justice model and a criminal justice model, respectively. In chapter 3, I compare the formality of case processing in each court type, and in chapter 4, I consider the evaluative criteria in each. The details from these two chapters build a case for a sequential model of justice in the criminal court that varies by stage of case processing, with a juvenile justice model used throughout both stages of juvenile court processing. In chapter 5, I compare the punishments given to adolescents in each court type. Here I show that despite the similarities across court types, adolescents in criminal court are still at a greater risk of serious punishment than adolescents in juvenile court.

In chapter 6, I discuss this argument and its implications for understanding the prosecution of youth in these two legal forums. I also consider an underlying and important intellectual issue: how individuals interpret and react to the behaviors of adolescents. I discuss public views of adolescents and actual behaviors of adolescents, and the distance between the two. Moreover, I speculate on why citizens support transfer laws so strongly, only to have court actors reintroduce juvenile justice to the prosecution of adolescents in criminal court. Understanding how adolescents are actually prosecuted is important for more than just an enhanced knowledge of courts, juvenile justice, or criminal justice. In addition, and perhaps more importantly, it offers a glimpse into how court actors view adolescents, reconstruct youthfulness, and rely on cultural beliefs to resolve the tensions between juvenile justice and criminal justice. Certainly, one of the best methods for understanding how society views and treats youth is to study how we punish youth.

Finally, in the concluding chapter, chapter 7, I offer lessons for juvenile transfer policy making. I discuss calls to increase and decrease the use of transfer to criminal court, and to abolish the juvenile court. The data I present throughout this book offer several concrete suggestions for dealing with adolescent offenders in ways that are consistent with cultural understandings of youthfulness, and that acknowledge how juvenile and criminal courts actually differ from each other.

2

Law and Context

One reason we currently know very little about the differences in the case processing and punishment of adolescents in juvenile and criminal courts is the difficulty of comparing similar cases across these two court types. Obviously, if we consider dissimilar cases, such as cases of youth arrested for homicide and prosecuted in criminal court to cases of youth arrested for aggravated assault and prosecuted in juvenile court, we would see enormous differences in how these youth are judged and what happens to them. Since a random assignment of adolescents to either a juvenile or criminal court would be entirely unethical, other methods must be used for assembling comparable samples across court types. There are two basic strategies one could use for performing this kind of analysis. One method is to compare cases of adolescents in the juvenile court to those of adolescents in the same state or county who are transferred to the criminal court. This is feasible in states that use a discretionary transfer process to select some cases for transfer to the criminal court and retain other, comparable cases in the juvenile court. One could match these cases across the two court types and select cases with similar offender and offense characteristics (e.g., offense severity, prior record, sex, age, etc.). Because they come from the same geographic area, these data would allow researchers to compare the matched cases while holding constant environmental (political, economic, and broader cultural) influences. Several current studies use this method to test whether transfer to criminal court deters crime by matching adolescents prosecuted in juvenile courts and criminal courts in a single jurisdiction, and comparing their recidivism rates.[1]

Yet this single-site method has a substantial potential problem because it introduces the possibility of comparing different groups of adolescents. If court decision makers are selecting for transfer to criminal court the most serious offenders (as defined by prior record or offense severity) or those deemed less amenable to treatment, then the criminal court cases in such a data set might be different from the juvenile court cases. The finding that the criminal court is more likely to sentence adolescents to incarceration might be an artifact of the greater severity of the cases or offenders that are selected for the criminal court, thus confounding the effects of court type with case-level characteristics such as offense severity. Since this very type of selection process is exactly how most discretionary transfer laws are designed to operate, one might assume that this sample selection bias is a recurring problem in single-site comparisons. In prior studies, researchers have minimized this bias through careful matching procedures for selecting pairs of cases in the two jurisdictions.[2] Yet one might argue that no matching procedure could reduce adequately the threat of sample selection bias when comparing a pool of cases selected for transfer to a pool of cases not selected.

The second strategy is to compare cases across states that have disparate boundaries between juvenile and criminal courts.[3] One can select cases across two states with different laws governing how, at what age, and for what offenses adolescents are transferred to the criminal court. These cases might demonstrate identical offender and offense characteristics, but are prosecuted in the juvenile court in one state and criminal court in the other.[4] Though it eliminates the problem of selecting dissimilar cases, this latter method has its own vulnerability. By comparing cases across different states, it is possible that one is comparing cases in court systems that are organized around different principles and norms other than simply their juvenile/criminal court boundary. Indeed, some of the myriad contextual factors that scholars like Eisenstein et al. have shown to shape case processing may vary across courts in different states.[5] Or, one may be comparing cases across geographic areas in which very different attitudes and criminal justice practices are prevalent. One could imagine, for example, that differences among outcomes of prosecuting adolescents in New York City and in a Midwestern or Southern city would be due to regional disparities other than simply jurisdictional boundaries. Selecting sites that are near one another and share cultural, political, and social structural characteristics greatly reduces the potential for regional distinctions. Additionally, paying careful attention to how contextual features of court communities vary across different jurisdictions, and how these variations shape processing, allows one to isolate the effects of court type on case processing and outcomes.

I use this latter strategy of comparing case processing across juvenile and criminal courts, as I compare the prosecution and punishment of adolescents in juvenile courts in New Jersey and in criminal courts in New York. I use qualitative and quantitative data to compare punishments, and qualitative data to compare formality of case processing and evaluations of adolescents across court types. Because the boundaries between juvenile and criminal courts vary between these two states, my comparisons include juvenile court cases in New Jersey and cases that *would* be in New York's juvenile court if not for New York's laws excluding certain youth from the juvenile court.[6]

The proximity and similarity of the sites I analyze reduces the primary vulnerability of this research strategy: differences in case processing due to regional disparities. Within New Jersey, I study the juvenile courts in three counties that border the Hudson River. These counties are among the three most populous in the state, and each includes large urban areas. Within New York, I examine the criminal courts in three boroughs (each of which is an independent county) of New York City. These six counties border one another (separated only by the Hudson River), are part of a single Census Metropolitan Statistical Area, and are matched along a variety of dimensions. They have similar crime problems relative to their positions in their respective states, and each is in the top five counties in its respective state in terms of homicides and the number of individuals sent to state prison.[7] Furthermore, according to 1990 and 2000 census data, the six sampled counties have similar rates of unemployment, poverty, female-headed households, and residential mobility.[8]

New York and New Jersey have similar criminal justice climates as well; the similarity of their sentencing laws demonstrates that the two states' criminal justice systems punish comparable offenders in a broadly similar fashion. For example, an adult who is sentenced for a first armed robbery may receive a maximum prison sentence of up to twenty years in New Jersey and up to twenty-five years in New York. In sum, the sample includes cases from two states within a similar social and criminal justice milieu. By collecting quantitative and qualitative data from these areas I reduce the likelihood of disparate environmental and organizational influences shaping my research results.

Divergent Court Boundaries

New York Criminal Courts

The starkly distinct laws guiding the boundaries between juvenile and criminal courts in these two states are the key to this book's comparative focus. The overall age of majority in New York is sixteen, that is, the criminal courts exclusively handle all arrests of youth ages sixteen and older. Additionally, in 1978 New York passed the Juvenile Offender Law (part of the New York State Crime Package Bill of 1978), which mandates that fourteen- and fifteen-year-olds (at the time of offense) who are charged with any of seventeen designated felony offenses,[9] and thirteen-year-olds charged with murder, are excluded from the juvenile court. While these individuals (I will refer to them hereafter as Juvenile Offenders, or JOs) can be waived back down to the juvenile court system, their cases originate in the criminal court system. The rules and procedures for prosecuting JOs match those of criminal courts in general, but the sentences legislatively prescribed for them are less severe (in terms of custodial sentence length) than those for adult defendants. As a result of New York's age of majority and the Juvenile Offender Law, *all* defendants aged sixteen and seventeen, and many aged fourteen and fifteen, are prosecuted in criminal courts.

The Juvenile Offender Law was created with the specific goal of providing increased penalties for youth committing serious offenses. In *Recriminalizing Delinquency*, sociologist Simon Singer describes the creation of this law as an organizationally and politically expedient response to increasing public fear about violent juvenile crime. Legislators expressed this fear through two avenues: an outcry over what was perceived to be or too lenient juvenile justice system, and a demand for greater accountability for violent youth seen as predators. For example, Singer quotes a televised 1976 New York senate committee hearing on juvenile crime, in which a detective describes how juveniles regularly attacked senior citizens:

These juveniles would work in a wolf pack—three, four, five at a time. It was not uncommon to have a ten-year-old placed in a bank to watch people cashing checks. When he found a likely victim he would go outside and signal the older kids. They in turn would follow this woman until she went to her apartment, with the hopes of pushing her in.[10]

The following exchange between Ralph Marino, the chairman of the Select Senate Committee on Crime, and a New York police detective illustrates how police and policy makers portrayed the juvenile justice system as allowing such victimization to occur by not holding offenders accountable for their actions:

> *Senator Marino*: Has it been your experience that when you were able to make an arrest, you were arresting basically young people?
> *Detective*: Yes. And not only that, we were arresting the same person over and over again. We would take him to Family Court, we would insist upon going to a judge. After court delays, maybe six or seven appearances, we got before the judge and we had a trial and the person was found guilty or, in Family Court, a finding of fact, we would leave the court convinced that the juvenile offender has now been prosecuted, found guilty, and will be dealt with by the Court. . . . [But] it was not uncommon to run into the same juvenile on the street a week later, and we had to ask him what happened in court.[11]

Partly on the strength of these perceptions, the Juvenile Offender Bill was passed by the senate with a vote of 50 to 2, and 125 to 10 in the state assembly.

According to Singer, though some politicians were ambivalent or reluctant in their eventual support of this measure, theories of deterrence and retribution helped justify this overwhelmingly popular law. Moreover, the law mandates transfer of jurisdiction from a juvenile court system whose purpose clause prioritizes rehabilitation, to a criminal court system for which rehabilitation or interests of the offender are not statutorily prescribed goals. Despite these retributive goals, New York's complex criminal justice system allows for more lenient sentencing for adolescents than for older offenders. Most defendants younger than nineteen are eligible to be designated as "Youthful Offenders" (hereafter YOs) by the criminal court judge presiding over their cases. Defendants convicted of anything other than a class A felony (e.g., murder) and who have no prior felony convictions in a criminal court are eligible for YO status if the judge can find mitigating circumstances related to the offense (e.g., no weapon was used, or the defendant was not the ringleader of the group committing the act). This designation officially replaces conviction and has significant consequences: YO cases are sealed and confidential, the punishment given to them is limited to a maximum of four years in prison, and the designation allows the judge to depart from the prosecutor's sentencing recommendation as well as the state's sentencing guidelines.

According to a recent report on case processing of JO defendants in New York City, 72 percent of JOs sentenced in 2000 received YO status.[12] Most defendants with YO status are sentenced to probation, though some are sentenced to relatively short periods of incarceration. If the defendant is not a YO, JO sentencing guidelines provide for sentences ranging from a minimum of five to nine years and a maximum of life in prison for murder, to a minimum of one to two-and-a-third and a maximum of three to seven years for a class C felony.[13] Sixteen-year-olds who do not receive YO status are not protected by the reduced sentences given to JOs, and are exposed to longer prison terms (equal to those given to older offenders).

Another important consideration for understanding New York's method of prosecuting adolescents is the specialization of youth courtrooms (called "youth parts" in New York).[14] In 1993, following the lobbying efforts of an influential judge and a grant from a private funding agency, New York City began to prosecute JOs in specialized courtrooms.[15] As a result, most JO cases that continue past the initial stage of arraignment (which takes place in a lower court before being transferred up to the [Felony] Supreme Court) are now prosecuted before a judge who specializes in JO cases. Other cases may be heard in these youth parts as well, but usually only if a co-defendant is a JO.

It is important to remember that, although JOs are prosecuted in specialized courtrooms, these are still criminal courts, not juvenile courts. Aside from the fact that the judges in these courtrooms deal mostly with cases of young offenders, there is no difference between these courtrooms and others within the New York City criminal court system. These courts are located in their counties' felony Supreme Court buildings, and they follow all of the same procedural rules as other adult courts. Other than the judges, no other participants (defense attorneys and prosecutors, mainly) specialize in cases of adolescents. Moreover, despite the fact that these judges preside over a specialized courtroom, they have no special training in this field and can be reassigned at any time; in fact, about one year after my field research in one county ended, the judge in that specialized courtroom was transferred to the civil court docket.

New Jersey Juvenile Courts

In contrast to New York, New Jersey maintains a traditional juvenile justice system. From its inception in 1929 to the present, juveniles charged as "delinquents" (i.e., accused of criminal or status offenses) who are below the age of sixteen (amended to eighteen in 1952) are adjudicated under the court of Juvenile and Domestic Relations.[16] In 1970, the New Jersey Supreme Court reaffirmed that "[t]he philosophy of our juvenile court system is aimed at rehabilitation through reformation and education in order to restore a delinquent youth to a position of responsible citizenship."[17]

The New Jersey juvenile court system's statutory mission changed in 1982, when the state legislature enacted a new juvenile code that recognizes the dual purposes of the juvenile court:

> This bill recognizes that the public welfare and the best interests of juveniles can be served most effectively through an approach which provides for harsher penalties for juveniles who commit serious acts or who are repetitive offenders, while broadening family responsibility and the use of alternative dispositions for juveniles committing less serious offenses.[18]

The new legislation includes "tougher" delinquency sentencing and jurisdictional transfer provisions, and permits the use of short-term incarceration, not to exceed sixty days, to deter future offending. It also creates a presumption for secure confinement in the juvenile system for youth charged with serious crimes such as murder, rape, and robbery.[19] The New Jersey juvenile code authorizes sentences of up to four years in prison for the most serious crimes other than murder,[20] and proportionally shorter sentences for less serious offenses.

New Jersey maintains a fairly traditional juvenile court, for which rehabilitation and punishment are both explicitly stated goals. The prosecution of all offenders younger than eighteen in New Jersey originates in the juvenile court. Juvenile court judges have the discretion to transfer individuals to criminal court, although prior research in the same counties finds that they rarely utilize this option.[21] New Jersey's juvenile court purpose clause statutorily prescribes a dual goal of rehabilitation and punishment. Of the five sections of the New Jersey juvenile court's stated purpose, the first reads as follows:

To preserve the unity of the family whenever possible and to provide for the care, protection, and wholesome mental and physical development of juveniles coming within the provision of this act.[22]

Sentencing in New Jersey juvenile courts reflects several tenets of a juvenile justice model. Judges have wide discretion with regard to the range of factors they consider when sentencing, and the types of sentences they prescribe. When a judge imposes a prison sentence, he or she can set any length of sentence within a maximum of three years for offenses other than homicide. Furthermore, judges are required by law to consider the interests of offenders in addition to factors such as severity of the offense and prior record. Hence, the New Jersey juvenile court system represents a classic penal-welfare compromise in which a goal of rehabilitation is prioritized and characteristics of offenders matter, yet offenders are punished for their crimes.[23] The following is the list of factors to be considered in sentencing adolescents. Note that all but the first two criteria are focused on the defendant's social background, development, and well-being:

1. The nature and circumstances of the offense;
2. The degree of injury to persons or damage to property caused by the juvenile's offense;
3. The juvenile's age, previous record, prior social service received and out-of-home placement history;
4. Whether the disposition supports family strength, responsibility and unity, and the well-being and physical safety of the juvenile;
5. Whether the disposition provides for reasonable participation by the child's parent, guardian, or custodian, provided, however, that the failure of a parent or parents to cooperate in the disposition shall not be weighed against the juvenile in arriving at an appropriate disposition;
6. Whether the disposition recognizes and treats the unique physical, psychological, and social characteristics and needs of the child
7. Whether the disposition contributes to the developmental needs of the child, including the academic and social needs of the child where the child has mental retardation or learning disabilities; and
8. Any other circumstances related to the offense and the juvenile's social history as deemed appropriate by the court.[24]

These very different laws for prosecuting adolescents make New Jersey and New York excellent case studies for comparing the prosecution and punishment of adolescents across juvenile and criminal courts. But understanding the differences between these laws is not sufficient background for comparing what happens in each court. One also needs to know how the contexts and organization of courts differ across these two jurisdictions. In the remainder of this chapter, I compare three important characteristics of the courts I study: (1) physical setting, (2) organization of court work, and (3) stability of membership. By offering a background description of the basic features of these courts, this chapter should help the reader understand my comparison of the models of justice across these two court types discussed in the following chapters.

My description of juvenile and criminal courts is based on the following research strategy (readers should consult the appendix for details of my research methodology). First, I collected quantitative data on case processing and punishments across New York's criminal courts and New Jersey's juvenile courts. I sample cases of fifteen- and sixteen-year-old defendants who are charged with aggravated assault (1st and 2nd degree), robbery (1st and 2nd degree), or burglary (1st degree) in 1992 or 1993 in three counties of New York City and three counties of northeastern New Jersey. Next, to compare the models of justice that guide case processing in both court types, I collected qualitative data on the processes and outcomes of prosecuting adolescents in juvenile and criminal courts. From October 2000 to April 2002,[25] I observed court proceedings and interviewed courtroom actors in two counties of New Jersey (where I studied juvenile courts) and two counties in New York (where I studied criminal courts). I assign the New York criminal courts pseudonyms of Brady and Brown County courts, and the New Jersey juvenile courts Pierce and Maxwell. In Pierce County, I studied each of four adjacent juvenile courtrooms, each with its own full-time judge, on the same floor of the county courthouse. In Maxwell County, I studied both of the two adjacent juvenile courtrooms. In Brady and Brown counties, I studied the one youth part that exists in each county.

I conducted interviews with judges, prosecutors, and defense attorneys who work in the two courts in the New York criminal court system and two courts in the New Jersey juvenile court system.[26] I perform thirty-two interviews across all sites. In addition to interviews, my qualitative data consist of field notes from observing case processing of adolescents in two courts from each jurisdiction. During eighteen months of regular court visits, I observed a total of 978 hearings.

New Jersey Juvenile Courts

Physical Setting

In contrast to the image of grand courthouses with wide marble stairways and marble columns, the two buildings housing the New Jersey juvenile courts are relatively plain ones that could just as easily pass for office buildings rather than arms of the State. The courtrooms are both small and unimposing. Each has a soft décor, with shielded overhead lights (rather than fluorescent lighting), and with fresh paint and carpeting in some. Because juvenile court hearings are confidential, spectators other than court staff or external sponsoring agents (e.g., social workers, probation officers) are not allowed in court.

Organization of Court Work

JUDGES

In New Jersey, judges are appointed by the governor. From the descriptions of many court actors with whom I spoke, this process is heavily influenced by negotiation within the state political apparatus and is used to reward attorneys through a patronage system. Some attorneys with whom I spoke even went so far as to accuse one juvenile court judge of obtaining a judgeship through large contributions to the governor's reelection campaign, another of utilizing family connections to obtain a judgeship, and a third of being connected to local organized crime. Though I doubt the legitimacy of these accusations, they illustrate that judgeships in New Jersey are at least perceived to be influenced by financial and social capital. Of course, like any political appointment, the appointment of judges in New York may be influenced by financial or social capital as well; however, unlike in New Jersey, no New York court actors ever raised this subject or even hinted at this possibility to me.

The New Jersey Administrative Office of Courts (AOC) supervises judges relatively closely (compared to the supervision of judges in New York). New Jersey judges are evaluated every few years through a standardized review process. Additionally, their supervisors review performance statistics, especially statistics of how quickly they dispose of cases, and may pressure them to move more quickly.

PROSECUTORS

There are two main organizational distinctions between the prosecutors' offices in the juvenile and criminal courts I studied. In one, due to the offices' administrative policies, the juvenile court prosecutors have less experience than the criminal court prosecutors overall. The second is the level of centralization of the prosecutors' offices. Relative to one another, the juvenile court prosecutors' offices I study are very decentralized with regard to discretion.

The prosecutors' offices in juvenile courts I observed use the juvenile court system as a training ground for newly hired prosecutors. Juvenile courtrooms are the first or second stop for prosecutors recently hired out of law school. These prosecutors gain experience and learn their craft while working with adolescent defendants before being transferred to criminal courts. The average age of prosecutor interview respondents in the juvenile court is thirty-five, and these respondents average only three years of experience in court.

For these prosecutors, working in a juvenile court is of lower status than working in a criminal court:

> *Prosecutor*: Here it is kind of like—it is looked down upon if you are in juvenile, because you know you have to work your way up. (#29)
> *Interviewer*: You said you're looking forward to being transferred out of juvenile. Is this because juvenile court is a less desirable place to work, or because it's the natural progression [to move up to criminal court]?
> *Prosecutor*: [It's] not less desirable, but there is no jury trial. The goal of assistant prosecutor is to be trying jury trials. I think that is the whole idea behind it. I think juvenile court—but I haven't been to adult court—but juvenile court takes a lot out of you. It is tough. You see the same kids coming back in, and in, and in. There is nothing you can really do! It is kind of heartbreaking to see these kids every day like that. It is very frustrating. (#27)

The lower status of juvenile court is partly due to the lack of jury trials, and thus no possibility of winning in dramatic fashion by convincing a jury through legal maneuvering (which the prosecutors perceive as glamorous). Furthermore, the lower status is partly explained by the difficult nature of the job (the frustration of seeing youth repeatedly involved in crimes), and the stigma of being the training ground for new prosecutors.

Yet despite their relative inexperience, these prosecutors have great discretion in handling cases. According to one of the more senior juvenile court prosecutors:

> *Interviewer*: When making these decisions, how does it work as far as your office goes? Are you required to seek approval from [the supervisor]?
>
> *Prosecutor*: We make a unilateral decision. Our juniors come to us because they are learning, but we don't because [our supervisor] trusts our judgment. Which is why she wants four senior people here within the trial section, who have been in the pre-indictment section, then the Grand Jury, then all that stuff and actually knew what charges were and what sort of punishment should be meted out. (#15)

According to a more junior juvenile court prosecutor:

> Juvenile is . . . frankly, a lot left up to our discretion. It really is. We can do it by what we think is right. (#27)

When they first begin working in the prosecutor's office, the juvenile court prosecutors receive daily advice from their supervisors, and the supervisor must approve all potential dispositions (sentences). But after a few months, the prosecutors earn the authority to fashion their own dispositions and are required to seek approval for dispositions of cases only for those in which incarceration might be a result. Because discretion of how to handle cases is left to these prosecutors after only a few months' experience, I consider these offices to be decentralized.

DEFENSE ATTORNEYS

Almost all defendants are represented by public defenders. In each New Jersey juvenile court, there is a single office for public defenders—in Pierce County eight attorneys in this office handle juvenile cases, and six in Maxwell County. In cases with more than one indigent defendant, a public defender represents one defendant and "pool attorneys" represent others. Pool attorneys are private attorneys who are paid by the county to represent indigent defendants in case of such a conflict with the public defender's office. It is extremely rare in the juvenile court to see defendants represented by private attorneys, though this occasionally happens.

The public defenders are a stable and consistent group who represent the vast majority of juvenile court defendants. These attorneys are stationed in the juvenile courtrooms rather than entering and exiting throughout the day for isolated cases (as in the criminal court). As a result, the defense attorneys' appearances are far more consistent in the juvenile than in the criminal court, where attorneys appear for specific cases and then leave to go to other courtrooms. Furthermore, the range of attorneys is far smaller in the juvenile courts because the public defenders handle almost all of the cases. The six or eight public defenders in each county, plus perhaps two or three frequently appearing pool attorneys, represent about 95 percent of all defendants. There is very little turnover among these juvenile court public defenders, especially in Pierce County, where the most junior among them has been in the office for over ten years.

The stability of public defenders allows them to organize as a coherent group and exercise power over other court actors. According to them, they present a ubiquitous and subtle threat to take more (or all) cases to trial. This threat to discontinue plea bargaining is much like a labor union's implicit threat to strike, and it is effective at achieving two crucial objectives. They are able to lower the bar with regard to going rates of punishment (so that sentences are more lenient across the board than they would otherwise be), and to prevent judges from straying from the plea agreements between the defense and prosecution in most cases. As one public defender told me in court (field notes):[27]

> The judges here are well trained. Some judges come here thinking that they'll be punitive, but they get tired of fighting with us on every case. The prosecutors are afraid to piss off the judges by arguing or fighting too hard, so we're able to force lenient dispositions.

Due to their experience and the stability of their appearances in court, the defense attorneys are able to exercise power in court with regard to controlling the pace of hearings and "winning" battles over dispositions.

Stability of Membership

According to scholars who have studied courts as local legal communities, the stability and familiarity of courtroom workgroups—also referred to as a robustness of shared pasts[28]—shapes court proceedings. It does so by enhancing the exchange of information (both explicitly in court and through informal networks), reducing uncertainty of others' potential actions, and facilitating the development of shared understandings of offenses and offenders (e.g., "going rates" and "normal defendants").[29] By this logic, plea bargaining is more frequent and more consistent in court communities with stable and familiar workgroups, with similar offenders receiving similar sanctions.

Overall, the courtroom workgroups in the New Jersey juvenile courts are very stable—much more stable than those in the New York criminal courts. The group of defense attorneys and prosecutors who work in the juvenile courts is very small. In each of the juvenile courts the same prosecutors work before the same judge every day, and one of a handful (six in Maxwell County, eight in Pierce County) of public defenders is in court and represents the vast majority of defendants on any given day.

The turnover of judges is uncommon in the New Jersey juvenile courts —most judges are secure in their positions and leave only through retirement. Among defense attorneys, turnover in the juvenile court staff is exceptionally rare. The turnover of prosecutors is higher than that of either judges or defense attorneys; prosecutors in the juvenile courts generally leave for the criminal courts once they receive sufficient training. Overall, then, in the juvenile court, the same people work together on a regular basis. They quickly learn one another's habits and personalities and usually form bonds of friendship or at least professional cooperation and compromise:

> As far as the resolution is concerned, what the disposition of the case is going to be, usually we try to . . . we try to compromise to sort of meet in the middle ground. I think that's where you can leave it at. These cases are compromises more often than not. It's not too often that either one side is going to get exactly what they want. (#26—defense attorney)

> [The public defenders] are a good group . . . at least the ones we come into contact with. We don't have as much contact with the group that is regularly over with [another judge], but the group we do have contact with is a pretty good group. (#31—prosecutor)

Though prosecutors and defense attorneys see themselves as representing different sides, there is undoubtedly a spirit of cooperation between prosecution and defense with regard to sharing "facts." One defense attorney told me that defense and prosecution often help each other by providing discovery materials (evidence they have collected) even when not required, or by allowing for continuances if needed by the other side. They may disagree on interpretations or accuracy of the facts, or on how much a case with given facts is "worth," but both sides work together by sharing information.

According to the juvenile court defense attorneys, building a rapport with prosecutors and judges enables them to work more effectively by earning respect and credibility. With such a rapport, the attorneys feel they are not second-guessed or questioned, and their opinions about what a case is "worth" (in terms of a reasonable disposition), or their arguments about the character of a defendant, are taken seriously. One attorney offered the following comments about the importance of maintaining one's credibility:

> The thing that we have most in this court is credibility. So I don't ever say that a kid with twelve armed robberies or something that has been here a million times . . . I don't say, "Please let him go." I don't make a pitch that is a baloney pitch. I know what the cases are and no judge is ever going to say, "Well, that's silly." In other words, I will never do anything to ruin my credibility with the court and neither will anybody else here. (#12)

Prosecutors as well are motivated to build rapport with defense attorneys to facilitate a shared understanding of appropriate responses to certain crimes, or "going rates," which in turn results in a speedier and less contentious flow of cases.

Of course, this cooperative nature and ability to predict one another's actions occasionally breaks down. Defense attorneys, prosecutors, and judges do not always agree with one another. Personality clashes may arise, since not all of these court actors like one another; but they know one another fairly well and (mostly) cooperate with one another. The most dramatic breakdown of communication or expectations comes when a judge rejects a plea bargain agreed on by the defense and prosecution. I only observed this occurrence once, when a judge refused to accept a negotiated plea because (in her words) the negotiated sentence made the court "look bad" by not punishing the youth for repeated noncompliance and delinquent activity. This led to a heated argument between the public defender and the judge, during which the judge stated, "When you have more control over yourself, let me know." At that point the judge left the courtroom for about five minutes. Normally this situation is avoided because the defense and prosecution learn to anticipate what the judge will accept, or because the judge tells them what he or she will accept as a sentence. This was an exception to the normally smooth cooperation of juvenile courtroom workgroups, but an interesting occurrence nonetheless.

New York Criminal Courts

Physical Setting

There is no question that the New York criminal courtrooms are more threatening architecturally and more imposing settings than any of the courtrooms within the New Jersey juvenile courts. Both criminal courtrooms are housed in large, marble buildings, with high ceilings, chandeliers, marble columns, and broad stairways leading to the entrances. Both courtrooms are large with several rows of seating for an audience, floors of gray linoleum tiles, and a dingy and official atmosphere. Overall, both counties have grand courthouses but dingy courtrooms, similar to those one might see on a television court drama.

An important distinction between the physical settings of the juvenile and criminal courtrooms is the presence of spectators. In contrast to the privacy of the juvenile courts, the spectator benches in the criminal courts are often filled at the beginning of the day by waiting defendants and their families. On an average "calendar" day, at least twenty to twenty-five people are seated in each of these two courtrooms at the start of the day's business.[30] Thus, an audience of interested spectators is present in the criminal courts.

Organization of Court Work

JUDGES

In New York, there are two methods by which a practicing attorney can become a judge and eventually preside over a criminal court youth part. One, he or she can be elected by a judicial selection committee to serve a fourteen-year term as a Supreme Court judge. Judges must nominate themselves to the committee and lobby by gaining all available community and political leverage; according to one of the judges, the four-teen-year term is almost always followed by reappointment. The second method is to be appointed by the mayor of New York City to serve as a lower criminal court judge for a ten-year term, and then be reassigned to the Supreme Court by the Administrative Office of Courts.[31] Once they obtain their judgeships, individuals are assigned to specific court parts (including the youth parts) by the Administrative Office of Courts (AOC).

The AOC supervises New York City judges and can reassign them to different positions within the judiciary. However, according to both youth part judges, this office provides very little supervision. The AOC does not instruct judges to operate in any particular manner on the bench, and would only be able to remove someone from office in the case of se-rious or illegal misconduct. Thus, the judges are supervised by an office that is not responsible for appointing them or renewing their appoint-ments and that exerts little supervision over them. As a result, they have a high degree of autonomy. According to one criminal court judge:

A[n] elected judge is a constitutional judge and it is a fourteen-year ap-pointment that can't be disturbed except for removal. The notions of punishment and the like for performance, unless we're talking about in-competence or deficiency or malfeasance, I've never heard of it. . . . But there is really no evaluative process to speak of. We never have a sit-down review where I'm told that I am deficient or that I have to improve in an area or there is some sort of written evaluation. It's not done. (#2)

PROSECUTORS

Though there is a wide range of ages and level of experience, the pros-ecutors (assistant district attorneys) in the New York criminal courts are older and have significantly more experience than the New Jersey juvenile court prosecutors. They are not in training, though most of them are at a relatively junior level within their offices. The average age of criminal court prosecutors I interviewed is forty-one years, with an average of ap-proximately eight years of experience; these figures are substantially higher than in the juvenile court (thirty-five years old and three years of experience). According to the prosecutors with whom I spoke, due to their relatively low pay many attorneys who begin their careers as prose-cutors eventually leave to become private attorneys, a potentially more lucrative position. Thus many prosecutors leave after several years, with the result of a fairly young crew of prosecutors (though not nearly as young or inexperienced as in the juvenile courts).

In contrast to the decentralization of prosecutors' offices in the juvenile courts, prosecutors in both Brady and Brown counties operate within a far more centralized office. Prosecutors from a single bureau of their counties' district attorneys' offices staff both of the youth parts I observed in New York. The supervisor of each bureau (a section of the district attorney's office) makes all decisions with regard to arguing for remand (preadjudication detention), considering dismissals, and requesting sentences. Unlike the prosecutors in the juvenile courts (who earn autonomy after a few months on the job), criminal court prosecutors must take any plea bargain offer to their supervisors for approval:

> If we already have a [plea bargain] offer set, and they counter with something, normally I would just go to [the supervisor] with the counter and say, "What do you think?" Sometimes if it is completely ridiculous, I don't even bother going to her. If it's something even I wouldn't accept. Then I don't bother and just say "no" myself. But if it's something that I would consider, then I go to [the supervisor] and ask her what she thinks and we take it from there. (#22—prosecutor)

> I've been a prosecutor for over six years now and it's not nice not to have any control over your [plea bargain] offers. I would hope that the office would have enough faith in my judgment that I would make appropriate choices and appropriate decisions. And I think I do, but the way our office is structured, I just have to say, our office's recommendation is whatever it is. (#23—prosecutor)

This centralization and lack of discretion inhibits teamwork and impedes plea bargaining, because the defense attorney negotiates with the prosecutor's office rather than with a single individual. This feature of the court also delays dispositions by adding levels of approval to the negotiation process:

> You can't negotiate one on one. [The prosecutors] don't have the authority to do that. When they go into the courtroom, the supervisor has told [them], "This is what the plea offer is." And to give you a perfect example, if the plea offer that they are recommending is two to four

[years, with] four years incarceration, and you have a client who is willing to take one and a half to three [years], they just can't say "fine." Which I think is absolutely ridiculous, especially with some of the senior people. You have somebody who has been in the prosecuting office five to ten years and they can't come down six months on a plea, something is wrong. . . . It makes the process slower. (#21—defense attorney)

In contrast to the juvenile courts—in which a plea bargain offer from a defense attorney can be accepted by a prosecutor and the case can proceed without delay—upon receipt of a plea bargain offer in the criminal courts, the case must be adjourned so that the prosecutor can discuss it with his or her supervisor.

DEFENSE ATTORNEYS

In the criminal courts there are four categories of defense attorneys working in each youth part. The distinction between them corresponds to how they are paid and to what organization they belong. In the first category are attorneys who work for the Legal Aid Society, which is publicly funded but an entity separate from the court system. The Legal Aid Society used to handle almost all cases with indigent defendants in the city until the mid-1990s, when a dispute with Mayor Giuliani left them financially weak and they lost their near monopoly of public defense. Now they handle about half of the cases, with no apparent pattern regarding which cases they assume and which they leave for other agencies.

The second category is the [County] Defender Services, which is an agency created in the past few years to help absorb some of the cases that the Legal Aid Society is no longer able to assume. According to a Legal Aid attorney:

When our funding was cut in '95, alternate providers [the County Defender Services] were set up so each borough has an alternate provider except in Staten Island where we were completely defunded. (#6)

The third category is 18B attorneys. The code "18B" refers to the statute that authorizes the courts to appoint these attorneys. These are private attorneys who register with the 18B office to assume cases with indigent defendants who are not assigned to either the Legal Aid Society or [County] Defender Services. Often this occurs because co-defendants may be represented by the two indigent defense agencies, and a nonaffiliated attorney is needed to prevent a conflict of interest between attorneys in the same agency representing different co-defendants on the same case. The state pays for the defense of these defendants, at a flat rate of $40.00 per hour for in-court time, and $25.00 per hour for out-of-court time.[32] A single office assigns these cases, with no distinction between cases of adolescent offenders and older defendants. All respondents with whom I spoke perceive this pay scale to be exceptionally low, and a recent series of critical articles in the *New York Times* described these attorneys as so underpaid that many are forced to take on hundreds of clients (with one attorney taking on well over a thousand) in order to sustain a living wage.[33]

Members of each of these three categories of attorneys assume cases by appearing in arraignment courts. Defendants who are arrested face a lower court arraignment within twenty-four hours of arrest; at this point attorneys are assigned to those who cannot afford to pay for private attorneys. Attorneys from the Legal Aid Society and each [County] Defender Service alternate in the arraignments. Legal Aid Society covers the majority of arraignments (usually about two-thirds), with [County] Defender Services covering most of the rest. Attorneys who take 18B cases also sit in on arraignments. Each 18B attorney agrees to cover a certain number of shifts per month and assume any cases that cannot be absorbed by the other two groups of attorneys.

The fourth category is private attorneys who are paid by the defendants themselves. This may be the only option for a defendant who is deemed by a judge (in a court hearing during which the defendant shows proof of his or her financial status) to be able to pay for his or her own defense. Most private attorneys charge one of two flat fees for their services; whether the case proceeds to trial or is disposed of by a guilty plea determines which of the two fees the defendant pays. Though no figures are available to illustrate how often defendants are able to hire attorneys, my observations and conversations with court staff suggest that about 90 to 95 percent of criminal court defendants are considered indigent and therefore are represented by one of the former three groups of attorneys.[34]

Stability of Membership

In contrast to the stability and familiarity of courtroom workgroups in the juvenile courts, there is little rapport building or sharing of information between defense and prosecution in the criminal courts. Because of the large populations of prosecutors and defense attorneys who may appear on different cases, the two individuals involved in any particular case sometimes have never met each other. As strangers facing each other, there is no incentive to build some rapport or help someone out (by sharing information or not opposing a continuance) in order to build a solid working relationship. Rather than having a small, consistent group of attorneys who work in the same courts every day, any of about twenty-five to thirty defense attorneys work sporadically in each criminal court youth part, and any of about fifteen to twenty prosecutors. Moreover, judges are also less integrated into the courtroom workgroups of the criminal courts than the juvenile courts because of this low level of familiarity.

There is one similarity between the two jurisdictions with regard to courtroom stability of membership: the patterns of staff turnover. Like the juvenile courts, the turnover of judges is uncommon in the criminal courts—most judges are secure in their positions and leave only through retirement. Judges can be promoted to supervisory or administrative judgeships, though this happens rarely due to the small number of such positions relative to the number of judges. Likewise, defense attorneys in the criminal courts demonstrate fairly stable careers with few career changes. Turnover among (usually low-paid) prosecutors in New York is more common; often they leave to look for more lucrative positions.

Court Differences within Court Types

Given the importance of local legal culture and local contextual factors in determining how courts act, one might expect substantial distinctions between the two different county-level courts in each of these two jurisdictions. However, overall, they are very similar to each other with regard to physical setting, organization of court work, and stability of membership. Only a few distinctions emerge in these courts.

New Jersey Juvenile Courts

One distinction between the juvenile courts is their method of training junior level prosecutors. In Pierce County, recently hired prosecutors work alongside a senior prosecutor in each courtroom for approximately six months or until a position opens up in criminal court, at which time the new prosecutors are transferred there. Yet in Maxwell County, all but one prosecutor are recent hires. Newly hired prosecutors in Maxwell are assigned to juvenile court after a brief assignment in appellate court, have no in-court supervision, and usually stay in the juvenile court for about a year—twice as long, on average, as junior level prosecutors remain in the Pierce County juvenile court. The one more experienced prosecutor in the Maxwell County courts is an older man who, according to court gossip, was demoted to juvenile court by his office in the hope that he retires (thus he is not a supervisor).

A second distinction between courts within the juvenile court system is the method of scheduling defense attorneys' appearances. In Pierce County, one member of the public defender's office is in each courtroom every day for the entire day. Each public defender schedules a few days per month before each judge in advance, and arranges to have his or her cases with that judge called on those days. In Maxwell County, public defenders stay in one courtroom for a week at a time and then have one week out of court for office work.

Significant distinctions emerge between the two juvenile courts with regard to the balance of power within each court's courtroom workgroup. This balance varies across each of the individual courts I observed, largely as a result of each judge's personality and approach to managing a courtroom. In the Pierce County juvenile courts, the balance of power rests with the defense attorneys. Defense attorneys in this court are very aggressive and well organized, as I describe above. They are able to exercise their power by lowering the bar with regard to "going rates" of punishment, and usually they prevent the judge from straying from their agreements with prosecutors. Defense attorneys in the Maxwell County juvenile courts are also well organized and use their influence to lower the going rates for punishments. Yet their influence is limited by one of the two judges in this court, the senior judge. The senior Maxwell County judge has a hard-nosed, punitive approach to dealing with adolescent offenders relative to the other juvenile court judge. This approach gives a significant advantage to the prosecution in this one courtroom. Here, the prosecutors know that the judge will reject a plea bargain he perceives as too lenient based on offense severity, giving the prosecutors the upper hand in bargaining and allowing them to dominate proceedings. However, the second judge in Maxwell County has a more lenient approach and softer disposition. This more junior judge is relatively more interested in background information such as the defendants' home lives and school records. As a result, the defense attorneys can offer mitigating evidence by presenting positive character assessments of defendants. When appearing before this judge, the defense attorneys have the upper hand in negotiation because they know the judge will reject a plea bargain he considers too harsh and can exert their collective influence over case processing.

New York Criminal Courts

One significant distinction between the two criminal courts is the consistency of prosecutors within the courtroom workgroups. In Brown County, a single prosecutor is in court every day and handles most of the mundane matters—all cases except for trials or special offenses such as rape, gang assaults and murders. Yet in Brady County a different prosecutor—albeit one from the same bureau consisting of approximately twelve attorneys—appears daily. Thus, the workgroup is somewhat more stable in Brown than in Brady.

In addition, the personalities of judges vary across the two courts in the criminal court system and thus shape the balance of power differently. In Brown County, the judge is a dominating figure who projects a strong aura of judicial authority while court is in session. He expresses his expectations clearly for all attorneys who work in his court, and voices his disapproval when attorneys fail in any way to meet his expectations. He demands that all attorneys arrive in his courtroom by 10:00 A.M., regardless of any other cases they may have scheduled on any given day. Other judges are more understanding of attorneys who must appear in several courts in a single day, and usually will make exceptions in order to accommodate the attorneys' busy schedules. In the following court field notes I demonstrate this judge's demeanor by showing how he treats an attorney who appears in court one hour late (field notes):

> [The judge begins the hearing by scolding the defense attorney for showing up late here this morning.]
>
> *Judge* (to defense attorney): Do you want to discuss the defendant first, or have your sanction hearing?
>
> [At this, the defendant looks at his attorney and laughs. The attorney has no coherent answer, but says he is ready to account for his tardiness, and he apologizes.]

Judge: Fine, then we'll conduct your sanction hearing now. Do you have an explanation?

Defense Attorney: I was in domestic violence court and had a very ill client. Because of this I was hung up. I intended to be here on time, or to call, but I had no opportunity.

Judge: Have we spoken about this before?

Defense Attorney: Yes.

Judge: You must show at 10:00 or call by then. I can't run a part like this. I accept your apology without a financial sanction, but next time there will be a "painful" sanction.

This judge often tells both prosecutors and defense attorneys to refuse any new cases while they have cases pending in his court, yet he has no authority to make this demand, and the individual attorney or prosecutor often has no say over this matter. Moreover, he subordinates both the prosecution and defense and dominates the flow of cases and decisions made in each case.

The other criminal court, in Brady County, is presided over by a judge with a more democratic style. As a result there is a very even balance of power, with court proceedings and outcomes shaped evenly by the judge, prosecutor, and defense. This judge's approach is very different than that of the Brown County judge. He runs a very relaxed courtroom and is far less demanding than the Brown County judge. For example, every day he asks the court clerks, security officers and stenographer when they wish to break for lunch, rather than unilaterally setting the court's schedule. Attorneys show up when they can, and the judge accepts this practice as long as they show respect to the court and make an effort to call in advance (though he still does not become upset when attorneys are unable to call first). Everyone working in the courtroom with whom I spoke recognizes his egalitarian approach. During several interviews with attorneys, the respondents noted that this judge is extremely fair, listens to everyone before making any decisions, and weighs the arguments of the defense and prosecution evenly.

Court Clientele

Despite the vast differences between the New York criminal courts and the New Jersey juvenile courts, there is one very important similarity:

their clientele. The adolescent defendants in each court are very similar. They are almost all poor and either African American or Latino/a, and the vast majority of them are male. Though I have no precise measurement of socioeconomic status of defendants, the fact that almost all are represented by public defense attorneys suggests that they are poor. And, during eighteen months of court observations, I observed fewer than five defendants who appeared to be non-Latino/a whites. Clearly, my ability to document ethnicity by skin color and name is far from perfect; but it is equally clear that the courts I study are primarily reserved for poor racial and ethnic minorities. Though girls do occasionally appear in court, their presence, too, is rare.

The homogeneity of defendants imposes a substantial restriction on my analyses. It seems likely that race, ethnicity, sex, and socioeconomic status might play a large role in how court actors ascribe youthfulness and culpability. Yet the lack of variation on these dimensions precludes me from assessing how large a role these factors play. This lack of diversity suggests that the prosecution of adolescents in the New York City area is a story about prosecuting poor, racial/ethnic minority males. As a result, to determine whether white or middle-class youth are treated differently by the juvenile and criminal justice systems, one needs to look earlier in the process: either at the decision to arrest or to formally prosecute. I return to this discussion in chapter 6, where I discuss the court actors' explanations for why there is no variation among their court clientele.

Conclusion

Understanding how case processing, decision making, and case outcomes vary across juvenile and criminal courts requires background knowledge of how the court communities in each jurisdiction are organized. Though none of the hypotheses that stem from the distinction between a criminal and juvenile model of justice are tested here, this chapter begins to show some validity for the idea that criminal courts and juvenile courts are very different environments. The criminal courts I study are far more imposing, physically, in that they are larger rooms that are open to the public and more chaotic; in contrast, juvenile courts appear to be administrative courts with soft lighting and a pleasant decor. If a goal of policy makers in creating juvenile transfer laws is to subject youth to a more formal and threatening physical environment, then they seem to have succeeded.

It is important to consider the symbolic element of courts and courtroom rituals. In his seminal article, "Conditions of a Degradation Ceremony," sociologist Harold Garfinkel reminds us of the symbolic power of courts, and their ability to use this power to degrade defendants from the status of citizens to that of offenders.[35] More recently, others demonstrate how courtrooms are designed to bewilder defendants and symbolically threaten them with the state's power.[36] Transferring youth to criminal court communicates a message to adolescent offenders—it tells them that their offenses have led them into an adult world without the protections of the juvenile court. This is precisely what one would expect, given the hypothesized distinction between the juvenile and criminal courts.

Yet the effects of symbolism can have their limits. Subjecting youth to a more physically imposing environment does not necessarily mean that transferred adolescents are prosecuted and punished in ways that depart from procedures and outcomes in juvenile court, just as a parent who raises his or her voice to scold a misbehaving child may not necessarily follow through with any punishment. Juvenile and criminal courts *look* different, but it remains to be seen whether they *act* differently. This is the subject of the remaining chapters.

3

The Process of Prosecuting Adolescents
How Formal?

When one thinks of the early twentieth-century juvenile court, the image comes to mind of an informal environment in which a juvenile chats with a judge and tells him or her is wrong, or what problems might have provoked his or her delinquent behavior. This scene is diametrically opposed to the contemporary image of a formal criminal courtroom in which a judge, raised on a dais, pronounces judgment on a defendant in cold, impersonal terms. By introducing adolescents into the criminal court, transfer policies cause these two images to collide. Yet we do not know where the criminal court prosecution of adolescents lies along this formality/informality continuum, or whether criminal courts are more formal than juvenile courts.

According to the conventional criminal justice model, formal due process rules guide courtroom interaction when adolescents are transferred to criminal court. Relative to juvenile courts, criminal courts are designed to be formal institutions in which an adversarial process protects both the state from guilty offenders (by ensuring aggressive prosecution), and the accused from wrongful conviction. Courtroom workgroups are limited to legally trained professionals in that they include defense attorneys and prosecutors who contest legal and factual issues while judges preside over cases, with hearings proceeding according to due process rules.

Of course, the functioning of criminal courts depends on some amount of teamwork and cooperation among these competing stakeholders. Much of the organizational literature on courts (discussed in chapter 1) looks at how prosecutors, defense attorneys, and judges work together, even while pursuing very different goals. This cooperation may involve the negotiation of common understandings of offenses and offenders, or the cooperative establishment of categories of "normal crimes" and "normal offenders."[1] These shared understandings allow courtroom workgroups to reach common ground and agree on appropriate dispositions for cases. Or, the cooperation among courtroom workgroup members may be more of a sort of collusion as described by criminologist Abraham Blumberg in *Criminal Justice*, whereby prosecutors, defense attorneys and judges help out one another in achieving professional goals and obligations. According to Blumberg, the use of plea bargaining allows each court actor to claim partial success while maintaining a large case flow. As a result, court actors work together to dispose of cases efficiently.[2]

Despite this level of cooperation, the procedural rules of criminal courts result in a relatively more formal style of case processing than found in juvenile courts.[3] The Progressive-era founders of the juvenile justice system dispensed with legal formalism in order to prevent formality from impeding the court's social welfare mission. Rather than having attorneys debate legal issues, the court founders envisioned juveniles talking freely about their problems with a judge and a probation officer. They believed that caring judges acting in the juveniles' best interests should be unencumbered by legal restraints as they attempt to uplift wayward youth. Moreover, the Progressives professed that without being limited by legal formalism, court actors could better address the underlying problems causing delinquency.[4]

Recent comparisons of juvenile and criminal courts also describe juvenile courts as relatively less procedurally formal. Criminologist Barry Feld, for example, repeatedly calls the juvenile court "a scaled down second-class criminal court" because juveniles are punished, yet they do not receive adequate legal representation or other necessary procedural rights. Feld argues that juveniles are often punished as severely as their counterparts in the criminal court, if not more severely. This happens because many juveniles are not represented by attorneys, and juvenile courts forego important due process protections in an attempt to rehabilitate delinquents. Thus, he claims that the less formal procedural nature of juvenile courts hurts defendants by denying due process protections available in criminal courts while allowing punishment similar to that handed out to adults.[5] Likewise, in his critical depiction of French juvenile courts, Jacques Donzelot describes this court system's relative informality:

The conventional confrontation between prosecutor and defense counsel, their rhetorical jousting, is thus relegated to the background by a new ordering of discourses, staggered according to a hierarchy of expertise [*hiérarchie technicienne*] that precludes any possibility of contradictory debate.[6]

In *In re Gault* (1967), the U.S. Supreme Court recognized the problems inherent in less formal procedures for the juvenile court. In this decision, the Supreme Court mocks the juvenile court as being "a kangaroo court" in which adolescents receive the worst of both worlds—punishment similar to that prescribed in a criminal court but without the advantages offered by due process in a criminal court. The Supreme Court decided that like criminal court defendants, juvenile court defendants who risk being sent to custodial facilities have several rights previously denied to them: the rights to legal counsel; to adequate, written, and timely notice; to cross-examine witnesses; and the privilege against self-incrimination.[7]

Even after the Supreme Court's decision that adolescents in the juvenile court must receive these procedural rights previously denied to them, one could (and many do) still argue that juvenile courts are procedurally less formal than criminal courts. For example, juvenile courts but not criminal courts involve defendants' families in case processing; relative to criminal courts, juvenile courts rely more on social workers and private treatment providers; juvenile courts are less wedded to a formal adversarial process; and most juvenile courts do not allow a right to trial by jury.[8]

Juvenile courts' courtroom workgroups include treatment professionals and other external sponsoring agents beyond the workgroup triad (prosecutor, defense attorney, and judge) to which criminal courts are traditionally limited. For example, in his seminal study of the juvenile court, *Judging Delinquents*, sociologist Robert Emerson finds that juvenile court communities include active participation from several external sponsoring agencies.[9] A network of interlocking social welfare agencies such as probation and mental health care providers are particularly prominent in his account. The interaction between courtroom actors and these sponsoring agencies results in complex relationships that shape prosecution and sentencing.

One would expect that transfer to criminal court would result in a much more formal style of case processing than found in the juvenile court, and that criminal court case processing is more adversarial, relies on a smaller courtroom workgroup with fewer external sponsoring agencies, and does not include defendants and their families in proceedings. Yet I find that the formality of case processing is not consistently different between juvenile courts and criminal courts. Rather, formality depends on the stage of case processing. During early stages of case processing, criminal courts follow a criminal justice model when prosecuting adolescents, but during the sentencing phase they follow a juvenile justice model.[10] Criminal courts thus follow a sequential justice model that incorporates elements of both juvenile justice and criminal justice. In contrast, the formality of case processing in juvenile courts resembles a juvenile justice model throughout all stages.[11]

New Jersey Juvenile Courts

Composition of Courtroom Workgroups

Aside from the judge, prosecutor, defense attorneys, and administrative court staff (e.g., bailiffs, clerks), several other sponsoring agencies participate in the prosecution of adolescent offenders in both court types. These external sponsoring agencies shape court proceedings by presenting information or proposing solutions to problems.

In the New Jersey juvenile courts, a wide array of individuals who are outside of the judge-defense-prosecution triad participates in case processing. These participants include representatives from the juvenile shelter (a residential facility for homeless or abused/neglected youth), the Department of Juvenile Justice (the state's juvenile prison agency), the Department of Youth and Family Services (a family-oriented welfare agency), the Department of Probation, and representatives from specific treatment or school programs. Representatives from these agencies are considered "regulars" by the court staffs—they come and go from the courtrooms frequently and without interruptions, despite the fact that the hearings (by rule) are closed to the public or to anyone not involved in the particular case. They wear identification badges and are known by all court staff, and as a result they are allowed full access in observing court proceedings. Usually, they sit in court and observe hearings before and after the case in which they are participating; during this time they chat with one another and with court staff. These participants may be involved in cases from beginning to end—they aid the courts by providing information at all stages of case processing. For example, one important contribution to juvenile court case processing occurs when probation officers, medical professionals, or mental therapists evaluate a defendant and report to the court on the defendant's likelihood of success in a pretrial diversion program. Depending on this evaluation, the judge might consider such a program as an alternative to preadjudication detention while the defendant's case proceeds.

One effect of the "regular" status of juvenile court external participants is that their goals are fairly similar to those of the court staff. They are members of the same penal-welfarist juvenile justice system. Because they seek to protect and treat juveniles, but also to control and punish, their goals match the court's statutory mission. These regulars readily report defendants' negative behavior for either of two reasons: to request the court's help in controlling the youth under their care, or to maintain credibility among the courtroom workgroup. These external participants are full members of the court "team."

Formality of Courtroom Interaction

Consistent with a juvenile justice model, the interaction of courtroom workgroup members in the New Jersey juvenile court is informal throughout case processing. This informality characterizes case processing from beginning to end in both county-level juvenile courts. In contrast to the criminal courts, in which court actors frequently submit written motions regarding admissibility of evidence and defendants' statements, court actors rarely file written legal motions in the juvenile courts. Rather, defense attorneys and prosecutors discuss their positions verbally in court. Veracity of police identification, for example, is debated in court during a probable cause hearing or a trial, rather than decided based on written motions. Even more frequently, defense attorneys use this type of issue informally during plea bargaining to suggest weaknesses in the prosecutor's case as a tactic to secure a reduced sentence:

> Winning 90% of the time is being able to convince the prosecutor that if it did go to trial they might not have such a good chance, as opposed to actually going to trial and winning the trial. So you look at the discovery when it's handed to you the day you show up for court and you say,

"Oh look, this is a search problem." Or, "Oh look, this is a Miranda problem." "Oh look this guy didn't do anything," or any kind of thing that can come up. (#10—defense attorney)

Legal matters such as formal arrest charges and identification procedures (e.g., how a witness identification lineup is conducted) are taken relatively lightly in the juvenile court, as illustrated by the following hearing (field notes):

> [When the judge asks for the status of the case, the defense attorney and prosecutor answer that they have failed to reach an agreement, and this case is going to trial.]
> *Judge*: I'm looking at the three cases pending against the defendant, and really this is only two cases, because two of them are inter-related. Do you have any questions?
> *Defendant*: Yes. I never saw a copy of the police report for one of the cases.
> *Judge* (to prosecutor): Yes, case number [ ]. Can you show her that police report?
> *Prosecutor*: There is no police report on that case, only the victim's statement. No report was ever filed.

In this hearing, not only is the number of charges pending an unsettled issue, but there is no police report on file for a case that is proceeding to trial—this lack of legal formality is in sharp contrast to criminal court proceedings. Overall, in the juvenile court far less time is spent on "legal housekeeping" than in the criminal court. Instead the judge, prosecutor, and attorney spend more time discussing the defendants, the offenses of which they are accused, and possible outcomes of prosecution. In other words, the subject of prosecution and its most likely outcomes are discussed in place of legal procedures.

Furthermore, the court actors in the juvenile court use a far more relaxed conversational style than in the criminal court and recognize fewer formalized status distinctions between judge, prosecutor, and defense. Consider, for example, the following interaction in court (field notes):

> *Defense Attorney*: This was either a disorderly persons or petty disorderly persons, so we request that he be released, now that he's been held this amount of time.

> *Judge*: This has come up before, raised by [another defense attorney], the argument that because it's a disorderly persons offense he can't be remanded. I respectfully disagree.
>
> *Defense Attorney*: Can I go get my statute book? I'd be happy to read you the statute.
>
> *Judge*: Sure, but I've got it right here.
>
> [The defense attorney leaves court for about two minutes then returns.]
>
> *Defense Attorney*: I'm sorry, judge, my statute book is in the office. Could I borrow yours?
>
> [The judge then prints out the statute for the defense attorney and for the prosecutor.]

During this hearing, the judge and defense attorney disagree about the meaning of a statute. In response, the attorney is sarcastic, challenging, and interrupts the hearing to fetch a book (which he cannot find) to support his argument. This informal level of interaction simply would not be tolerated in the criminal court. Either criminal court judge would have become very angry at the disrespectful tone of the defense attorney, his sarcastic offer to read the statute aloud in court for the judge, and his act of leaving the courtroom to fetch his book. Yet this judge remains calm, prints out the statute, considers the argument, and then sorts through the disagreement rather than reacting with hostility to this disrespectful act.

Although there are few people in the courtroom at any one time, and the courtrooms are small, the juvenile court judges allow people to converse with one another during hearings. Defense attorneys waiting for cases to be called frequently chat with each other, or even negotiate with the prosecutor while a case is being heard. This occasionally occurs while the prosecutor is participating in a hearing; he or she may make a statement to the judge, then turn around and have a side conversation while the defense attorney speaks. The judges and court officers allow this behavior as long as the side conversations remain quiet and the people involved in the hearings can perform their duties without significant interruption.

Roles of Defendants and Their Families

In the New Jersey juvenile courts, case processing resembles a participatory, family-oriented model that incorporates defendants and their families. Both parents and defendants are primary courtroom participants throughout the cases, beginning with the defendant's first appearance in court. The court requires that a parent, or a suitable substitute such as an aunt or uncle or a family friend, attends all hearings. If a parent knowingly fails to appear for his or her child's hearing, the judge issues an arrest warrant for that person. Once hearings begin, the parents either stand (in Pierce County) or sit (in Maxwell County) directly next to the defendant. The judge actively seeks the participation of both the juvenile and his or her parents, as the judge asks either the defendant or the family (or both) direct questions. For example, most juvenile court judges routinely ask parents, "How is he (she) behaving at home?" Furthermore, parental consent is a vital component of court dispositions—judges will not send a defendant home to a parent who refuses to accept him or her back—and the presence of a parent frequently determines whether the judge releases or detains the defendant at the first court appearance.[12]

Judges often consult with defendants about how they are doing and what they want to happen as a result of their court cases. The following interaction is typical of juvenile court hearings (field notes):

Judge (to mother): There's a proposal to change the detention status. Who else lives with you besides the defendant?

Mother: Me, my other son, [his name], and my boyfriend.

Judge (to defendant): What's your mother's boyfriend's name?

Defendant: I don't remember.

Judge: What other adults are in this household?

[Mother answers]

Judge (to mother): Does he listen to you?

Mother: Yes.

Judge: Do you want to take him home?

Mother: Yes.

Judge (to defendant): How often do you see your Dad?

Defendant: Almost every day.

Judge: That's terrific.

Judge: Here's my solution. He goes home and is under house arrest. He can only leave with his mother, father, or a grandparent. And no female visitors under sixteen.

As this interaction shows, the defendant and his mother are intimately involved in juvenile court case processing even during the early stages.

This juvenile court clearly reflects a juvenile justice model of case processing, with a courtroom workgroup including external sponsoring agents, informal interaction, and participation of defendants and their parents.[13] Moreover, these characteristics are consistent throughout all stages of case processing. For example, probation officers or treatment professionals assess defendants to prepare for sentencing as well as to find alternatives to preadjudication detention. One important contribution to case processing by probation officers is to give the court pre-disposition reports on defendants for sentencing. Judges order these reports for cases in which incarceration is likely, such as when a plea bargain has been reached that involves a custodial sentence, or when a defendant loses at trial for a serious or violent offense. Pre-disposition reports summarize the defendant's prior court history, school achievement and attendance, family background and living situation, the reports of any counselors or therapists who evaluate the defendant, and a sentencing recommendation by the probation officer.

New York Criminal Courts

Unlike the situation in the New Jersey juvenile courts, criminal court case processing is not consistent throughout case processing in New York. During the initial phase of case processing, up until sentencing, the criminal court does resemble a rather formal style of case processing that conforms to a criminal justice model. Yet during the sentencing phase, this process abruptly and noticeably changes and becomes less formal. In fact, case processing resembles a juvenile justice model rather than a criminal court model during the sentencing phase.

Composition of Courtroom Workgroup

Before the sentencing phase in criminal court, the courtroom workgroup is limited to three participants: the judge, defense attorney, and prosecutor. No other court professionals or members of sponsoring agencies, such as social workers or counseling professionals, participate in this early phase. The only exceptions are when police officers or other witnesses testify under oath about the actual offense, or the involvement of the department of probation in establishing a defendant's guilt for a violation of probation.

Yet during the sentencing phase of case processing, the courtroom workgroup expands to include external sponsoring agents in a way that resembles a juvenile justice model. Often, the judges or defense attorneys request the involvement of representatives from treatment program agencies during the sentencing phase. These individuals represent agencies that offer a wide variety of services, such as mental health assessment, emotional counseling, drug treatment, employment counseling, or anger management therapy. A number of privately operated agencies in New York City offer these services, and both judges incorporate them into the courtroom workgroups during sentencing. The participation of these external agents in hearings consists of submitting written memos, detailing defendants' compliance with program rules and defendants' emotional or behavioral progress, and participating in discussions about defendants. Their memos offer details about the defendants' court histories, school backgrounds, families, and home lives, as well as diagnostic reports and recommendations to the court. The program agency representatives fully participate—along with the defense attorney, prosecutor, and judge—in all court hearings during the sentencing phase.

Relative to one another, only one difference arises between Brady and Brown County criminal courts with regard to external sponsoring agencies' participation in sentencing hearings. In Brown, the judge incorporates representatives from several different treatment program agencies. In fact, on several occasions the judge told me that his biggest wish for his court is to have a central directory that lists all possible treatment programs, which would allow him to choose from among several options. To help further his objective of incorporating a wide range of programs, he hosts quarterly meetings with representatives from probation, the district attorney's office, and all program agencies he can recruit to attend the meetings. In contrast, the Brady County judge relies primarily on the department of probation to supervise defendants, attend court, and submit reports about the defendants. Other program agencies might assume a few cases in this court, but the majority is handled by probation. Despite the more narrow range of external sponsoring agencies, the Brady County judge uses probation representatives for the same function for which the judge in Brown County uses other agencies: to supervise the defendant, offer treatment and counseling services, and report on the defendant's behavior and compliance with court orders.

Although the courtroom workgroups of these juvenile courts and criminal courts are very similar during the sentencing phase, there is still an important distinction between them. Relative to the close-knit community of the juvenile court workgroups, the external sponsoring agents who participate in criminal court sentencing hearings are "outsiders" who visit the court community. Because the criminal courtrooms are larger and more crowded, external sponsoring agents are unable to interact with court staff as easily as those in the juvenile court. Rather than chatting with all court actors upon arrival as in the juvenile court, a criminal court external participant will arrive in court, silently find a seat in the audience, come forward when his or her case is called, and leave afterward. As a result, relative to the interaction in the juvenile court, the external participants in the criminal court are more purposeful—they come for the cases in which they are participating and they leave directly afterward. In addition, their participation usually consists primarily of the introduction of written reports into the court record, rather than the casual verbal interaction among regulars that occurs in the juvenile court.

Furthermore, in contrast to the juvenile court, in which external sponsoring agents share the court's dual mission of helping and punishing youth, most external sponsoring agents in the criminal court are dedicated to treatment rather than to punishment.[14] The social workers and treatment clinicians who staff these agencies have little incentive to report negative behavior or to pursue social control objectives, unlike the regulars in the New Jersey juvenile court. Treating adolescents as opposed to punishing them resonates with the criminal court external sponsoring agents' professional orientations as social workers. Hence they are not as well integrated into courtroom workgroups as their counterparts in the juvenile court, though they do participate fully in hearings during the sentencing stage. The treatment programs they represent are run by private agencies but are funded by the state based on their enrollment, thus they often compete with one another to recruit defendants. Consider the following statement by a criminal court prosecutor concerning the disincentive of private treatment programs to report program violations:

We have found over time that most of the programs, and I don't know if it's because they rely on a number of kids to be in the program for them to keep their funding, I don't know what the reason is, but [they] never [report a violation of court orders for] anyone. (#3)

Formality of Courtroom Interaction

As prior research and political rhetoric predicts, and in contrast to the informal interaction of the juvenile court, courtroom interaction in the criminal court prior to sentencing is entirely focused on an adversarial debate between the prosecution and the defense. This debate focuses solely on the evidence against the defendant. Hearings follow a typical pattern whereby the defense attorney submits written legal motions concerning evidentiary and policing issues: whether the defendant is properly arrested, whether a witness identification lineup is properly conducted, or whether the evidence assembled by the police is legally collected. The prosecutor takes an adversarial stance and argues against the defense attorney's motions, and the judge mediates between them by ruling on either side.

During these debates the prosecutor and defense attorney each estimates the strength of the other side's case and decides how to proceed. For the defense attorney this information informs his or her recommendation to the defendant of whether to plead guilty, and if so, for how lenient a sentence he or she can negotiate. For the prosecution this information determines whether to offer a more enticing plea bargain or, occasionally, to dismiss the case. The judge mediates the negotiations by prodding each for information, ruling on motions, and suggesting resolutions to disagreements. Consider the following statement by a defense attorney concerning the adversarial stance between prosecution and defense and the lack of cooperative communication:

> A judge will listen, particularly a judge in a part like that [the youth part]. I think he's there to listen. But sometimes these [assistant district attorneys] they don't want to hear anything about what you've got to say. (#1)

Prior to sentencing, hearings follow a typical pattern whereby the prosecutor presents evidence to strengthen the state's case against the defendant, the defense attorney challenges the prosecutor's case by pointing out weaknesses in the quality of the evidence, and the judge ensures that statutes regarding evidence and case processing are properly followed and defendants' rights are respected. However, this, too, abruptly changes once cases reach the sentencing stage of case processing, at which point an informal and more cooperational style of interaction emerges. According to a defense attorney,

> We've had cases where it was incredibly adversarial up until we were able to provide a psychiatric report and then it becomes collaborative. Sometimes I think often the relationship changes as the case progresses. They almost always start adversarial because the prosecutor has a victim and we have a client and until we can humanize our client. (#6)

When describing the sentencing process, one youth part judge stated:

> You certainly like to develop an atmosphere in your courtroom, which I think I do, that this is a serious matter and you get people on board and try to use your influence to get them to work together and we do. (#16)

At this point, court actors cooperate with one another as they collectively fashion appropriate sentences for defendants. Of course, the prosecutor typically lobbies for a harsher sanction than requested by the defense attorney. But, the distance between their views is smaller and their differences are more nuanced than when debating the dichotomous outcome of guilt versus innocence during the earlier phase.

The language used in New York criminal court sentencing hearings is far less formal than the ceremonial language of hearings during the early stage of case processing. The judges openly make character judgments, a hallmark of juvenile court case processing that Emerson highlights in *Judging Delinquents.*[15] This character evaluation in criminal court occurs in most cases with which the judge thinks the defendant has not complied with his or her previous court orders. For example, during one hearing I observed a probation officer inform a judge that a defendant awaiting sentencing is a suspected gang member. The judge responded by telling the defendant that most gang members "wind up dead or sent up for a long time," and continues by saying "you're stupid if you want to be in a gang." In another hearing the judge told a defendant, "One to three years in prison is a lot for a fourteen year old, isn't it? From my vantage point you're on a fast track to hell. You're throwing your life away." This type of judgmental discourse is a sharp contrast to the formal discourse prior to sentencing, in which guilt or innocence is discussed strictly in legal terms.

Roles of Defendants and Their Families

Unlike the juvenile court, during the early stages of New York criminal court hearings defendants' families have no direct involvement in court cases—not unless they are needed as witnesses or to establish the age of a defendant. An attorney may refer to a defendant's family as capable of caring for the defendant and helping him or her show up for court appearances, but families have no direct participatory role. Other than their initial plea of guilty or not guilty, criminal court defendants themselves do not speak until either the allocution of a plea bargain or the beginning of a trial. In fact, regardless of whether or not defendants are in handcuffs (about half are), almost without exception all defendants stand silently with their hands behind their backs. If a defendant wants to add something (which itself is rare), he or she whispers it to the defense attorney. If a defendant tries to address the judge directly, the judge stops him or her and tells the defendant instead to talk to the attorney, who then relays any information to the court.

Again, though, during the sentencing phase in the criminal court, there is a significant shift away from this absence of defendants' participation. Once guilt has been established and the court begins to consider sentencing, defendants (though still no parents) participate in court proceedings. This may take either of two forms. One, the judge may ask the defendant direct questions in order to evaluate character features, such as the defendant's willingness to participate in a treatment program or to determine the level of remorse. Two, the judge may have a direct exchange with the defendants in an attempt to communicate to them the wrongfulness of the acts of which they have been convicted.

Often, the judge admonishes defendants during sentencing. Consider the following transcript of a hearing in which a defendant pleads guilty to robbery by recounting how he and a co-defendant stole a woman's handbag while displaying a handgun. This passage vividly displays the informal interaction between judge and defendant during sentencing. This style of interaction is in stark contrast to the formalistic legal language and lack of interaction between judge and defendant prior to the sentencing stage. After asking the defendant several questions about the incident, the judge continues:

Judge: Did your mom ever have somebody stick a gun to her head?

Defendant: No, your honor.

Judge: How would you feel if somebody did that to your mother, took her paycheck, she can't buy food or pay the rent?

Defendant: I'd be angry.

Judge: Why?

Defendant: Because.

Judge: What if it was somebody that needed money to get on the bus really bad?

Defendant: It doesn't justify to do what we did.

Judge: I don't understand. Why not?

Defendant: We wasn't thinking when we did it.

Judge: How much thinking you got to do to stick a loaded automatic twenty-five caliber gun in somebody's head to get car fare? How much thinking does it take? This lady is forty-three years old. She is no different than your mother, probably the same age as your grandmother a few years ago. Just people minding their own business. Now, when you look at your mother now and see how she must feel knowing that her son participated in a gunpoint robbery, can you see the shame you brought on her? So how do I know you are not going to do this again?

Defendant: Because I learned my lesson.

. . .

Judge: Tell you what I am going to do, Mr. [ ]; you are getting this break, but I promise you that if you slip up on this case, I guarantee you I will sentence you to the maximum that I can. And you're very young to be doing three and a third to ten years, but that's exactly what I'll do. So if you really learned your lesson, learning that lesson is going to include 100 percent compliance with the terms of this agreement. You are not going to cut school. You are not going to be using any drugs. I am going to have you tested to see that you're drug-free. There will be curfew in place every day of the week. Your life is going to change quite a bit from this day forward so that you can walk freely out this door. If you slip up, I am going to send you away for the maximum. Okay? If you don't slip up, you may get out of this without being a felon.

In this dialogue, the judge shames the defendant by personalizing the offense and asking how the defendant would feel if this act had been perpetrated against his mother. Furthermore, he points out to the defendant that his mother feels shame because of his criminal actions. The judge also threatens the defendant with a severe sentence of several years in prison in case the defendant does not comply with his requirements and restrictions. The judge's comments are personalized and emotive, they are delivered in a hostile tone, and they imply that the offense was a foolish act and the defendant a fool for committing it.

This admonishment is marked by the judge stepping out of his official judicial character and engaging the defendant in language that resembles street talk more than legal jargon. It is clearly an attempt to communicate to the defendant in language that the defendant can understand: the judge "disses" the defendant. The admonishment is very noticeable because the judge's tone and mode of interacting with the defendant are vastly different than both the formal language and the lack of interaction between judge and defendant before the defendant's admissions of guilt.[16]

Such a bifurcation of case processing allows the New York criminal court to produce a hybrid form of justice by using a sequential model of justice—a criminal model early on, then a juvenile model during the later stage of case processing—in the degree of formality. As I demonstrate in the following chapters, a sequential model of justice implies more change than one sees in adult cases during plea bargaining, when adversarial proceedings can become more cooperative as court actors negotiate punishments.[17] When criminal court actors proceed to sentence cases with adolescent offenders, they do so while acknowledging adolescents' immaturity and seeking solutions to cases that may help defendants and their future life chances. Rather than seeking administrative efficiency through negotiating solutions to cases, they often take extra measures and time in an effort to help and nurture these youth.

Conclusion

When we contrast the sequential model of justice in the criminal court with the consistent juvenile justice model of informal case processing in the juvenile court, we begin to see how transfer of adolescents to criminal court does not automatically produce wholesale changes in how they are prosecuted. Instead, criminal court decision makers filter transfer policies by selectively applying a modern conception of youthfulness to criminal court case processing. During early stages of case processing, they follow laws dictating formal procedures as they establish guilt or innocence. But once guilt is established and the sentencing phase begins, court actors incorporate a vision of malleability and reduced culpability for youth into case processing. They then follow a juvenile justice model by relying on social workers, using a less formal and more personal style of interaction, and including the defendants in case processing. This allows court actors to follow the law, yet still deal with adolescents in ways that recognize their youthfulness even though they are in a criminal court.

Of course, given the evidence I have presented thus far, one could argue that this is simply a matter of increased discretion and reduced formality of case processing during sentencing generally, and not rooted in the court actors' conceptions of youthfulness. Yet as I show in the following chapters, criminal court decision makers do in fact view youth as less culpable for crimes than adults, and they state their intention to introduce this concept into the sentencing phase of case processing. Certainly, their level of discretion is enhanced during the sentencing phase, yet the manner in which they choose to use this discretion is important. I find that they intentionally use their discretion during sentencing to do what they believe is appropriate given the age of the defendants, and to reintroduce some aspects of juvenile justice.

Finding that the formality of case processing in juvenile and criminal courts is very similar during the sentencing phase helps us understand how these two types of courts actually compare to each other. Earlier empirical research has neglected to consider whether juvenile and criminal courts are as different as the distinction between a criminal justice and juvenile justice model would lead one to predict. Instead, we normally assume that the two types of courts are very different environments that use different logics, practices, and philosophies in dealing with delinquent adolescents. If this is not the case, then why do we bother to change our laws and transfer more youth to the criminal court?

One possible explanation for why we transfer youth to criminal court is that it offers a Durkheimian solidarity-enhancing ritual. Emile Durkheim argued that by drawing visible and public boundaries between acceptable and unacceptable behavior, and by punishing those who have offended collectively set rules, society restates and enhances its collective identity and sense of cohesion.[18] Perhaps when we transfer youth to criminal court we voice our public indignation at perceived (but not always actual) increases in juvenile crime. A dramatic case like Lionel Tate's might seem like a good example. Lionel's crime and prosecution were sensational, making national news at each hearing. Anyone concerned with the idea that younger and younger youth are committing increasingly severe crimes and getting away with them—a view poorly supported by empirical reality, but which a majority of the public holds[19]—might take solace in the life sentence Lionel originally received. But Lionel's case, though it is a good illustration of how ideas of youthfulness complicate the criminal court prosecution of youth, is not a representative case. Most youth—and all of those whose cases are discussed above—are transferred to court in relative obscurity. Because of changes in how youth are transferred, with direct file and legislative exclusion replacing judicial transfer, most decisions to transfer youth to criminal court are now made by prosecutors or legislators, not by judges in court. Furthermore, many transferred youth are not being prosecuted for violence, but for repeated property or drug offenses.[20] Recent expansions in transfer policies mean that we increasingly use this option for less severe offenses, which leads to the criminal court prosecution of youth whose cases never appear in a newspaper and about whom the general public has little concern.

Although transfer laws may serve some solidarity needs, they are also expected to serve more instrumental functions in cases of individual adolescents. Transfer laws are designed to subject youth to a criminal justice model instead of the juvenile justice model of juvenile court. Youth who are transferred are assumed to be prosecuted in a more formal environment. Yet when we compare the formality of juvenile and criminal courts, we see that reality does not quite match rhetoric. Thinking in terms of juvenile justice and criminal justice has some merit, as early stages of case processing conform closely to these models. But during the sentencing phase, this distinction breaks down, and we begin to see the limitations of commonsense understandings about the differences between juvenile courts and criminal courts. Simply stated, they are not as different, or at least not as consistently different throughout case processing, as one might expect.

This sequential model of justice is consistent with Simon Singer's analysis in *Recriminalizing Delinquency* about the beginnings of New York's transfer system.[21] Singer argues that this law was about politics and organizational convenience rather than a wholesale change in actual court practices. In response to the public's fear of juvenile crime and perception that the juvenile court was ineffective in handling violent youth, the New York legislature passed the Juvenile Offender Law. The law offered legitimacy to a juvenile justice system perceived as failing to protect the public, but resulted in less change than one might have expected. In the same jurisdiction, I offer empirical evidence to support Singer's argument with reference to how criminal courts make their decisions. New

York can claim to have one of the toughest transfer statutes in the nation, but this does not mean that criminal court decision makers no longer perceive adolescent defendants as youthful.

As I continue to illustrate in the following chapter, this sequential model of justice is a case of court actors "filtering" transfer laws. Criminal court actors follow rigid formal procedures early in case processing, but then they allow their ideas about adolescence to reshape their dealings with adolescents' cases during sentencing. These ideas lead them to bring in social workers and other external sponsoring agents, to incorporate defendants into case processing, and to follow a less formal procedural model overall. This allows them to follow their concepts of youthfulness by dealing individually with each youngster and responding to the particular needs and issues of each one in a way that might be helpful; these were the goals of the original juvenile court.

This chapter has also addressed our understanding of how and when court actors exercise discretion, an important part of understanding how courts go about their duties. Most prior studies find that the level of discretion exercised in the juvenile and criminal justice systems decreases as cases move from arrest to sentencing. With each stage of case processing —including arrest, the decision to prosecute, the decision to detain pretrial, conviction, and sentencing—oversight increases while decision-making options and individual-level discretion seem to decrease. As evidence of this shift, searches for racial/ethnic or gender bias tend to find larger disparities earlier in the process rather than at sentencing.[22] As an example, consider the difference between the latitude a police officer has in deciding whether or not to arrest an adolescent, and a judge who must sentence an adolescent based on legislatively prescribed criteria.

Yet my argument so far shows contrasts in what we know about discretion in the justice process. I argue that when adolescents are prosecuted as adults, court actors are able to introduce their ideas of youthfulness at the sentencing stage rather than in the early stages. Though this finding may run counter to expectations, these two perspectives are not necessarily contradictory. It is important to distinguish here between processes and outcomes. So far, I have been discussing the processes used in prosecuting adolescents in criminal court. Once they receive a case, court actors are unable to alter *how* they do things early in the process. The importance of a fair and impartial prosecution for every defendant precludes judges from allowing any shortcuts or circumvention of a rigid adversarial process. But once the sentencing phase begins, there is much more leeway for a change in procedure and for making the types of changes that resemble a juvenile justice model rather than a criminal justice model. Thus, it is important to understand how court actors use their discretion to alter the process of prosecuting adolescents, and not just the outcomes, as most earlier research has done.

One important question raised by the findings in this chapter is whether the filtering of case processing to incorporate ideas of youthfulness is desirable. As I have argued above, policies mandating transfer of large numbers of youth are counterproductive and counterintuitive. Finding that criminal court actors filter these policies in ways that seek to avoid some of their intended consequences strengthens this argument by illustrating how these policies do not fit with how court actors seek to solve tough cases. But, given that transfer policies are widespread, popular, and are unlikely to be weakened any time soon, do we want criminal court workgroups to reintroduce a juvenile justice model of case processing? Given that no study comparing recidivism in juvenile and criminal courts finds that transfer prevents crime, and some find that it might increase crime (see chapter 1), one might respond to the question by arguing that the public is best protected from crime if most adolescents (other than the most violent or recalcitrant offenders) simply stay in the juvenile court. But it is entirely unclear whether reintroducing a juvenile justice model of case processing to the criminal court changes this conclusion, because every comparison of recidivism between juvenile and criminal courts assumes that the models of justice vary between courts. Perhaps criminal courts that rely on a sequential justice model are better at preventing recidivism than other criminal courts. This is possible, but it is equally likely that the criminal courts studied in earlier research have acted similarly to the criminal courts I study here, in that they also rely on a sequential model of justice; thus the prior research may already be studying courts that incorporate such a model, but still fail to deter crime among transferred youth. If criminal court actors, generally, are swayed by widespread culturally inscribed beliefs rather than (or in addition to) local norms or laws, then one would expect few differences across courts or over time. As I demonstrate in the following chapters, given the similarity among views about youthfulness among all participants in this research project, it is likely that this is indeed the case.

A second question that remains unanswered is how defendants perceive what happens to them in criminal courts. Some evidence suggests that despite the bravado they may show, adolescent defendants are unsure of what goes on in court.[23] A recent study by legal scholar Richard E. Redding and public health researcher Elizabeth J. Fuller found that transferred youth are unaware of transfer laws and of the likely penalties for their crimes, and that they overwhelmingly perceive transfer laws as unfair.[24] Does the inconsistency of a sequential justice model enhance this perception of unfairness and confuse defendants even more? For several months, they are told not to utter a sound while their cases are before judges, and then at some point they can get in trouble for *not* participating in hearings. Perhaps this switching of gears, from a criminal justice model to a juvenile justice model, only adds to the confusion and alienation of youth before the court.

Furthermore, a sequential justice model suggests that it is counterintuitive to prosecute large numbers of adolescents as if they were adults. It may be good—if we trust criminal court actors to make sensible decisions, at least—that court actors can filter case processing to reintroduce elements of a juvenile justice model. Yet this filtering illustrates that our transfer policies are not consistent with the realities of adolescence and adolescent crimes. Adolescent offenders are not adults, and most of them do not need to be prosecuted as if they are adults. Criminal court actors understand this, even if policy makers do not act on this understanding.

4

Judging Adolescents
What Matters?

It is understandable and reasonable that the public wants to be protected from violent and predatory youth; this desire is a primary incentive for implementing transfer policies and punishing these adolescents more severely than they might be punished in juvenile court. But what does this suggest about how they should be judged, and particularly how our modern conception of reduced culpability for youth should enter into the punishment equation? Does this enhanced accountability mean that youth who commit violent acts are simply more mature than other youth? Does it mean that they are still immature, but that they no longer deserve to be judged with their immaturity in mind? Or does it mean that society no longer cares about immaturity when punishing criminals? Certainly, one would think that the answer to at least one of these questions is "yes," in that criminal courts are more focused than juvenile courts on the severity of offenses, and less on the characteristics of defendants—or at least this would be the case if the rhetoric behind transfer policies were true. This distinction between juvenile and criminal justice is one of the very reasons for transferring youth to criminal court, since the notion of prosecuting and punishing youth in the criminal court presumes that adolescents who commit serious offenses are fully culpable for their crimes, despite their age. The idea behind the phrase "Old enough to do the crime, old enough to do the time" suggests that the potential immaturity and developmental incompleteness of adolescents (relative to adults) are discounted when they are prosecuted in the criminal court. Such a disregard of adolescents' youthfulness is antithetical to the notion of parens patriae that guided the creation of the juvenile justice system.

Earlier research supports the idea that, relative to each other, criminal courts use offense-oriented evaluative criteria and juvenile courts use offender-oriented evaluative criteria to prosecute and punish adolescents.[1] Of course, juvenile courts still consider the offense, but they do so in ways

71

that take individual offenders and their future welfare into account in addition to considering the safety of the community. Though no prior research directly tests this claim, policy makers who advocate juvenile transfer policies explicitly endorse the goal of using an offense-based punishment system for adolescents in the criminal court.

However, as the case of Lionel Tate demonstrates, juvenile justice considerations can creep into the criminal court process in different ways. Recall that Lionel was convicted of homicide because of the severity of his actions, which is consistent with a criminal justice model in criminal court. But then the Florida Appeals Court struck down the conviction because of "Lionel's extremely young age" and his inexperience, which is more consistent with a juvenile justice model than a criminal justice model. Understanding when and how criminal court actors judge youth with these different criteria in mind is important, since it tells us whether the act of transferring youth to criminal court meets its goals.

In order to test this hypothetical difference between judgment of youth in juvenile and criminal courts, we must consider how courtroom workgroup members collaboratively arrive at understandings about adolescent defendants. In both juvenile and criminal courts, courtroom workgroup members work together to develop common typifications of offenses, offenders, and "going rates" of punishment. Dating back to work in the 1960s by sociologist David Sudnow,[2] researchers have shown that common understandings of "normal crimes" and what these crimes are "worth" (i.e., appropriate punishments) mirror workgroup norms and focal concerns, and allow courtroom workgroup members to reach mutual understandings and dispose of cases efficiently.[3] Given the theoretical difference between the offense-based criminal justice evaluative criteria and offender-based juvenile justice evaluative criteria, one might expect distinctions between shared typifications that mirror this contrast.

Finally, it is also important to consider how distinctions among evaluative criteria might correspond to the distinct professional roles within each court community. Scholars who study the professional socialization of court actors in both juvenile and criminal courts repeatedly conclude that the goals and interests of court actors' professional roles shape their methods and criteria for evaluating defendants.[4] Because prosecutors' immediate professional objectives (secure convictions, protect the community) are very different from those of defense attorneys (obtain dismissals, protect clients' rights), these two types of court actors should be socialized into holding different conceptualizations of the evaluative process.

This framework suggests that prosecutors prioritize the harm inflicted by a defendant, while a defense attorney might conceive of a defendant's social history as the most important evaluative criterion, irrespective of court type.

To analyze differences in evaluating adolescents across the two types of courts, I consider two features of court evaluation: criteria discussed in evaluating adolescents; and shared understandings of offenders, offenses, culpability among adolescents, and punishments. I find that court actors consistently rely on a juvenile justice model in juvenile court, but that in criminal court the evaluation of youth varies with the stage of case processing. Again, I find that the initial stage conforms to a criminal justice model, but that as cases progress, things change, and case processing begins to resemble a juvenile justice model. Thus, mirroring the previous chapter, I find a juvenile justice model in juvenile court, but a sequential justice model in criminal court.

New Jersey Juvenile Court

Evaluative Criteria

In the juvenile court, courtroom interaction focuses on individual offenders in addition to, rather than solely on, the offenses that led to each juvenile's arrest. Court actors discuss defendants' personal lives early and often during court proceedings, and consistently throughout each stage of case processing. Consider the following courtroom interaction, which is typical of many juvenile court hearings. The hearing begins with the judge establishing the defendant's address, date of birth, and the charges pending against him, and continues as follows (field notes):

Prosecutor: Your honor, the state requests remand because of the seriousness of the case.

Defense Attorney: Your honor, I ask for his release. Unlike the other co-defendant, he has no prior contact with the [juvenile court] system. His parents are here and would like to take him home. There was a gun displayed in this offense, but it wasn't pointed at anyone. And there were adults involved. Maybe he can be given in-home detention?

Judge: I don't think he's even in school is he?

Defendant's father: If he isn't, we'll make him go.

Judge: I can't release him. . . . Part of the problem is that he's not in school, he's got all this time on his hands, and he's running around at 11:00 at night. He's involved in what everyone agrees is a very serious offense. I can't release him unless there's some structured program in place. He's not obeying his parents, am I right?

[Father nods yes.]

Judge: I can't release him, not with him not listening to his parents. And of course he's innocent until proven guilty, but I can't let him go. . . . Does he have a drug or alcohol problem?

[The parents both say no.]

Judge: Do you use drugs?

Defendant: No, I just smoke some [marijuana] blunts.

Judge: So that I have it for next time, what was the school situation?

Defendant's mother: Sometimes I send him and he doesn't participate.

Defendant's father: Bottom line is he doesn't want to go. We're trying to get him into the job corps. He's got an appointment for an interview.

Judge: Good, keep trying and tell me what happens next time in court. Because something's got to happen.

This hearing demonstrates how the defendant's behavior at home, including his drug use and his behavior at school, are paramount topics of discussion even in the early stages of a case. The only discussion during this hearing of the actual offense or the evidence against the defendant comes during the defense attorney's early request to have the defendant released from detention. Following that, the judge asks about the defendant's family and discusses matters not relevant to the offense at hand. This case is typical, in that juvenile court workgroup members routinely discuss a broad range of topics rather than only debating evidentiary and legal factors to determine legal sufficiency for conviction. Judges, prosecutors, and defense attorneys discuss offense severity and circumstances surrounding the offense (e.g., number of co-offenders, prior arrests, level of injury of the victim) in addition to the defendant's family, home life, education, drug use, employment, and perceived attitude.

Often, offender-oriented factors are introduced into the court record by the defendants themselves and by their families. Judges routinely ask defendants' parents about the defendants' behavior and obedience at home, their peers, and their school attendance and performance. Parents' and defendants' participation introduces peripheral issues that might be considered irrelevant in a criminal court. These issues provide the courtroom workgroup with personal, extralegal information about defendants, and arm the court with greater knowledge of the defendants and their personalities beyond legal issues related to the alleged offenses.

The opportunity—and often the necessity (by demand of the judge)—for parents to report on their children sometimes causes parents and defendants to "hang themselves,"[5] or to make statements that the prosecution uses to demonstrate negative character traits. The situation gives frustrated parents an audience to whom they can complain about their disobedient children. The parents, too, are under court order to appear before the judge or risk a warrant for their arrest. Sometimes parents feel stigmatized by this necessity and react defensively by portraying themselves as good parents, and their children as disobedient.[6] This search for validation as parents can lead to the detention of their children, or even a more severe disposition of the case. Consider the following excerpt from a Pierce County hearing (field notes):

Judge: How's his behavior at home?

Mother: Bad. I've been trying to get help for over a year. He doesn't listen to me. I've had to pay off two drug dealers that he owes money to. He cusses me out and gives me a lot of problems. I need help.

Judge: I'll give you help.

[Judge then starts to order the defendant to be detained, and the mother interrupts.]

Mother: I don't want him locked up, I want help.

Judge: I'm trying to help. You can't control him. I can have him evaluated in the youth house.

Mother: I don't want him locked up.

Judge: Do you want to take him home?

Mother: I don't want him locked up. I want him on a campus where he can go to school and get an education and get some help. Can you put him on house arrest? I want help. [Mother starts to cry.]

Judge: Can you deal with him at home?

Mother: Yes, I can deal with him. [Still crying.]

Judge (to defendant): Look at your mother. You caused this.

Defendant: I didn't cause nothing.

Judge: Send him to the youth house.

In this hearing, the judge detains the youth as a result of the mother's plea for help, despite her repeated plea not to "lock up" her son.

In contrast, some parents request that the judge detain their children. For example, in the following excerpt from a Pierce County hearing, a mother and her boyfriend requested that the defendant be detained (field notes):

Judge: Who is this?

Mother: My boyfriend.

Judge: Does he live with you?

Mother: Yes.

Judge: For how long?

Mother: About one month.

Judge: How do you get along with him [the defendant]?

Boyfriend: We get along well. I try to be a role model for him, especially because his father ran out. He was doing better with me for awhile.

Judge: What do you think should be done with him?

Boyfriend: I think he should be off the streets. He's uncontrollable and won't listen to me or to his mother.

Judge: So then what should be done?

Boyfriend: I guess you could put him in a program, or in jail for a little bit.

Judge: Should we keep him locked up until the thirtieth and see if his attitude changes? This is for you too, Ms. [].

Mother: Yes.

Boyfriend: I think that's good, but what if he violates probation again?

Judge: If he violates again, then he'll get picked up and come back to court. If he still violates we'll lock him up. How long has he been in?

Mother: Two weeks.

Judge: Well then, it'll be a month. Maybe his attitude will change.

Mother: He has a lot of bad influences around him.

Judge: I know that. That's what I'm doing—I'm trying to keep him away from them. We'll keep him locked up until the thirtieth, but you should visit him.

This hearing is extraordinary not just as an illustration of how parents are involved in cases, but of how heavily judges may weigh these requests. In this case, the mother's boyfriend had a profound influence over the course of events, even though he was not related to the defendant and had been a member of the household for only one month.

Additionally, a judge's interpretation of parents' behaviors (rather than their verbal responses) can have a significant effect on his or her decision making:

You also have the opportunity here to talk to and observe their parents during the course of the proceedings, which is an equally powerful tool in predicting whether or not they are going to be appropriate candidates for probation, and maybe decide what conditions you need to impose. You might be parents who are . . . for example, today we had one that was a clear enabler versus somebody who is realistic and understands that in order to help. It's a case-by-case determination based on your life experience, eventually. (#9)

In addition to the disadvantage they may face by their parents' participation, adolescents may hurt their cases by displaying bravado or defiance to authority. In response, the judge usually detains or incarcerates the defendant. Even when neither defendants nor parents act out in court, they might give responses that are interpreted by judges as slow witted or unremorseful. These mannerisms may simply be a result of their lack of understanding of what is going on, or fear of the punishment they may face, and can be misinterpreted by the judge. According to judges, defendants' bad attitudes can influence a decision of whether to detain a defendant pretrial:

A lot of decisions, the kids were mouthing off all the time and they are defiant and they show that attitude as soon as they walk in the court, that's a kid you're going to have to deal with. He is going to be defiant no matter what you do. Actually, with the females—they have an attitude about them. . . . Most of those kids have already been on the streets for a long time, and parents don't control them at all, and by the time we get them it's almost too late. If they've already learned to live on their own at the age of fifteen or sixteen years old, [then you] place them in an institution and they run away from it. But a kid's attitude has a lot to do with whether I keep them in custody or not. It has nothing to do with what I do with them at trial, because you don't consider that. Whether he stays in custody, that's a big factor, his attitude and his way of speech and the way he conducts himself. The way he deals with the parent standing next to him. (#7)

Though each of the above cases led to punitive action by the courts, this is not always the case. For example, defense attorneys can sometimes use information about the defendant's character or home life to obtain more favorable final dispositions for their clients:

Interviewer: When you're arguing why a juvenile shouldn't be incarcerated, what are the reasons you would normally give?

Defense Attorney: Anything I can come up with. . . . If you can come up with anything in their life. I happen to know that Judge [], for instance, used to box when he was young and I have a kid who has been to the gym and can pronounce the name of the gym that he goes to, and I might bring that up as almost an aside and then the judge will take the bait and run with it. So you will do little things like that if you know. . . . there are certain things with [another judge], too. (#25)

The involvement of defendants and their families may have positive consequences for the defendants. Their involvement may "humanize" them by portraying them as children in need of the state's help, as normally well-behaved adolescents who followed delinquent peers into criminal activity, or as "good kids" whose criminal acts are isolated incidents. The parents may react constructively to the pressure the court places on them by offering positive reports of their children and requesting that their children be returned home. A parent who asks for his or her child's release from custody and can promise close supervision at home is more likely to secure the juvenile's release than a parent who fails to lobby in this way. In addition, although parents' involvement carries risks, these risks often are mediated by the attorney, who can present the information in a way that might benefit the defendant.

Typifications of Offenses, Offenders, and Punishments

As scholars such as David Sudnow and Robert Emerson have demonstrated through earlier court ethnographies, court actors develop typifications of offenders and offenses that help them make decisions in court.[7] By coming to see categories of defendants as "normal offenders," or categories of offenses as "normal offenses," they remove uncertainty from their decision making and rely on patterned, shared understandings of cases.

How court actors create and enact typifications of offenses relies in large part on the range, volume, and nature of cases in each court. Both of the juvenile courts process very high volumes of cases. According to supplementary data provided on request by the New Jersey Administrative Office of Courts, the Pierce County juvenile court disposed of 6,566 new juvenile delinquency cases in fiscal year 2002, and the Maxwell County court disposed of 2,447 cases. These are distributed to four judges (only three of whom work full time) in Pierce and two in Maxwell. And the caseloads of these courts are very diverse. Adolescents of any age under eighteen appear here, and all offenses are represented. Some case screening does occur—an intake officer diverts some less serious cases to a separate agency prior to any court appearance, and prosecutors screen cases for legal sufficiency as well. However, the range of cases heard in these courts is large—much larger than in the New York youth parts (see below).

Though there is a large range of the types of cases heard in the juvenile courts, court actors rely on three general typifications of offenses: drug offenses, car thefts, and violence. According to the court actors in each juvenile court, the cities in which the courts are located each have a flourishing drug trade. These drug businesses often employ poor inner-city youth as drug sellers, who subsequently comprise a significant proportion of each court's caseload:

> In the state of New Jersey we have mandatory drug laws for adults. If you get arrested and you are charged with possession with intent to distribute drugs within a thousand feet of a school, you have to spend mandatory time in state prison. Now in [the central city of Pierce County], there are only one or two places in the entire city of [ ] you can go where you're not within a thousand feet of a school. So if you are over eighteen, you do time. Juveniles, it doesn't apply. So what happens is the adults go out, they find them and they send the juveniles out. You've heard me say this in court. That they think nothing is going to happen. And it does happen. And you've also seen me in court ask them, "Do you use drugs?" [They answer:] "No." They are out there trafficking. It's a very difficult problem. (#9—judge)

As his statement makes clear, this judge sees a frequent pattern of drug dealers using juveniles as part of a calculated plan, whereby these dealers know that the juveniles will receive less severe sanctions than other potential street-level drug sellers. In court this judge asks each adolescent charged with selling drugs if he or she has a drug problem—when the adolescent denies a drug problem the judge chastises him or her for being "caught up" in the drug business, and tells the offender that older drug dealers are using him or her as a pawn.

Auto theft is the second type of "normal" offense in the juvenile courts. Northeastern New Jersey has a reputation as a hotbed of auto theft activity, and the juvenile court workgroup members take this offense seriously. When sentencing auto thieves, one of the judges routinely adds a statement he does not make to other offenders: "This is an offense to everyone in [city name], not just the owner of the car. This is the type of thing that makes people not want to come to [this city] or work here." These offenders also comprise a significant proportion of the court's caseload. According to one of the public defenders,

> It doesn't take long to evaluate a case. Most of our police reports are two to three pages. You can tell right off the bat if you have a good case or a bad case. Many of them deal with cars and many deal with drugs. Those are primarily the two kinds of cases we handle. (#12)

Violent offenses comprise the third broad offense category in the juvenile courts. Violent offenses can be somewhat typical as well, since a number of them are before the court at any one time. Yet these cases stand out for being more serious than auto thefts and drug offenses, which are considered "normal" offenses. Thus these cases receive somewhat greater attention and a more individualized consideration by the courtroom workgroups.

When considering typifications of normal offenders, the results are less compelling and clear than the distinction among offenses. In his study of the juvenile court, Robert Emerson found that court actors evaluate defendants with regard to their attitudes and "moral characters," perhaps even more so than factors related to their criminal offenses, which are interpreted as cues that can help one understand a youth's moral character.[8] Certainly some character evaluation occurs in the New Jersey juvenile courts, but this is far less important than a defendant's prior arrest record and current offense. These are indeed cues that the defendant may be dangerous, but the juvenile court actors react to these cues actuarially, not affectively. Relatively severe punishments are given to adolescents because they have demonstrated that they will not respond well to lenient treatment, not because of their moral character, as Emerson describes.

When character evaluations do come into play, they usually benefit defendants. This is because the courtroom workgroup members stereotype most defendants by assuming they are poor, come from single-parent families (or foster homes, or homes of other relatives like grandparents), and are uneducated:

The poorer the person, usually the less parental guidance they receive. A lot of our kids don't have a father. The mothers are on public assistance. And I think that's a contributing factor. The father is dead. You read a lot of predisposition [reports]: "My mother's in jail, my father is in a drug rehab, and I'm being raised by my grandmother." So what you see your parents do, you do. I don't think it's necessarily race. I think more economics. (#11—defense attorney)

Though there may be some truth to these attributions of poverty, especially since almost all defendants are represented by public defenders (and are hence poor), it is important to note that the court actors hold to these stereotypes and assume most defendants fit them. As a result, when adolescents appear before the court with two parents and a positive attitude, they are more likely to evaluated positively. Consider the following sentencing hearing (field notes):

Defense Attorney: This is his first arrest. He's never been in trouble before. He does well in school and is planning to graduate soon.

Judge: Have you had any problems with him?

Defendant's mother: Never before.

Defense Attorney: The fact that his whole family is here is a good sign. I'm convinced that this offense is aberrational. He says he wasn't participating, but he was with others who were.

Judge (to defendant): Do you know what aberrational means? Your attorney just said it about your offense. It means it was out of character. What do you want to do after you graduate?

Defendant: Go to college.

[They discuss where he might go, and where he has applied.]

Judge: This isn't a crime of violence, and he doesn't present a threat to himself, to the community, or to property. He comes from a good family. I think the fact that he's never been in trouble before by this age is commendable. I think he might be hurt by a prior record, so I'll give him a diversionary program. If he successfully completes the program, I'll dismiss the case.

This transcript exemplifies two court dynamics. One, it reveals the judge's assumption that most similarly situated (African American inner-city) youth are arrested during their adolescence. This becomes apparent when the judge states, "I think the fact that he's never been in trouble before by this age is commendable," as if not being arrested deviates from a norm. Two, it demonstrates that having a positive attitude, a desire to continue with one's education, and a supportive family are interpreted as positive indicators that the offense is aberrational. This second dynamic is important, because it suggests the use of a social-class bias in sentencing youth. An intact family and progression to higher education may be potential markers of social class, which, as this hearing demonstrates, clearly benefits the defendant. These markers are interpreted by all court participants as indicating a youth with potential: an adolescent whose future life achievements would be hindered by a juvenile record. Given the extreme poverty of the community in which the courts are located, and the lack of educational opportunities facing most defendants who appear before the court, it is easy to see how court actors might make these assumptions. But these assumptions can create an unfair advantage for middle-class youth based on the financial status of their families.

In addition to typifications of offenses and offenders, juvenile court actors also collaboratively establish understandings of individual adolescents' culpability, or blameworthiness, for their offenses. Historically, this understanding is a central part of juvenile court case processing, since the guiding principle of the country's first juvenile courts was the idea that juveniles are less culpable, or blameworthy, for offenses than adults. This idea, rooted in a *parens patriae* tradition, follows from the belief that serious crimes committed by young offenders may reflect developmental deficiencies in autonomy and social judgment, suggesting a reduction in their culpability.

Overall, each of the juvenile court workgroup members I interviewed expressed a *parens patriae* notion that adolescents have less than an adult-level capacity to make decisions about whether or not to commit crimes, and should not be held responsible for their offenses in the same way or to the same extent as adults. Aside from some subtle differences between judges', prosecutors', and defense attorneys' understandings of the components of adolescents' culpability, there are many shared understandings among the three types of court actors. Each of them believes that culpability is something that can be measured only individually, as it varies by individual juvenile rather than progressing in finite stages. Moreover, all agree that adolescents should receive reduced punishments and more rehabilitative services relative to how adult offenders are treated. Here is how one prosecutor sees it:

Prosecutor: We have a system that effectually values rehabilitation more than punishment. That means the system works to take all of those questions you just asked into consideration. When you say the ability to understand the complexity of what is going on, or work with their attorneys or something like that, that is why they have to have their parents or guardian present because nothing can be done outside of a parent's or guardian's presence for that reason. I feel like the system has all of those things worked into it. It already recognizes the problems and the questions that you are asking.

Interviewer: Other than a parent or guardian present, how else does it take those things [elements of reduced capacity relative to adults] into consideration?

Prosecutor: Like I said, the system already starts with the whole intake process, the review process. So every time they come into court or meet with the intake officer or do something with their parent's involvement right there and their attorney is present, they are taken by the hand with each step and told, "This is what you have to do in order to not be in trouble again or not come back here again." They are made fully aware of what they have to do. "Don't get into trouble anymore. Don't get into fights at school. Don't get suspended. Don't mouth off to the teacher." And, really, how much more can you say it with ABC language than the way it is? There is really no other way to do it any better. (#29)

This understanding is mirrored in the following statement by a judge, which exemplifies the child-saving mission of the original juvenile justice system:

I find myself doing the same things that judges that I appeared before did twenty to twenty-five years ago. You basically try to save the kid. As a public defender I tried to save the kid. But you also had to defend constitutionally; legal rights were protected. Here I'm more concerned about doing the right thing for the kid's best interest and trying to rehabilitate him and try to save the kid. (#7)

The juvenile court actors share a basic conception of adolescents having a reduced capacity for decision making relative to adults. During my interviews I asked each respondent a series of closed-ended questions concerning several distinct capacities for decision making, and asked each respondent to compare the capacity of the average fifteen-year-old to that of the average adult. All respondents in the juvenile court indicate that adolescents are very different from adults with regard to all capacities for decision making included in the closed-ended questions as well.

Despite these broad similarities in how they think of culpability, prosecutors, defense attorneys and judges begin to disagree with how one should hold adolescents accountable for their offenses while also recognizing their immaturity. A clear trend is apparent, whereby defense attorneys operationalize the level of culpability according to the adolescent's understanding of the consequences of their criminal behavior, and prosecutors consider culpability in terms of offense severity.

When asked whether or not adolescents have an adult-level, or mature, capacity to make decisions about whether or not to commit crimes, most of the juvenile court defense attorneys say "no." They indicate that adolescents are very different from adults with regard to all capacities for decision making included in the closed-ended questions as well; the average response score, on a scale of 1 to 4 (with 1 meaning that adolescents are very different than adults, and 4 meaning they are similar), from these defense attorneys is 1.9. The following response is typical of their expressed beliefs on the reduced maturity of adolescents:

> Kids do things because they're stupid and they are stupid because they are uneducated. They are not stupid because they lack intelligence. . . . [They] lack the ability, like you said earlier, to make judgments, to think abstractly, to realize what tomorrow will bring and also I do think many of them are unable to walk in the shoes of another. I just don't think they realize the permanence of their actions, including killing somebody. (#8)

Defense attorneys cite the reduced ability of adolescents to make sound decisions about committing crimes as a primary reason why adolescents should not be punished as adults. Rather, they should receive more rehabilitative services than offered to adults, and given second chances rather than held accountable in the same way or to the same extent as adults. These attorneys consider adolescence to be somewhat of a "training period" during which youth should be offered opportunities to make mistakes without paying serious consequences for them,[9] though with punishment to communicate wrongfulness and teach proper behavior. A typical response from a defense attorney is as follows:

Interviewer: What are the components of being responsible and being held accountable by the criminal justice system?

Defense Attorney: It is ability to comprehend what you did. And understanding the outcome. A lot of times that really will turn on a medical, psychiatric evaluation. (#11)

The responses of prosecutors to questions of maturity and culpability are somewhat more complex than those of defense attorneys. When asked outright, several of the prosecutors say that adolescents do have a mature capacity to make decisions about whether or not to commit crimes. However, when I asked these prosecutors the closed-ended questions about distinct decision-making capacities, their responses contradicted their earlier answers, showing the underlying belief that adolescents are in fact very different from adults. The average response score of juvenile court prosecutors to the scaled questions about similarity of adolescents and adults is 2.1, which mirrors the responses of the defense attorneys. Moreover, these prosecutors state the belief that adolescents are influenced by peer pressure, fail to look ahead to the future, and lack the overall judgment of typical adults.

This contradiction, between claiming that adolescents have a fully mature capacity to make decisions and that their judgment is less well developed than that of adults, was acknowledged by one prosecutor.[10] She began to laugh at her responses to the scaled questions when she realized that they contradict her previous general statement that adolescents have a mature capacity for decision making. According to her, the interview questions were "ruining her system." While laughing, she said that the questions caused her to rethink her earlier response. Others failed to notice or to comment on this apparent contradiction:

Interviewer: In general, would you say that adolescents have a level of mature capacity to make decisions about whether or not to commit crimes?

Respondent: I think they do, I think they have that capacity. The question is whether they think forward like adults. So I don't know whether that's the same, or—do you follow me on that? They may not necessarily think forward or think about the consequence. Though they know whether it is right or wrong, but they don't necessarily think about the consequences. So, I think it is different. (#27)

Another prosecutor, when asked under what circumstances youth should be held responsible for their criminal actions, seemed confused and stated that he "had never thought about it before." Remarkably, a legal professional responsible for initiating proceedings to transfer youth to the criminal court had failed to ever consider what such an action means, or under what circumstances it should be taken.

Apparently, prosecutors' professional socialization into the role of punisher seems to foster the uncritical acceptance that defendants are able to make mature decisions about their behaviors, even when this is in conflict with their other beliefs about youthfulness. To settle this potential incongruity, prosecutors tend to rely on their professional socialization. Generally, the prosecutors evaluate culpability based on whether adolescents understand the difference between right and wrong, and on the severity of offense, rather than based on nuances of development and maturity. The following is a typical response from juvenile court prosecutors about culpability:

> *Respondent*: I think it depends on the nature of their conduct. I certainly think at a very early age children acquire a sense that killing is wrong. I don't know. I can't . . .
> *Interviewer*: Does that mean a kid who does a more serious offense should be held to a more mature standard than a kid who does a less serious offense?
> *Respondent*: Probably. Yeah. (#14)

However, the prosecutors also express the belief that adolescents' level of culpability is lower than that of adults, regardless of other factors.

And, as one might expect, the judges' stated perceptions of maturity and culpability are midway between those of the prosecutors and defense attorneys. The opinion of one of the two interviewed judges on the culpability of adolescents resembles those of the defense attorneys and the other judge thinks more like the prosecutors. The former believes that adolescents are very different from adults with regard to all facets of decision making; the latter says that they have a mature capacity to make decisions about criminal behaviors overall but still rates them as very different from adults when answering the closed-ended questions about distinct decision-making abilities. Thus, judges offer views that accommodate both perspectives. One judge states that responsibility is determined by the following wide array of factors:

The nature of the offense. The circumstances of the offense. The kid's background. You have to know something about the background. Is this a kid with a real serious mental problem? You've got to look at that. (#7)

As these examples show, there is some consensus among the diverse courtroom workgroup members concerning the shared understandings about offenses, offenders, and culpability that juvenile court workgroup members rely on to make sense of adolescents' cases. Usually, the end products of these collaborative understandings are sentences for youth. As one might expect, this phase as well is guided by shared typifications, or "going rates," of punishment. The going rate of punishment follows a very predictable pattern of escalating sanctions. This pattern is evident when searching through individuals' case files, and when observing court proceedings.

The progression of sanctions is driven by a combination of prior record and offense severity. For all offenses other than severe violence (violence leading to serious injury of the victim), on a first offense the juvenile is diverted from court before coming before a judge; on a second offense a judge diverts the case to a counseling program; on a third offense the judge sentences the defendant to a review period of six to twelve months (after which, if the offender has been compliant and not been rearrested, the case is dismissed); and on a fourth offense the defendant receives probation. Probation might be given more than once, though with continued criminal involvement offenders graduate to the two other available sanctions: suspended sentences (probation with an added threat of a prison term) or incarceration. A defendant's prior record primarily shapes this pattern, though the progression can change based on the severity of offenses, where severe offenses involving violence will escalate the progression, and petty offenses hinder the escalation.

All juvenile court actors with whom I spoke acknowledge the use of this punishment progression during sentencing. For example:

The kid is supposed to move up in progression. So defense attorneys want that. You don't want to start with the worst penalty. The kids move through a progression of sentences. You give them an opportunity. (#27—prosecutor)

Yes, there is a progression. We joke about it a lot because a lot of times defense attorneys will be like, "he didn't get [a less severe sentence]." Honestly, the first offer is a dismissal. I have dismissed cases where there was no evidence, if I don't think this [the alleged offense] is what happened. We will dismiss. After that, it is just diversion and intake where we take it out of the court system, put [them] in a program and they don't have a record. The next step is a review where they plead guilty, placed on a [review period], and as long as they follow conditions and don't get reinvolved, the case is dismissed. . . . If the kid has had a prior [arrest], even if it is for a diversion, I make an exception because he already had one chance at reforming the conduct, even if he had a diversion beforehand and he successfully pleaded that. The diversion is technically a review period for six months. . . . Other distinctions that I make personally are home burglaries. I give probation instead of review just because I find it is a more serious crime. There is also crime where there is more of a chance of injury and becomes more serious such as if there is an assault and there is a weapon involved whereas it may have been a review from just fighting and beating somebody up; but he pulled out not even a knife or gun because obviously then I am looking at probation. That is more threatening. There is the danger someone is going to get hurt. (#30—prosecutor)

According to these prosecutors, they offer a progression of sentences through plea bargaining, and this progression changes based on prior record and severity of the offense.[11] Some prosecutors discuss this progression of dispositions as a strategy for allowing defendants second chances that would not be offered to adults:

That is the general progression. It is not like we collaborate on that. It's like we will give them chances really. That is what juvenile [court] is all about, trying to give them chances so they rehabilitate more so than punish them. (#29)

Defense attorneys also describe this gradual escalation of sanctions. According to one public defender, they rely on this progression because it allows them to predict what the prosecutor and judge will accept as a sentence:

That's the prosecutor's philosophy. That prosecutor's philosophy is you got a drug offense; the first time, if it's not a serious drug offense, the first time he goes to the [drug counseling] program, the second time he gets an adjourned disposition. The third time he gets probation. The fourth time he gets a suspended sentence. The fifth time he may get an outpatient or he may have gotten an outpatient along the line. The fifth time or the last clear chance he may get an inpatient drug program. Or he may not even have a drug problem and he may get a residential program. And the sixth time is jail. Now the sixth time you may have a good case. Or somewhere along the time you may have a good case so everything is just stayed. (#12)

As the final stop of this progression, prison is only used as a last resort option of the juvenile court.[12] Prison is reserved for offenders who are extremely violent, or offenders who have exhausted all other less severe court dispositions:

Generally by the time you are ready to send a kid to [the state training school (prison) for boys], you've been through just about every plea, or the majority of pleas . . . they've been through every aspect of the system that you can offer unless, of course, they have done something absolutely horrific from the outset—like killing somebody or coming close to killing somebody. But usually [when] we are looking for [training school], the kid has gone through intake review, probation, drug treatment programs whether out-patient or inpatient, on to residential [treatment programs] . . . and a lot of the times they have gone through several residentials. They have exhausted every other remedy they can have, and at that point in time there is literally nothing else to do. Usually the kids who go to [the training school] fit that profile. (#31—prosecutor)

To tell you the truth, the kids that get sent to [the training school] run the whole system and have been given the benefit of anything we have available to us, and actually as it stands we send fewer kids to [the training school] than a lot of other smaller counties do. Fewer capital cases anyway. Kids have exhausted all the programs, probation hasn't been successful, the outpatient programs haven't been successful, the residential programs for the juvenile justice have not been successful. At that point, the kid is usually a serious offender and that's when they go. We have really run out of resources. We try to keep them out of there. (#7—judge)

Thus, more so than normal offenses, there are normal dispositions in the juvenile court. The court actors share an understanding of what sentences should be given for which offenders, based primarily on prior record and offense severity.

New York Criminal Court

Evaluative Criteria

During early stages of case processing, the members of the criminal court workgroups debate the evidence rather than discussing other, personal information about the offender. A strict preoccupation of the "facts" governs all courtroom interactions. According to one defense attorney,

> Obviously the first order of business is what are the facts. And the DA has his or her witnesses and they have one version. I have my client and possibly other witnesses and I wouldn't say always but quite often the version of the facts is totally different. (#18—defense attorney)

Of course, "facts" here are pliable things, in that they are open to interpretation and often they have different relevance for the various court actors. For example, a prosecutor might focus only on the severity of an act committed by a group of adolescents, while a defense attorney might attempt to restrict the conversation to her client's relatively small role within this group of offenders. Yet these different interpretations center almost entirely on the evidence against defendants, and not their backgrounds, personal characters, or behaviors unrelated to the offense at hand.

Courtroom observations reveal a routine pattern for this interaction during the early stages of nearly every single case, illustrated by the following typical dialogue. In the following interaction, the prosecutor and defense attorney debate the evidence against the defendant and the severity of the offender's prior record, with a focus on adjusting the defendant's bail (field notes):

Judge: Do the people wish to be heard on bail?

Prosecutor: Yes your honor. The defendant has been indicted on a second crime while out on the first. Both are violent offenses.

Defense Attorney: Your honor, his father is here in court and is interested in the case.[13] I was at the indictment for this second case and saw that bail was set with knowledge of both cases, therefore there's no new development and the bail shouldn't change.

Judge (to prosecutor): What are your facts on this case?

Prosecutor: The victim was on a train, when the defendant and three others approached him with a weapon. They punched the victim and took his money and his Metrocard. The defendant and three others were then apprehended on the train. The police recovered fifteen dollars and a Metrocard.

Defense Attorney: About the property recovered. The weapon that was recovered, a knife, was found on the train tracks. But, the defendant never left the train, nor did his co-defendants, so they couldn't have put it there.

Judge: I think the bail set in criminal court is inadequate, given the defendant's number of contacts and the seriousness of this case.

Defense Attorney: He only has these two arrests, both are close together. . . .

As this representation of routine interaction shows, the prosecution and defense compete with one another to establish a case for guilt or innocence. To build a case, the prosecutor describes the physical and circumstantial evidence against the defendant. To weaken the prosecutor's case, the defense attacks the veracity of the evidence against the defendant, describes the defendant as a minor participant within a group rather than a primary offender, or downplays the severity of the offense (e.g., by describing an assault as self-defense). The judge oversees this process, ensuring that it is conducted in accordance with the law. Unlike in juvenile court proceedings, during the early stages of case processing in the criminal court court actors restrict their discussions and debates to evidentiary, legal factors—what they refer to as the "facts"—rather than personal characteristics of the defendant.

Again, however, the progression of cases into the sentencing phase brings significant change. Once the sentencing phase of case processing begins, the criminal court workgroups begin to follow more of a juvenile justice model by discussing offender-oriented factors. One method of introducing characteristics of offenders into the court's discussion is for defense attorneys to share a defendant's personal background with the court in order to portray the defendant as a person, not just a criminal offender. Attorneys introduce the characteristics of their defendants to proceedings in an attempt to present mitigating circumstances, which they hope will "humanize them" and secure reduced sentences. According to one defense attorney, her strategy for dealing with difficult cases, or cases in which the evidence is strong enough for conviction and the offense is severe, is

> to make excuses for the person. They've had a hard life so far, been abused, if they've been neglected, if you can capsulate them from the blame, then there's a chance to make people understand where they're coming from. Try to humanize them. (#5)

Other criminal court defense attorneys say that they introduce into court the potential future consequences to the defendant to avoid a prison sentence. These discussions focus on what might happen to the defendant if incarcerated, not about the defendant's prior life:

> Well, the pitch is usually to me that my experience has been that any young man that spent any significant amount of time incarcerated is going to come out the worse for it, not the better. Because I don't care if it's [a local juvenile detention facility] or Attica or whatever it may be, it becomes survival of the fittest and a kid who can't survive is going to learn to be tough and he's going to learn a certain edge, I think, that he may . . . may serve him no purpose down the line other than to defend himself on the street and get into fights and things like that. (#1)

> *Interviewer*: What reasons would you usually give for why an adolescent shouldn't be incarcerated as a final sentence?
>
> *Defense Attorney*: That incarceration is not rehabilitative or remedial and long periods of incarceration are unduly harsh for most of the defendants that I work with. (#4)

As both of these examples illustrate, defense attorneys introduce the rehabilitative goal of protecting the future welfare of the defendant into the sentencing calculus, thereby introducing elements of a juvenile justice model into the criminal court sentencing process.

Another method of introducing offender characteristics into the court's discussion is through the external sponsoring agents who participate in sentencing hearings. At this point, the external treatment program representatives assume a considerable role in proceedings (see chapter 3). The judges use these programs to gather information on the defendant's home life and educational background, and to fashion a treatment program that fits each defendant's individual needs. By sending defendants to counseling programs prior to final sentencing, the judge enrolls them in programs that supervise them. These programs then send representatives to court who can report on defendants, including their educational background; occupational skills; mental, learning, or behavioral disabilities; and family support and supervision. The judge uses this information in deciding on each defendant's status, as in the following hearing (field notes):

> [The defense attorney reads a report from the educational program in which the defendant has been participating while remanded (incarcerated while waiting for final sentencing). The report says that the defendant has shown outstanding achievement and a great attitude. The defense attorney then argues for the defendant to be released to his own recognizance, because remand is inappropriate given his compliance and success in the program.]
>
> *Judge*: Who would care for the defendant if I released him, since his Mom is in the Dominican Republic?
>
> *Defense Attorney*: His older siblings would—they're in their mid-twenties.
>
> *Judge*: I don't think that would be adequate supervision, so I won't [release] the defendant [from custody].
>
> *Defense Attorney*: Your honor, we'd like you to reconsider. The [outpatient program agency] found the defendant to be acceptable, and they'll take him if you release him.
>
> [The judge asks the defense attorney and prosecutor to approach. He considers releasing the defendant to the program, as requested by the defense attorney.]
>
> *Judge*: But I think that [program agency] alone would not be enough supervision, though, because they don't do curfew checks. This defendant would need a closer watch.

A judge who considers the level of care and supervision, curfew, and presence of parents in the house is characteristic of a juvenile justice model, but not of a criminal justice model in which the severity of offense and length of prior record primarily guide decision making.

As these examples illustrate, during the sentencing stage offender-relevant factors arise as prominent factors for consideration, as court actors begin to discuss offenders' characters, social, educational, and family backgrounds, and the future consequences of court actions. However, this inclusion of individualized juvenile justice criteria occurs only when the judge (who has extensive discretion in sentencing) perceives the defendant as deserving leniency. According to the judges, most adolescents deserve leniency and second chances. Usually the leniency is only denied if court intervention has failed on several prior occasions, or if the offense is so severe (e.g., murder, rape, or aggravated assault resulting in permanent injury) that protecting the community outweighs the judge's desire to rehabilitate. Thus, a juvenile justice model is applied during sentencing in the criminal court to "normal" cases[14] but not to the most severe cases, for which "last resort" punishments are saved.[15]

Typifications of Offenses, Offenders, and Punishments

The criminal court youth parts process relatively few cases of adolescents. The caseload of each part is at or around sixty cases at any one time, with approximately one hundred cases disposed of per year.[16] Because of their status as specialized youth parts, most of the cases the parts handle are classified as "Juvenile Offender" (JO) cases. This means that most defendants are aged fourteen or fifteen, and charged with a serious felony (from the list of JO eligible charges). Moreover, because of the case screening performed by the prosecutor, only serious cases remain in these courts. These youth parts process other cases besides those of JO defendants, but usually only if they involve co-defendants of JO defendants. As a result, these defendants tend to be young as well. Hence, these workgroups deal with much smaller caseloads and a narrower range of cases than the juvenile court workgroups.

In contrast to the typifications of normal offenses in the juvenile court, criminal court actors rely on fewer shared categories. There is little variation among the offenses prosecuted in these criminal courts. Only serious felonies appear in these youth parts, due to the exclusion of the designated felony offenses from the juvenile court and the prosecutors' screening. With little variation among offenses, there is little need for court actors to form conceptual categories into which they can sort them.

Furthermore, as I describe in chapter 2, there is less stability and familiarity among the criminal court workgroups than the juvenile court workgroups, which hampers their relative ability to develop shared conceptualizations of offenses.[17]

When considering typifications of offenders, the evidence from the criminal court is about as thin as the evidence from the juvenile court. As with the New Jersey juvenile court, there is very little diversity of defendants in the New York criminal court (see chapter 5 for quantitative data descriptions). This relative homogeneity makes it very difficult to assess how criminal court actors assess defendants' personalities. In fact, because fewer personal or social characteristics of defendants are discussed in the criminal court than in the juvenile court prior to sentencing, the characterization of defendants' "moral characters" is even less frequent than in the juvenile court. When defendants are described as atypical, this description usually centers on the offense rather than the offender.

Though the data on this subject from court observations are sparse due to the homogeneity of defendants, criminal court actors offer comments that resembled the stereotype of defendants held by juvenile court actors:

Most of the kids I see have parents who are both in jail, grandmother is raising them. They witnessed someone being killed. Bad. (#20—defense attorney)

I think when you grow up in a place like [Brady County], it's hard not to get arrested. If you are asking me what causes people to commit crime as opposed to people being arrested. . . . When you live in a place where you see cops on the street arresting people all the time, it just becomes part of your way of life. When I pick a jury and we ask people, "Do you know anyone who has ever been arrested or convicted of a crime?" Everyone does. And so when that becomes the norm, it almost becomes normal to commit crime or get arrested. So something about the socialization . . . (#19—defense attorney)

These comments suggest that court actors in the New York criminal court may hold views similar to New Jersey juvenile court actors about the average or "normal" adolescent defendant. The stereotype is of a poor African American male who has a high probability of getting into trouble with the law at some point during his youth. Conforming to this expectation is not unusual, though youth who do not conform to this stereotype may have an advantage. Again, this state of affairs has significant implications for how courts deal with cases of youth of varying socioeconomic levels. As I argued earlier in this chapter when discussing the juvenile court, the expectation of poverty may be of substantial benefit for middle-class defendants. Criminal court actors might view middle-class youth as having fewer negative influences than the typical lower-class youth and thus have a greater potential for future success.

Of course, as I argue throughout this book, shared understandings of offenses and offenders among courtroom workgroups are filtered through workgroup members' shared sense of adolescents' blameworthiness. Perhaps surprisingly, attitudes about reduced culpability of adolescents held by criminal court actors mirror the views of juvenile court actors. Workgroup members in both jurisdictions express similar views about adolescent decision making and culpability. Interviews and court observations in the criminal court suggest that the mission of *parens patriae* guides court actors' beliefs; I find that in the criminal courts of both counties, the court community members perceive adolescents as less able to make decisions about whether or not to commit crimes than adults, and most court actors perceive adolescents as less culpable for crime than adults. Furthermore, the court actors believe that the factors that cause adolescents to commit crime differ from those causing adult criminality. Moreover, the criminal court actors give almost identical responses to the closed-ended questions regarding adolescents' decision-making capacities as the juvenile court actors. Though these general responses are fairly consistent across each professional group and in both criminal courts, there are some distinctions between prosecutors, defense attorneys, and judges.

Recall that in the juvenile court I find a general agreement about adolescents' culpability among different court actors, but prosecutors have a more offense-based idea of what culpability means than defense attorneys or judges. This distinction is shown in the criminal court outcomes as well. Both criminal court judges who preside over the youth court parts express judicial philosophies that closely resemble premises of juvenile justice. One of these judges identifies himself in public as a "child saver," expressing that he "wants to save as many children as possible."[18] In this self-identification he borrows language from the Progressive-era founders of the juvenile justice system, who envisioned judges as paternal figures who would prevent delinquency through reform-oriented court intervention. This judge also borrows for himself (unknowingly, I assume) the title of Anthony Platt's book, *The Child Savers*, which Platt uses derogatively to criticize the Progressives' efforts to control immigrant and lower-class youth. The judge states that he approaches his decision-making role with the understanding that young adolescents are "works in progress," and that one must take into account their mental development and maturity as well as other individualized assessments. His stated views are clear examples of the notion of *parens patriae* applied to contemporary juvenile justice. In response to being asked how he would ideally like to handle cases of adolescents, he replies:

> If I was going to do social engineering, I suppose what I would do is create a system where the courts would deal with these issues, the Family [Juvenile] Court and the Supreme [Criminal] Court, would be permitted access to impaneled and certified experts in child psychology, child behavior, mental health, where assessments could be done that would be state-of-the-art to evaluate the child's cognitive skills and educational level, where we would have the benefit of a full analysis of the capacity of the individual in front of us and access to expertise at will. And then we can do what is appropriate based on a better understanding [of] who is in front of us. (#2)

This response bears a striking resemblance to the positivist philosophies stressed by the Progressive-era founders of the original juvenile justice system.

The other criminal court youth part judge offers similar sentiments—if not as strongly worded—about giving youth a second chance and attempting to help them rather than simply punish them. With regard to their reduced culpability, he states:

> I don't think they are functioning on the same level as adults. The punishment is not as severe and for a crime that an adult commits I give a fourteen-year-old probation and I wouldn't dream of giving a twenty-two-year-old or twenty-five-year-old probation for the same crime because I think youngsters are influenced by peers. I don't think their sense of decision-making and maturity and responsibility and understanding is fully developed. Also they act sometimes impulsively. I think these are all mitigating factors and they certainly have a certain level of conduct. Give them a second chance . . . depending on the seriousness of the crime. I don't think they function like an adult. (#16)

The defense attorneys who work in the criminal court likewise profess a belief in the reduced culpability of adolescents relative to adults. These attorneys work with both adolescent and adult defendants, and all attorneys with whom I spoke indicate that their adolescent clients are less mature and less able to understand the consequences of their actions than their older clients. All of them believe that, as a result, these defendants should receive a "youth discount" rather than be punished as if they are fully responsible citizens.[19] According to one defense attorney:

> I don't think they [adolescent defendants] have a[n adult] level of maturity. They should have some sort of recognition and understanding that what they are doing is right or wrong but when you're talking straight maturity, particularly inner city kids, I would say they are not anywhere at the maturity level of an adult. (#1)

Most of the prosecutors who work in the New York criminal court also express beliefs that adolescents are less culpable for crime than adults. The supervising prosecutors for both the youth parts are former New York City public school teachers, and both view adolescents as very different from adults. Both state that most adolescents who commit crimes should be supervised and receive therapeutic services rather than punished as if they are adults. These prosecutors offer statements that adolescents are indeed less mature than adults and—unless their crimes are severe enough to necessitate incarceration to protect the community —should be given individualized treatment rather than punished based solely on their offenses. For example, one supervising prosecutor states that plea negotiations for adolescents should focus on "the best thing for the kid [defendant]." And, regarding the culpability of adolescents relative to adults, she states:

> You might be stupid enough when you're fourteen to do something reckless and kill someone and I don't know that you should be held criminally responsible for that, because you're acting like a teenager. (#3)

This is a supervising prosecutor in the criminal court suggesting that a fourteen-year-old who kills should be held less responsible than an adult who kills! This statement is a direct rejection of the concept of adult justice for adult acts.

Such sentiment is not limited to a single prosecutor, but is shared. Other prosecutors offer similar comments about adolescents' reduced maturity and corresponding level of culpability:

> Because they can't defer gratification and they are not goal oriented and they don't think. They don't have the thought processes of adults. And I recognize that. . . . They should be held accountable for adult activity but I don't think the consequences should be the same. (#17)

However, as with the juvenile court prosecutors, a few criminal court prosecutors offer contradicting arguments with regard to adolescents' culpability. All respondents state that adolescents' capacities for decision making are lower than the average capacity of an adult, and that adolescents are less cognizant of future consequences of their behaviors. Yet some prosecutors continue by saying that adolescents who commit serious crimes should be held responsible for those crimes at an adult level, regardless of their reduced cognitive capabilities:

> And kids of fourteen, fifteen years old, that committed these crimes, but you know what, they are old . . . I think if they are old enough to commit crime, they are old enough to understand the ramification of any plea bargain or any disposition and if they have an attorney who will explain it to them. And Judge [] is excellent in explaining to them the criteria for any disposition. It's like, "If you can do the crime, you can do the time." . . . And unfortunately, I've seen a lot of these juveniles, they are fourteen, fifteen years old, they look like they are twenty years old and it's physical maturity, it's the lifestyle that they live. . . . They seem to be so much more mature at such a young age, it's probably a result of the life they live. And certain crimes, it's evidence how serious it is. And at fourteen, fifteen years old. So they really should be able to understand the ramifications of what they are doing and they also need to know this is not something they can continue to do and therefore they are being punished. (#23)

Others state that criminal court prosecution is a good crime control strategy *because* adolescents are less mature, and that punishment helps teach adolescents how to behave:

> *Prosecutor*: I would say most of the offenses that I have here, I feel like this person should be treated as an adult and I feel it is appropriate that they

are in court. Most of them are gunpoint robberies. There is a lot of those. It's like Chinese delivery guys and things like that and I think it is appropriate that those people be dealt with as adults in Supreme [criminal] Court. So to the extent that the system now sends those kinds of cases up, I think it's fine.

Interviewer: What distinguishes them as appropriate?

Prosecutor: Part of it is, to put a gun in the hands of a kid, is a frightening thing for society, for the community. *Especially a kid who I don't think necessarily understands what it means to kill somebody or the danger inherent in putting a gun to somebody's head.* [emphasis added]

Interviewer: So that danger necessitates criminal court prosecution?

Prosecutor: I should hope that it makes them understand the severity of what they've done a little bit more than going to Family Court. Yeah. That this is really serious. And we mean business, that this is not appropriate conduct. And we're not just going to call you a juvenile delinquent and put you in foster care for a year and give you some counseling. (#22)

Ironically, according to the prosecutor quoted here, an adolescent's lack of understanding of the consequences of his or her actions makes it even more imperative to prosecute the adolescent in criminal rather than juvenile court. The adolescent's lack of maturity makes that adolescent very dangerous, and protection of the community necessitates harsh punishment for him or her.

As these examples illustrate, most court actors in both court types and across professional roles agree that adolescents fall short of an average adult's ability to make decisions about whether or not to commit crimes. Most agree that adolescents are therefore less culpable for their offenses than adults, though a few prosecutors suggest that the need for punishment proportional to an adolescent's offenses outweighs the mitigation of reduced understanding or maturity.

These attitudes about culpability have greater impact during the sentencing phase than in earlier stages of case processing. Because the evaluation of adolescents in the sentencing stage of the New York criminal court focuses primarily on offenders and their needs rather than offenses, the courtroom workgroup members' perceptions of reduced culpability for youth influence this stage of case processing. Their attitudes do not change as a function of case processing, though unlike in the offense-driven earlier stage of case processing, they are able to implement these beliefs during the sentencing stage.

Finally, the cumulative effect of how criminal court workgroup members evaluate and perceive adolescent defendants is reflected by how they arrive at sentences. This process, too, is a collaborative one that relies on shared understandings of "going rates" for offenses. Similar to the juvenile court, in the criminal court shared typifications of punishments play a significant role in evaluating defendants during the sentencing stage. I find that instead of categorizing punishments based on an incremental progression (like the juvenile court), the criminal court workgroup members make distinctions based on two primary factors: the defendant's role in the offense, and the level of injury that results from the act.

The criminal court actors recognize that adolescents often commit crimes in groups, and that peer pressure often leads adolescents into illegal activity:

> I don't know about kids these days. I think that there's a lot of peer pressure that they are dealing with. Just even gangs are just taking over the schools. And they are almost dictating patterns of behavior for these other students. It's almost either "I join them or they are going to beat me up or they are going to rob me." It's just a matter of doing things to survive, even though they may know it's wrong. (#23—prosecutor)

Whether the defendant is a leader or a follower in the criminal act is a very important determinant in the interpretation of an offense. Court actors have sympathy for adolescents who simply follow other youth. As the above statement by a prosecutor illustrates, they perceive these youths to live in such rough social environments that they might have to commit crimes in order to escape victimization. Of course, these adolescents must still be taught to avoid such influences and find other ways to get by, but they deserve some sympathy and leniency. However, the youth who lead others to commit crimes deserve harsh punishment, for these are the ones that corrupt others and create the criminal situation in which others get ensnared. By leading the offenses, these youth demonstrate greater blameworthiness than their followers.

The second factor by which court actors evaluate the suitability of punishment—the level of injury—allows decision makers to sort offenses based on the amount of harm caused by defendants:

> On certain cases I would say I am willing to take more of a risk, on certain types of young people because I think I've learned that some kids

can in a short period of time do some things that get them in trouble that maybe if they get the right type of help. And some other things, I've learned. My wife is a social worker and also a Ph.D. and she works with kids. She sees things. I'm not saying I know what she knows but we discuss these things occasionally in terms of her profession and I think I may have a better handle on it but still a lot of times it's difficult. You want to help them, you want to help somebody, but you're concerned. . . . And one of the things I've learned is that when you see a youngster who's actually hurting other people, doing violence, it really sets off an alarm. This is a whole area of psychology and social work that tells you that there is a big difference between stealing some things or even robbing someone, but not hurting them. Robbing from them but not hurting them. And actually doing physical harm. I think it always sets off alarms and a lot of times it really concerns me that some kids may have, unfortunately, the capacity for violence that I cannot afford them any help really. (#16—judge)

This judge uses the level of injury inflicted as an indicator of a defendant's psychological well-being, as well as a marker of danger to the community. Offenders who are more disturbed are more dangerous, and according to court actors these adolescents must receive serious sanctions in order to protect the community. This thought process might be shortsighted in that it leads to incarceration for disturbed youth rather than getting them the help they might need, but it follows a logical rationale of protecting the community by removing dangerous youth from it.

These two factors, the defendant's role within a criminal group and the level of injury inflicted, combine to form an *imprisonment threshold* in the criminal court. Whether or not adolescents go to prison depends primarily on the subjective interpretation of these factors. Defendants who have hurt others physically and who cannot claim peer pressure as a mitigating factor face near certain imprisonment in the criminal court. The following transcript illustrates this imprisonment threshold at work (field notes):

[There are two co-defendants, each with an attorney. Each defendant is charged with two incidents of robbery and assault. The judge begins the hearing by stating the facts of the case that have been presented to him.]
Judge: The defendants beat the shit out of a forty-year-old. He gets kicked, hit on the head, hit in the chest, and his wallet removed. . . . This would

appear that all defendants were acting in concert. The victim ran from them, and they chased him and ran him down like a dog. With the other case they chased him, got him in a choke hold, and hit him with a bottle. . . . In terms of disposition, this just isn't a [youthful offender status] and probation case. I'll look it over, though. . . . This is a pack of wolves. . . . In the second case they pulled out a razor and said "give it up or die."

[One of the attorneys argues repeatedly with the judge that they shouldn't go to prison.]

Judge: The fact that Mom and Dad are nice people isn't going to work on this. . . . The fact is that [one co-defendant] is the heavy on this case, that he's the most culpable, so I can't take him out of the case. . . . So what I'm saying is that I won't give him [youthful offender status] and probation for belting a forty-year-old man on the head.

Attorney 1: According to the indictment the victim was OK, he only had a bruise.

Judge: Here's how it works. When you start using violence with a robbery, you go to jail. That's how it works in this part. If you get violent with a robbery, you've got problems, personal and legal problems. I'm not talking about sending him to state prison for long periods of time. But I am saying he can't get [youthful offender status] and probation. Instead of asking for probation, you should be arguing for [youthful offender status] and one to three years [in prison]. Probation just isn't going to work.

[Attorney 1 continues with his argument that the injury was minor.]

Judge (to Attorney 1, with a raised voice): I've heard enough from you.

Attorney 2: Your honor, this was a street fight, not a random robbery.

Judge (with a dramatically changed tone—much softer): Oh, I didn't realize that. I don't see it like that, but maybe it is. [To prosecutor:] Does that fit with what you know?

Prosecutor: Your honor, I don't know if it was a street fight, I'll ask the [Assistant District Attorney] handling this case.

[The judge ends the hearing by rescheduling to learn if this was a street fight or a random robbery.]

Initially in this hearing, the judge understands the crimes to be offenses in which innocent victims are injured, and angrily rejects the defense attorney's argument that the injury is too minor to warrant concern. Yet when the judge hears that these acts may have occurred during a group fight with other adolescents, he leaves the door open for reconsidering his interpretation of the offense and downgrading its significance. A group fight implies that peer pressure is involved, that the defendants acted as part of a misbehaving gang of youths rather than calculating criminals, and that the victims are not innocent bystanders. These possibilities change the judge's understanding of the context of this offense and cause him to revisit his hastily formed conclusion that the defendants must serve prison time.

In the above hearing, the judge mentions youthful offender (YO) status (see chapter 2). The judge's decision to ascribe youthful offender status is tantamount to deciding on the imprisonment threshold. If a defendant does not receive YO status, he or she most likely goes to prison for a sentence set by state law. If he or she does receive YO status, the judge can opt either to place the offender on probation or send him or her to prison for a maximum of one and one-third to four years, a significantly shorter sentence than the defendant would receive without YO status. The majority of YO cases receive probation. However, judges occasionally do use YO status to imprison a defendant but to give a lower prison term than mandated by sentencing statutes. Cases in which the judge gives YO status *and* a prison term straddle the imprisonment threshold: they are serious enough to necessitate some prison time, but not so serious that the defendant should be imprisoned for a long sentence and left with a felony conviction. The following transcript of a sentencing hearing for such a case demonstrates how the judge struggles with the competing considerations that place this defendant on the imprisonment threshold (field notes):

> *Judge*: Miss [ ], you weren't the prime person in this incident, but you participated in a terrible, terrible act. The victim in this act will be permanently affected by it. If this was done out of friendship, or trying to belong, then you need to think about why you do what you do. The victim had a gun to her head, she was burned, she was sodomized with a broom, and she was raped by several people. You think about what happened. [There are gasps in the audience as the judge recounts the offense.] . . . I'm satisfied that your role in this was minor, but not so minor as to constitute a defense. This is because you were young, only fifteen years old. This is sufficient reason to give you YO status. . . .
>
> *Judge* (for the record, not directed at the defendant): The interests of justice wouldn't be served by giving her a felony record. I'm sentencing the defendant on two counts of sodomy in the first degree, with a sentence of one year [in prison] on each, to run concurrent, and YO status.

In this case, the defendant's lack of direct participation (she helped plan the offense and lure the victim, but not participate in the actual event) and her youthfulness convince the judge to sentence her to only one year in prison, and to give her YO status, despite the horrendous nature of the crime.

Conclusion

In this chapter, I contradict taken-for-granted assumptions about the differences between what happens in juvenile court and in criminal court. Academics and policy makers alike assume that adolescents are evaluated with a more offense-oriented lens in criminal court than in juvenile court. Here I show that although this comparison holds true in the early stages of case processing, it breaks down during the sentencing phase. It is true that the evaluation process of adolescents during the early stage of case processing in the New Jersey juvenile court is very different from the New York criminal court, just as the earlier literature and hypothesized distinction between juvenile and criminal justice predict. Yet during sentencing, evaluations of adolescents in the two courts are more alike than the conventional distinction between juvenile justice and criminal justice would lead one to believe. In the juvenile court, adolescents are evaluated according to a juvenile justice model throughout all stages of case processing: court actors express a belief in evaluating individual offenders with an eye toward rehabilitation, offender-oriented factors are discussed in court, and court actors conceive of youth as less mature and less criminally culpable for offenses than adults. Yet in the criminal court, I again find a bifurcation of case processing. Initially, only offense-relevant factors are discussed, but then offender-relevant factors take center stage during criminal court sentencing hearings. Again, the data demonstrate a sequential model of justice in the New York criminal court.

One important reason for these similarities is the shared perception of culpability for adolescents among both juvenile and criminal court decision makers. The belief that adolescents are less responsible for their crimes than adults—even for homicide, according to one prosecutor—is shared by criminal and juvenile court workgroup members alike. This should not surprise anyone, since this belief fits a modern conception of childhood that pervades our cultural consciousness and that initially gave rise to the first juvenile court. But what might be surprising is how criminal court decision makers filter their sentencing practices through this belief in reduced culpability. Shared ideas about culpability clearly inform the shared understandings of punishments, including who should be punished and how severely, in both courts. These understandings shape what happens in court; actual practices of the juvenile court throughout case processing, and in the criminal court during sentencing, reflect this notion of individualized treatment and reduced culpability for youth. When discussing these ideas that inform their practices, no criminal court decision makers indicated that their practices as officers of the court preclude them from acting on the belief in reduced responsibility for youth. Instead, all discussed how they collaboratively reach agreements based on their shared conceptions, which include the widespread belief that youth are less mature and less culpable for their actions than adults. Clearly, this belief in reduced culpability for youth does not end with the transfer of adolescents to criminal court.

The similarity I find in the evaluation of adolescents in juvenile court and criminal court again suggests that a distinction between a juvenile justice model and a criminal justice model has limited value. This distinction clearly articulates the differences between how adolescents are judged during early stages of case processing, but it breaks down when the sentencing phase arrives. However, as I discuss in the following chapter, the distinction between these models of justice more aptly characterizes differences in punishment rates. This raises an important question: How much does it matter that the process of sentencing adolescents in juvenile and criminal courts is very similar, especially if the outcomes are different across court types?

Comparing the process of prosecuting youth does not have the bottom-line appeal of comparing practical outcomes like incarceration rates, but it is valuable for an understanding of how our juvenile justice policies actually work. If the only aspect of prosecuting youth that matters is the final punishment they receive, then why not simply raise the punishments in juvenile court to match those given out through the criminal court for transferworthy youth? One answer to this question is that transfer of youth to criminal court is intended to offer a different mode of evaluation for youth. Policy makers intend transfer to criminal court to carry symbolic and practical value beyond the eventual punishment. Transfer should communicate to youth the severity of their misdeeds, and that they have committed crimes so severe that they no longer deserve to be thought of as children: instead, they are simply criminals. As I argue throughout this book, however, the message that transferred adolescents no longer deserve to be thought of as children is simply not consistent with cultural understandings of youthfulness. As a result, court actors send an inconsistent message to adolescent defendants, transfer policies are not implemented as intended, and we see the lack of efficacy of policies that lead to a large number of youth in criminal court.

Of course, the worthiness of juvenile transfer policies might go beyond what happens in court. As I discussed in the previous chapter, transfer laws potentially have a broad solidarity-enhancing effect by defining public enemies and drawing boundaries between acceptable and unacceptable behavior. As Simon Singer has shown with the creation of New York's Juvenile Offender Law,[20] one can also understand the value of transfer laws from an organizational or institutional perspective; transfer laws legitimate, or provide "cover" for juvenile justice systems under attack from the public because of perceptions that they are too lenient. Aside from these more diffuse symbolic and political purposes, though, transfer to criminal court is designed to achieve certain results, and one of the most important of these results is to subject youth to more offense-based evaluative criteria than found in juvenile court. In this chapter I illustrate that this result is not well achieved, at least not in the sentencing phase of criminal court processing.

As a final consideration in this chapter, I return to one of the unanswered questions raised at the end of the previous chapter: Is it desirable for criminal court actors to filter case processing and reintroduce ideas of reduced culpability for adolescent offenders? It is very difficult to answer this question with the available evidence. Though we have strong and consistent evidence that transferring large numbers of youth to criminal court either has no effect or increases recidivism, we do not have a very good understanding of why. It is unclear whether this is a result of harsher penalties given out by criminal courts relative to juvenile courts, or because of prosecution procedures for adolescents. If subsequent research finds that these procedures help shape recidivism, then it would seem desirable that criminal courts adopt a juvenile justice model of evaluating adolescents because this practice partially mitigates (but does not eliminate) the potential harmfulness and counterintuitiveness of transfer policies. Yet as I discuss in chapter 7, even with a sequential model of justice in place, the criminal court is a worse forum for prosecuting most adolescents than the juvenile court.

Regardless of whether it is desirable, however, the filtering of criminal court case processing might be inevitable. Several studies have found that filtering by courtroom workgroups serves to match broader cultural scripts. The widespread agreement I find among different court actors and across courts and court types suggests that the ideas of youthfulness that lead to filtering are broadly shared. These results should indicate that the process I describe in the New York criminal court occurs, at least to some extent, in other jurisdictions as well.

5

Punishment for Adolescents
What Do They Get, and Why?

Deciding on appropriate punishments for adults who commit crimes is a process fraught with uncertainty, not to mention racial/ethnic, gender, and social class inequities. This uncertainty only grows when youthfulness is added to the equation, and when we try to find appropriate punishments for adolescent offenders. The recent expansion of transfer policies across the United States begs the question: Should youthfulness matter when punishing adolescents who commit serious crimes?

Policy makers who create transfer policies promote them as a means to provide more severe punishments for violent and chronically offending youth. Court type is thought to be an important predictor of punishment severity because the range of punishments in the criminal court's portfolio includes more severe sentences than in the juvenile court's, and because incarceration is prescribed more frequently than in the juvenile court. Scholars, as well, assume that the punishment of adolescents in criminal and juvenile courts generally supports the distinctions among punishments between a criminal justice and juvenile justice model; this distinction holds that criminal courts pursue a sanctioning goal of retribution and prescribe relatively severe punishments, whereas juvenile courts pursue a goal of rehabilitation rather than punishment and prescribe more lenient punishments such as probation rather than incarceration.

The few published studies that analyze punishment severity across court type report equivocal results with regard to whether adolescents in criminal courts receive more certain or severe punishment than adolescents in juvenile courts. Some early research suggests that when juveniles are transferred, they may appear to be less serious offenders than older, more criminally experienced defendants.[1] Judges accustomed to punishing older, hardened offenders may balk at giving the same punishments to juveniles, and thus give reduced sentences to adolescents transferred to criminal court. A greater number of studies and most recent research, however, has found that youth transferred to criminal courts are detained pretrial, convicted, and incarcerated more often than youth in juvenile courts.[2]

In addition to affecting the severity of punishment, court type also may shape the sanctioning goals court actors follow when punishing adolescent offenders. The creation of the juvenile justice system at the turn of the twentieth century was fueled by the Progressive-era reformers' desire for adolescents to be sentenced with the goal of rehabilitating them rather than for retribution. In contrast, the recent spate of laws mandating transfer of youth from the juvenile to criminal court was motivated in part by the wish to apply more retributive and proportional sanctions in the punishment of violent adolescents.[3] It seems reasonable to predict, then, that juvenile court actors are more likely than criminal court actors to attempt to rehabilitate adolescents, and that criminal court actors are more likely than juvenile court actors to seek strict proportionality and retribution. Certainly, policy makers and scholars both assume that transfer to criminal court leads to more punitive sentencing in the criminal court than in the juvenile court.[4]

Using both quantitative and qualitative data, I answer two central questions in this chapter: (1) Does court type affect punishment severity when controlling for other relevant factors? and (2) Does court type affect the sanctioning goals of courtroom workgroups? To answer the first of these questions, I compare the punishment outcomes of prosecuting adolescents in juvenile and criminal courts. Using the quantitative data from 1992–1993 cases (see chapter 2) I test the degree to which the punishment severity differences between adolescents processed in the New York criminal court and the New Jersey juvenile court reflect the distinction between juvenile and criminal justice models. To answer the second question, I use qualitative data to test the degree to which the sanctioning goals held by courtroom workgroup members in the two court types reflect these two models.

The results of these analyses add a new wrinkle to the book's argument. Until now, I have been building a case for the surprising similarity in the approach used by criminal court and juvenile court actors, or at least how the differences between these two court types is smaller than one would expect during the sentencing phase of juveniles' cases. But this is not true when it comes to the actual punishments handed out. As predicted by both policy makers' rhetoric and the distinction between a juvenile justice model and criminal justice model, adolescents transferred to criminal court do indeed receive substantially more severe punishments than those in the juvenile court. For this one goal of jurisdictional transfer, the policy meets its mark by giving more severe punishments to youth than they might receive in the juvenile court.

However, consistent with the results of the previous chapters, I also find that juvenile court actors and criminal court actors have very similar punishment goals. Both sets of court actors seek to rehabilitate as many youth as they can, and to give most youth reduced punishments relative to those for adults. I find that the cultural construction of youthfulness still pervades the punishment process, but that its impact is restricted by the statutory sentencing laws and limited sentencing options for adolescents within the criminal court. Facing relatively harsh sentencing laws and few options other than incarceration, criminal court actors are more punitive than juvenile court actors, even if both have similar goals.

This leads me to revisit the question: Why should we care about the goals of criminal court actors and the process of prosecuting adolescents in criminal court, especially when the adolescents receive harsher punishments there than in juvenile court? Finding similarities in goals or processes might not comfort the adolescent who serves prison time as a result of being transferred to criminal court, but it is crucial for understanding how youth are perceived and judged. Comparing outcomes—to which the prior research has been limited—is insufficient for understanding what happens when youth are transferred. We also need to consider *how* these outcomes are reached, for both theoretical and policy considerations. This allows us to judge how closely transfer policies meet their goals, offers an opportunity to improve on a policy that partially misses its mark, and offers a view of how cultural conceptions can and do lead to filtering of case processing.

Quantitative Sample Descriptions

Table 5.1 displays a description of the offense and offender characteristics for the entire sample, and separated into the two court types (see the Appendix for summary statistics). Though the cases from each court type are very similar, they differ in a few important ways. The offender characteristics in the sample include age, sex, and race of defendants. As table 5.1 shows, there are greater proportions of sixteen-year-olds, minority defendants, and male defendants in the criminal court subsample than in

TABLE 5.1 *Offense and Offender Characteristics of Cases,*
Total Sample, and in Each Court

		Total Sample (n = 2223) %	Juvenile Court/ New Jersey (n = 1048) %	Criminal Court/ New York (n = 1175) %
Offender Characteristics				
Age:	15	33.9	46.9	22.2
	16	66.1	53.1	77.8
Sex:	Male	86.1	82.7	89.1
	Female	13.9	17.3	10.9
Race/Ethnicity:	White	8.9	13.3	4.9
	African American	56.1	54.4	57.5
	Latino/a	29.7	26.4	32.6
	Other and Unknown	5.3	5.9	4.9
Offense Characteristics				
Offense Type:	Robbery	53.6	24.9	79.1
	Aggravated Assault	29.2	43.9	16.2
	Burglary	17.2	31.2	4.7
Associated weapon charge		38.2	34.6	41.4
Preadjudication detention		45.7	41.3	49.9
Presence of prior arrests		56.0	66.8	46.3
Arrested during case processing		26.5	36.5	17.5
Previously incarcerated		10.0	3.9	15.4
Arrest warrant executed		13.2	18.6	8.5

the juvenile court subsample. The two court types show roughly similar breakdowns of racial categories, though there is a larger proportion of white defendants in the juvenile court than the criminal court, with this difference offset by a larger proportion of Latino and Latina defendants in the criminal court.

The offense characteristics in the data set include the offense type at case filing, use of a weapon in the offense, imposition of preadjudication detention, prior arrest record, arrests during case processing, previous incarceration record of the defendant, and ordering of an arrest warrant for the defendant during case processing. The juvenile court subsample contains a greater percentage of individuals who have prior arrest records, are arrested during sampled case processing, and have arrest warrants issued during case processing.

Another noticeable difference between cases in the two courts is the distribution of offense types at case filing. The juvenile court cases are nearly equally divided among the three sampled offense types, but the criminal court cases consist of mostly robbery cases. This is the result of the sampling process, with cases selected based on their representation within each state's court system. Thus, sample disparities occur because of the natural variation between the two populations sampled. This sampling method includes the most serious fifteen- and sixteen-year-old offenders in each state not including adolescents who are arrested for homicide or sexual assault.[5] In addition to including offense types as control variables in the multivariate analyses, to ensure further that accurate comparisons are made between comparable groups of cases, I conducted additional multivariate analyses using the entire sample as well as separately for robbery cases.

Comparing Punishments

Descriptive Comparisons

As figure 5.1 illustrates, preadjudication detention is more likely for adolescents prosecuted in the criminal court than in the juvenile court. With regard to punishment severity as measured by an intermediate punishment (detention), the criminal court prescribes more severe punishment and thus reflects a criminal justice model relative to the juvenile court.[6]

Figure 5.2 continues with the descriptive comparison of the two court types by comparing frequency of court action and imposition of different sentences. I use the term "court action" rather than conviction because the meaning of conviction is not clearly equivalent across the two courts. Both court types have middle-ground adjudicatory options that are ambiguously defined as convicted or not-convicted. In New York, this option is called *adjourned in contemplation of dismissal,* and in New Jersey it is called an *adjourned disposition.* These options in both states are identical in content; they involve a suspension of the case for a specified period of time. If the defendant is not arrested during that time and complies with all court orders (e.g., attending school regularly), the case will be dismissed after the time period. An important distinction between them is that in New Jersey, the juvenile must plead guilty to the charged offense in order to receive this disposition, thus it is clearly a sentence fol-

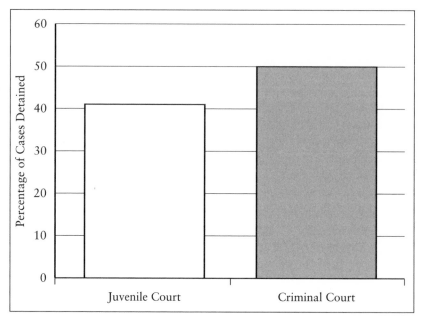

Fig. 5.1. Preadjudication detention rates (%) among juvenile and criminal court cases.

lowing a conviction. Yet in New York, the resolution occurs without any plea or admission of guilt. Thus, technically this same disposition involves a conviction in New Jersey but not in New York. For the sake of comparing the practical actions of each court type, I include both as sentencing options, because in both court types the court supervises the defendant rather than dismissing the case outright.

Overall, a few patterns emerge. One, the criminal court takes action in a greater percentage of cases than the juvenile court, as illustrated by the far-left bars in figure 5.2 for "any court action." This is further support for the theoretical contrast between a juvenile and criminal model of justice, by showing that the criminal court is more likely to give some punishment than the juvenile court. To pursue further empirical inquiry into why the criminal court takes action in more cases, one would need additional data—which were not available—most importantly the quantity and quality of evidence against the defendant, level of injury to the victim, and the relationship between the offender and victim.

Figure 5.2 also displays the different sentencing patterns of each court type in cases where some court action is taken. As predicted, the criminal court is significantly more likely to incarcerate defendants, and the juvenile court is more likely to impose other sanctions (primarily probation or a suspended sentence). Hence, when measured by the sentences allocated in each court type, the criminal court prescribes relatively more severe punishments than the juvenile court.

Finally, figure 5.3 compares the average custodial sentence lengths, in months, for those who are incarcerated. The average custodial sentence length in the criminal court is nearly three times greater than the average in the juvenile court, with an average of 9.5 months in juvenile court but 27.2 months in criminal court. This figure clearly demonstrates that adolescents sentenced to incarceration in the criminal court are sentenced to significantly longer prison terms than adolescents incarcerated in the juvenile court.

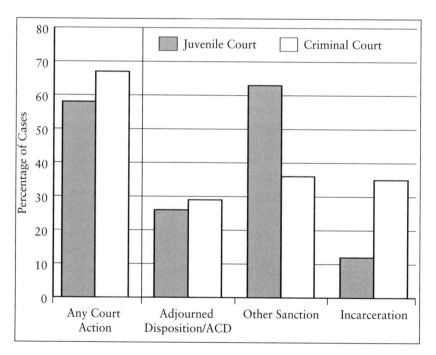

Fig. 5.2. Rates (%) of any court action and sentencing options among juvenile and criminal court cases.

Fig. 5.3. Average prison sentence length, juvenile and criminal court cases.

Multivariate Tests

Next, to determine the impact of court type on sentence severity while controlling for characteristics of offenders and offenses, I estimated multivariate equations predicting a dependent variable of incarceration. I used incarceration as a dependent variable, because the decision to incarcerate is perhaps the most crucial sentencing decision. It offers a clearer comparison of court types than would other sentencing decisions, which may have different meanings across jurisdictions, or may be enforced by different personnel and in different ways. Of course, incarceration is not always the same, in the sense that prison terms given by juvenile and criminal courts differ from each other in terms of duration, type of institution, and conditions of confinement. Yet on a basic level of comparison, imprisonment is a fairly similar punishment in both systems, in that it always involves deprivation of liberty through coercive means in custodial institutions.

In order to adjust for the potential bias introduced when cases are censored at the conviction stage, I used Heckman two-stage probit models to predict incarceration (see Appendix). Using this method, I estimated two separate models. The first model predicts the probability of receiving a custodial sentence for the total sample, using the independent variables. The second model restricts the analysis to only robbery cases, to test whether the results from the first model are the result of the greater proportion of robbery cases in New York.[7]

The details of these analyses and the resulting regression coefficients are listed in the Appendix. In figure 5.4 I present the estimated difference in the predicted odds of incarceration between juvenile and criminal courts, while controlling for the independent variables. The first comparison in figure 5.4 includes all cases, and the second comparison includes only robbery cases—the two model results are nearly identical. Using juvenile courts as a contrast, figure 5.4 illustrates the increase in probability of incarceration in criminal court. According to the multivariate probit models, the odds of incarceration are 8.82 times greater when prosecuted in criminal courts rather than in juvenile court, or 8.24 times greater when looking only at robbery cases, while holding constant offender- and offense-oriented independent variables.[8] In both of these multivariate models, type of court is statistically significant and the best predictor of incarceration. These results clearly demonstrate that sentencing is more punitive in the criminal court than the juvenile court.

This distinction between juvenile and criminal courts is consistent within each type of court as well. Mirroring the results presented in earlier chapters, no significant differences are found across counties within the juvenile court system or the criminal court system. Each county-level juvenile court incarcerates a much smaller percentage of adolescents than any of the three county-level criminal courts. Moreover, multivariate tests fail to find significant sentencing differences within each court type. Rather than attributing the results to county-specific court contexts, the different punishments seem to be the result of jurisdictional transfer.

Sanctioning Goals

At this point, I turn back to qualitative data to analyze the sanctioning goals held by court actors in the two court types. According to a juvenile justice model and a criminal justice model, one would expect that court actors' sanctioning goals in the criminal court are more punitive than in the juvenile court. If this were the case, I should find that a sanctioning

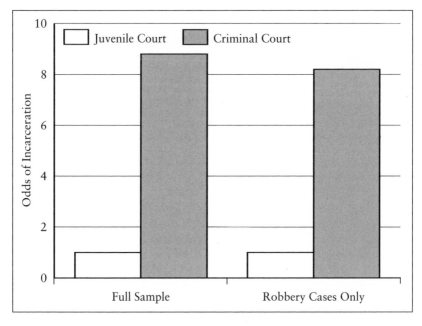

Fig. 5.4. Estimated odds (juvenile court = 1.0) of incarceration in juvenile and criminal courts, for full sample and robbery cases only.

goal of retribution or incapacitation guides sentencing in the criminal court, and a sanctioning goal of rehabilitation guides sentencing in the juvenile court. This might explain why the rates of incarceration are so much higher in the criminal court than the juvenile court.

As I illustrated in chapter 2, the statutory goals of each jurisdiction are very different from one another. The New Jersey juvenile court follows a dual statutory mission of community protection and rehabilitation; court actors are instructed to consider a defendant's best interests and future welfare in addition to protecting the community. In contrast, the New York criminal court is not statutorily guided by any rehabilitative goal such as the defendant's future welfare or best interests. Rather, New York law establishes goals of retribution and incapacitation for sentencing in the criminal court.

However, this statutory distinction of sentencing goals may or may not correspond to actual sanctioning goals held by courtroom decision makers in the criminal and juvenile courts. In fact, I find that despite the very different statutorily prescribed punishment goals across the two types of courts, court actors view adolescents very similarly across the two court types and seek very similar ends to cases. Once again, I find that they do their best to filter case processing and circumvent the law to reintroduce notions of juvenile justice to criminal court case processing. Of course, as the previous section of this chapter has illustrated, the punishments given are not similar in juvenile and criminal courts. Clearly, an alternative explanation is necessary for why the punishments are very different across court type. The explanation is this: the differences in sentencing are a result of the constraints placed on criminal court actors' discretion by sentencing laws, courtroom norms, and limited sentencing options, but not necessarily because of the court actors' wishes.

New Jersey Juvenile Court

Overall, I find that juvenile court actors in each professional role do indeed follow the statutory dual mission of rehabilitation and punishment. Each court actor I interviewed in the juvenile court expressed a belief that sentencing in the juvenile court should not only attempt to rehabilitate juveniles, but also protect the community by incarcerating "last resort" cases:[9]

When you do juvenile [court], it's a lot different than doing adult [criminal court]. With adult, you really are just dealing with crime and punishment. With juvenile you're dealing with rehabilitation. And when I look at the police report, I am thinking only as a lawyer, who is trying to win a case. When I speak to the parents, I am thinking more of social worker part of my job, where I have the best interest of the child at heart, trying to work towards his rehabilitation. What is wrong with the kid? What is his background? (#25—defense attorney)

This isn't an adult [criminal court] where you are looking for the idea of retribution and punishment before rehabilitation. In juvenile, you are looking at rehabilitation first. (#30—prosecutor)

There is a little bit more expectation [in the juvenile court than in the criminal court] that these kids are going to have several shots at some sort of rehabilitation and not just punishment straight out from the beginning unless they have done something horrifically awful from the get-go. (#31—prosecutor)

The juvenile court's statutory mandate requires that defendants are evaluated with an eye toward whether or not they can be treated through education or counseling. The following court transcript illustrates the juvenile court's focus on treatment through a medical model, as prescribed by the Progressive-era founders of the juvenile justice system (field notes):

> *Judge*: [Defense Attorney], you and I have discussed this many times before. You know I don't believe in outpatient treatment without inpatient treatment. He's messed up before, how do I know he won't do it again?
>
> *Judge* (to defendant): What drugs are you using?
>
> *Defendant*: Angel dust and marijuana.
>
> [The judge then lectures the defendant on telling the truth, asks again, and defendant says same thing.]
>
> *Judge*: Tell me the truth. Understand that we're asking in order to help you, so we know how to help you. If you go to the doctor with a heart problem, you wouldn't lie, you'd be honest so that he could help you.
>
> [The judge then sentences the defendant to probation for eighteen months with an outpatient program.]
>
> *Judge*: If you come back, you better bring a toothbrush!

Thus the juvenile court actors approach punishment with a presumption of finding a disposition that meets the treatment needs of the defendant.

Because they are linked to the state's family welfare system, the juvenile court has many noncustodial sentencing options that can be prescribed in an attempt to rehabilitate. Agencies that are well connected with the juvenile courts—with whom they even share office space on the same floor in both courts—are able to provide the court with alternatives to incarceration. The Office of Probation, the Division of Youth and Family Services, and other state-funded agencies offer counseling and treatment programs that the juvenile court uses as noncustodial punishments. In chapter 2 I described personnel from these agencies as "regulars" in the juvenile court who interact freely with courtroom workgroups and are very involved in case processing. These agencies provide services such as anger-management counseling and workshops encouraging youth to avoid drugs. When adolescents are sent to these programs, they are required to abide by rules such as curfews, drug testing, and regular counseling sessions.

Despite the noncustodial options available in juvenile court and the statutory goal of achieving rehabilitation, punishment is still a consideration. The sentencing statutes make both goals explicitly clear. Juvenile court actors give serious consideration to harsh punishments such as incarceration in order to protect the community from predatory youth when they believe it is necessary:

> I think the purpose [of juvenile court] is twofold, to get them the help that they might need. At least for me it's twofold. And obviously punitive in nature. I don't think anyone will deny this, sentences often reflect the nature of the crime. So while certainly the advocates for the juveniles are for rehabilitation, you can go just about anywhere . . . there are many different types of outlets for rehabilitation. Not all of them are at [the state juvenile prison] or [residential juvenile justice commission] programs. So obviously the system recognizes the need to keep the community safe and the need to punish offenders. (#14—prosecutor)

This dual goal of rehabilitation and punishment is mentioned by several court actors in interviews, and even stated in court (field notes):

> *Judge* (to defendant): Given that there are two purposes to the juvenile justice system, punishment and rehabilitation, you're to be put on probation. This is an offense for which an adult would almost certainly go to prison.

The sanctioning goals of juvenile court actors are consistent across the two courts I studied and invariant across the stage of case processing. As the above statements by court actors make clear, juvenile court workgroup members take seriously the statutorily defined dual purpose of the juvenile court: to punish and to rehabilitate. Both of these goals guide their apparent behaviors in court, suggesting that the juvenile courtroom workgroups do indeed pursue a juvenile justice model of rehabilitative sanctioning goals.[10]

New York Criminal Court

Perhaps surprisingly, the criminal court actors pursue a similar goal of rehabilitating adolescents. Recall how criminal court workgroups bifurcate case processing into two phases, whereby they practice elements of a criminal justice model during the early stages but a juvenile justice model during the sentencing stage. As part of this bifurcation into what I have called a sequential model of justice, the courtroom workgroups pursue a goal of sentencing deserving youth (who are below the imprisonment threshold) to treatment-oriented sentences. This is best displayed by the comments of a criminal court youth part judge who calls himself a "child saver," stating that his goal is to "save as many children as possible."

This sentiment is shared in varying degrees by court actors in both criminal courts and in each professional role (prosecutors, defense attorneys, and judges). Though most criminal court actors do not phrase their goals as "rehabilitative" or "treatment oriented," they offer the goal of reduced punishment for youth relative to the sentences given to adults. Recall from chapter 4 the comments by criminal court actors, including prosecutors, that adolescents are less culpable for their offenses than adults; one prosecutor is even quoted in chapter 4 as saying that an adolescent who kills is not as culpable for the crime as an adult. As a result of this belief, criminal court workgroups actually pursue a juvenile justice model of rehabilitative treatment—or at least reduced punishment relative to the punitive sentences given to older offenders—relative to a criminal justice model of punitive sanctioning goals that one might anticipate.

This raises an interesting question: If criminal courtroom workgroups pursue rehabilitative sentencing goals, why is punishment more severe in the criminal court? Adolescents prosecuted in the criminal court are significantly more likely to be incarcerated, controlling for offense and offender characteristics. According to the criminal court judges themselves, this disparity in punishment severity is a result largely of the sentencing options available to them. Criminal court actors claim to be hampered by a lack of sentencing options, relative to the sentencing options of juvenile courts. These court actors expressed to me repeatedly their frustration over the disparity between noncustodial options in the juvenile and criminal courts. The criminal courts do not have as many liaisons with treatment agencies or professionals as juvenile courts, nor do they have as many treatment-oriented dispositions available to them. According to one criminal court judge:

> Family courts and juvenile courts have more options [than the criminal court]. They have more options to provide help in a number of ways, plus when the court's goal is not punishment, but rather rehabilitation, you can expedite cases. . . . Some kids that you would like to—some of these kids need what's called a structured setting, which is a euphemism for "well, they can't be on probation at home, because that's not a structured setting." It means there's not enough structure in the

family of this child, even coupled with a supervising probation officer to provide an appropriate place to supervise the kid. So then a structured setting to a family court judge could mean places that are short of jail, that provide all sorts of services that are not, you know, a jail. For me there is no such place. I have—there is nothing intermediate to me. . . . There is no state [treatment] facility [short of prison] where I can mandate the kid. A family court judge does have facilities where the judge says I'm mandating that someone take this kid. . . . The state doesn't have these intermediate things for these juveniles that we choose to treat as adults. (#16)

The relative lack of intermediate sentencing options is a severe constraint on the criminal court judges' decision making. It is interesting to note that this lack of punishment options for adolescents is one of the constraints that caused a perceived need for a juvenile court in the late nineteenth century. With no sentencing options that incorporated goals of individualized rehabilitation, and with few available punishments other than adult prisons or juvenile reform schools, Progressive-era reformers sought a separate court for adolescents that would allow treatments suited to each individual case.[11] Ironically, we have now partially dismantled the juvenile court by transferring increasing numbers of youth to criminal court, and again the judges responsible for punishing these youth feel constrained by a lack of intermediate sentencing options that may be available through the juvenile court but not the criminal court. In other words, as a result of contemporary transfer policies, we now face the same dilemma faced by judges over one hundred years ago.[12]

The lack of sentencing options available in criminal court is not only something that criminal court judges talk about—their actions, too, reflect this constraint. In response to their limited sentencing options, criminal court judges sometimes get creative. In chapters 3 and 4 I discussed how judges invite external sponsoring agencies into the court during sentencing in an attempt to incorporate principles of juvenile justice into case processing. Expanding the courtroom workgroup in this way is an intentional attempt to devise intermediate punishments for adolescents. Judges can demand that youth complete treatment programs with varying restrictions and requirements, using both inpatient and outpatient programs. The judges thus attempt to overcome their limited sentencing options by inviting external sponsoring agencies into court during the sentencing stage of case processing, but they report that this is insufficient to match their rehabilitative sentencing goals. Another creative response to the limited sentencing options is the admonishment I described in chapter 3. By admonishing adolescents with tough talk, and then sparing them from prison, judges attempt to add teeth to probationary sentences and thereby carve out an additional sentencing option that is short of prison but is more punitive than probation alone.[13]

Scaled Responses of Sanctioning Goals

To examine further the sanctioning goals of courtroom workgroups in each court type, I collected surveys from each interview respondent (see Appendix) that asked what, in their opinion, sentencing goals or ideas *should* influence sentencing of adolescents. In table 5.2 I report the mean responses to survey questions asking respondents to evaluate how important sentencing goals or ideas should be. The numbers in table 5.2 are the average responses to scaled questions of how valuable each sanctioning goal should be on a scale of one to four, with one being not important at all and four being very important. The respondents rated each goal independently, rather than ranking the goals relative to one another.

Table 5.2 illustrates that juvenile court actors value several goals in near equal proportions. Juvenile court decision makers express ideas that correspond to the statutory mandate governing the jurisdiction's sentencing criteria: an equal emphasis on both a defendant's future welfare and crime control. The only goals not rated as important by juvenile court actors are just deserts, retribution, and (not including prosecutors) maintaining moral order by establishing right from wrong. Contrary to the expectation that criminal court actors will hold more punitive goals, the criminal court respondents offer similar accounts of the sentencing criteria that should be prioritized as the juvenile court respondents. Mirroring the survey results from the juvenile court respondents, criminal court respondents rate almost all of the goal options as important. The only exceptions to this are retribution, and making an example of the offender as a general deterrent. Overall, it seems that both juvenile court actors and criminal courts actors follow goals of both punishment *and* rehabilitation when sentencing adolescents.

TABLE 5.2 *Survey Responses to Factors That Should Be Considered When Punishing Adolescent Offenders*

	Juvenile Court Mean Responses			Criminal Court Mean Responses		
	Judges	Defense Attorneys	Prosecutors	Judges	Defense Attorneys	Prosecutors
1. Offenders' Needs						
Treatment/ rehabilitation	4.0	3.9	3.5	4.0	4.0	3.0
Recognizing emotional or other needs of offender	3.0	3.7	3.0	2.5	3.4	2.4
2. Crime Prevention						
Preventing the individual from committing future crime	3.0	3.4	3.8	4.0	3.3	4.0
Making an example of the offender in order to prevent crime in general	3.0	1.9	3.3	1.5	1.1	2.0
Protecting the community	4.0	3.4	3.5	4.0	2.4	3.8
3. Punishment & Justice						
Retribution—"an eye for an eye"	1.0	1.1	1.5	1.0	1.0	1.4
Just deserts— providing the most appropriate legal punishment to fit the crime	2.0	2.3	3.3	3.0	1.9	2.8
Finding a morally fitting punishment	1.0	1.4	3.0	3.5	2.0	3.2
4. Due Process						
Fairness and equal justice for all defendants	4.0	4.0	3.8	4.0	3.4	4.0
Protecting the legal rights of the offender	4.0	3.7	3.3	3.0	3.9	3.2
5. Victims/Moral Order						
Looking after the rights and needs of the victims	4.0	2.7	3.5	3.5	2.1	3.6
Maintaining moral order by establishing right and wrong behavior	1.0	1.6	3.0	3.0	1.9	2.8

Older Offenders in Criminal Court

As I have been arguing, criminal court actors filter case processing to introduce principles of juvenile justice into the criminal court, and thereby accommodate their belief in the reduced culpability for youth. If this is true, then one would expect to find that adolescents in criminal court receive more lenient sentences than older offenders in criminal court. Though this project seeks to compare case processing of similarly situated adolescents across court types rather than within only the criminal court, I offer supplemental data to compare how adolescents fare in criminal court relative to adults in the same court. These data describe the court outcomes of all defendants in the three New York City counties from which the original quantitative sample comes, aged seventeen through twenty-one, prosecuted for aggravated assault, robbery, and burglary in 1992 and 1993. This supplemental sample was provided by New York's Department of Criminal Justice Services.

In figure 5.5, I show the proportion of cases resulting in incarceration, among those that were convicted for the original sample (age fifteen–sixteen) and for each age cohort from the supplemental data. To the left of the line is the cohort of the original sample, which serves as a reference against the new data set. This figure clearly demonstrates that as offenders age, incarceration becomes more likely. Given differences between these two data sets, I was unable to subject them to more stringent analyses; yet this supplemental analysis lends additional support to the thesis that adolescents in criminal court are still judged as if they are juveniles, not adults, and is consistent with the ideas I have developed throughout this book based on comparisons of adolescents in juvenile and criminal courts. Additionally, this result is consistent with prior studies finding that age has a curvilinear effect on sentencing among adults, with both young and older adults receiving less severe sentences than adults around age thirty.[14]

In contrast, a recent study by criminologists Megan Kurlychek and Brian Johnson used more recent and thorough data to show very different results.[15] Kurlychek and Johnson found that adolescents transferred to criminal court receive harsher sentences than older offenders (aged eighteen to twenty-four), in that adolescents are more likely to be incarcerated than eighteen to twenty-four-year-olds, and they serve longer prison terms when they are incarcerated. They rely on the focal concerns perspective to explain this relationship,[16] with the increased punishment

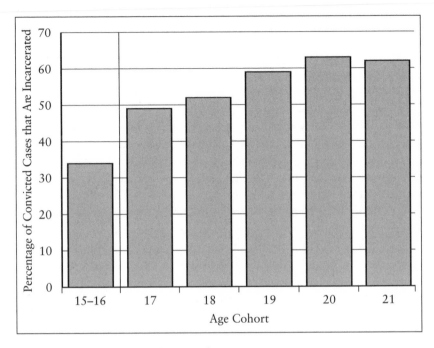

Fig. 5.5. Incarceration rates by age cohort.

for juveniles described as the result of either public pressure to get tough on supposed "juvenile super-predators," or because judges use juveniles' transfer to criminal court as a cue indicating their dangerousness and culpability. Admittedly, the descriptive bar graph I offer here is a far less robust test than their rigorous statistical analyses.

Despite the disparity between my argument (that youth in criminal court receive leniency because of their youthfulness) and the results of this recent study, the two sets of results may not be entirely contradictory. As Kurlychek and Johnson hypothesize, a prior decision to transfer these youth to criminal court may serve as a cue of the youths' dangerousness.[17] My data do not include cases with any prior transfer decision-making juncture, since the youth are either excluded from the juvenile court (at age fifteen) or above New York's overall age of majority (at age sixteen); as a result, New York criminal court judges know that youth are in criminal court because of the broad reach of the state's statute rather than because a prior decision maker perceived any particular individual as too dangerous for the juvenile court. Thus, the difference in findings may be the result of different modes of transfer. Additionally, the differences in our results may be because of differences in the areas studied. Kurlychek and Johnson analyze the entire population of cases in Pennsylvania's criminal court system (up to age twenty-four) from 1997 to 1999, rather than restricting their analyses to a particular area within the state. Given the diversity and large size of Pennsylvania—a state that includes Philadelphia (part of the Northeast corridor, and less than two hours from New York City), the traditionally blue-collar Pittsburgh, and rural areas in between—the effects of youthfulness on criminal court sentencing may vary significantly within the state. Kurlychek and Johnson do not control for regional variation in their analysis, so it is unclear whether this is the case. In contrast, the criminal court cases I analyze are all from the same area—New York City. It is entirely possible that their results are driven by a small number of outlying regions, and that an analysis of only Philadelphia cases might look very similar to the results I discuss above.

Conclusion

With regard to punishment severity, I find that adolescents prosecuted in criminal court are much more likely to be detained pretrial, given any court action (analogous to conviction), and sentenced to incarceration than adolescents in the juvenile court. And, among adolescents who are incarcerated, those in the criminal court receive much longer sentences than those in the juvenile court. These results are clear from both descriptive comparisons and (for likelihood of incarceration) multivariate analyses controlling for offense and offender characteristics.

In this chapter I also analyzed the effect of court type on sanctioning goals. Although the criminal and juvenile courts follow disparate statutory goals, with the New York criminal court statutes suggesting sanctioning goals of retribution and incapacitation, and the New Jersey juvenile court statutes suggesting goals of rehabilitation and community protection, I find that the individual court actors in both court types hold similar sentencing goals. That is, courtroom actors in both the juvenile court and the criminal court pursue a juvenile justice model of sanctioning goals by seeking to rehabilitate youth, or at least to offer reduced sentences relative to those given to older offenders.

This result may be surprising, given the robust effect of court type on sentencing, with much more severe punishments in the New York criminal court. I find that the mismatch between the sanctioning goals of court actors within the criminal court (holding a juvenile justice model of rehabilitative sanctioning goals) and the actual punishments prescribed by the criminal court (a criminal justice model of severe punishments) is, to some extent, a result of the constrained sentencing options within the criminal court. By finding similar sentencing goals, this research again contradicts taken-for-granted assumptions about the difference between juvenile and criminal justice. Again it seems that, at least with regard to the sentencing phase, and despite different punishments given, there are more similarities than assumed by policy makers and researchers alike between the approach used by criminal court and juvenile court actors in processing juvenile cases.

Again we see the awkwardness of contemporary transfer policies. Rather than maintaining the vast majority of adolescents in the juvenile court, which has greater expertise on adolescent criminality and where more intermediate punishments are available, New York prosecutes large numbers of fourteen- and fifteen-year-olds and all sixteen- and seventeen-year-olds in criminal court, where court actors want to pursue a juvenile justice model but feel constrained in their sentencing options.

It is important to keep in perspective the relative nature of these comparisons. Adolescents prosecuted in juvenile court are much less likely to be incarcerated than adolescents in criminal court, but this does not mean that the juvenile court has no bite to it. Court actors in both juvenile and criminal courts view incarceration as a last resort for adolescents, but one they are willing to prescribe for youth who have either committed serious violence or exhausted other, noncustodial options. These results contradict the arguments of some critics of the juvenile court, who portray it as an institution that gives no punishment.[18] Certainly, punishments are more likely and more severe in criminal court than juvenile court, but both court types are willing to prescribe incarceration in cases for which they cannot find alternative solutions. In other words, I find that the imprisonment threshold is lower in the criminal court than the juvenile court, but that youth can still be punished severely in the juvenile court.

The distinction between a juvenile justice model and a criminal justice model is more accurate when comparing punishment than when comparing formality of case processing or the evaluation of adolescents, in that youth in criminal court certainly receive harsher punishments than those in juvenile court. If we are only concerned with whether the courts hand down severe punishments, then these models of justice would be valid. But this distinction between criminal justice and juvenile justice is incompatible with the process of punishing youth and how and why court actors make punishment decisions. Criminal court decision makers *want* to prescribe rehabilitative punishments for youth and prevent most adolescents from going to prison, but their sentencing options are constrained.[19]

These differences in punishments between court types suggest that transfer policies matter. Laws mandating transfer of youth to criminal court are not merely symbolic, rhetorical, or solidarity-building rituals, nor are they only ways to enhance the perceived legitimacy of the juvenile justice system. This does not mean that transfer laws cannot perform these functions; they can and they do. Additionally, however, by leading to more severe penalties for transferred youth than for youth in juvenile court, transfer laws have a real impact on how we punish adolescents. As a result, we have a system for prosecuting adolescents that works in off-setting ways. Criminal court decision makers view transferred youth as adolescents who are less culpable for their offenses than adults, and they reintroduce elements of juvenile justice to criminal court case processing. But then the limited sentencing options result in harsher penalties for youth in criminal court. These penalties seem to be less than those given to older offenders in the criminal court, but still much more severe than what the juvenile court gives to similar offenders.

The conclusion in this chapter also demonstrate the importance of court context. Throughout my analyses I have shown that the type of court (either juvenile or criminal) matters much more than the local legal culture or organization of court communities. Yet organizational and structural context still matters substantially, as we have seen in this chapter. Sentencing patterns are influenced by the facts that counseling programs and other external sponsoring agencies are more deeply embedded in juvenile courts than in criminal courts, and that there are more non-custodial options available to juvenile court decision makers than to criminal court decision makers.[20]

6

Children in an Adult World

Over one hundred years following the creation of the juvenile court, an institution made necessary by the growing realization that adolescents are different from adults and require different responses when they commit crimes, we are now prosecuting an increasing number of adolescents in criminal courts. We refer to this practice as the act of "prosecuting juveniles as adults," but it is unclear whether these youth are in fact dealt with as if they are equal to adults.

Based on the existing literature and political rhetoric, one would assume that different models of justice—the juvenile justice model and the criminal justice model—guide case processing in the two types of courts. In the preceding chapters I assessed the validity of these models of justice, which leads me to conclude that the prosecution and punishment of adolescents in the New Jersey juvenile court fits the juvenile justice model very well. In contrast, I find that criminal courts approximate a criminal justice model during the early stage of case processing, and a juvenile justice model during the late stage for all dimensions other than punishment severity (formality, evaluation, and sentencing goals). Because the criminal court reflects a hybrid form of justice that incorporates elements of both juvenile and criminal justice at different stages of case processing, I call this a sequential model of justice.

The results of my research beg the question whether sequential justice is a product of prosecuting adolescents, or if it is simply a feature of criminal court case processing for all defendants. It is possible that adult defendants as well are prosecuted in a formal environment in which only offense severity is considered during early stages of case processing, yet during sentencing the court operates with a less formal style, considers characteristics of offenders as mitigating evidence, and pursues a rehabilitative sentencing goal. This possibility acknowledges that laws are unable to repress the application of substantive justice within criminal courts. As prior research demonstrates, formal rational guidelines intended by policy makers to limit court actors' discretion get filtered by court actors in ways that allow them to introduce substantive concerns. In other words, judges, prosecutors, and defense attorneys find room within rigid procedural laws to do what they think is right based on individual defendants, rather than blindly following laws that limit their discretion.

There is no doubt that, to some extent, substantive justice permeates sentencing in all criminal courts. But the sequential model of justice I have described is different from this more widespread phenomenon. The sequential model is distinguished by its understanding of youthfulness, which guides the criminal court workgroups. During the sentencing stage, court actors do not simply take into consideration who the defendant is, or whether he or she is employed. They also look at adolescent defendants' development, family lives, and social and educational backgrounds. They bring in social workers to determine if the defendant might be helped by treatment or counseling. They allow notions of youthfulness to guide sentencing for all but last-resort cases, considerations that are not taken into account for adults.

In chapter 5 I briefly presented data comparing sentencing of fifteen- and sixteen-year-olds with sentencing of older offenders. These data suggest that at least the outcomes of cases are not the same for all defendants in the criminal court, and that adolescents are punished less severely than adults. More convincingly, however, the qualitative data I have presented throughout this book illustrate that the methods and reasons for a sequential model of justice hinge on perceptions of youthfulness. The "child-saving" orientation of criminal court actors suggests that the case processing of adolescents is different from that of adults. In their statements to me, the criminal court decision makers cite adolescents' immaturity and reduced culpability as their reason for evaluating individual characteristics of offenders and trying to offer rehabilitative sentences. Their actual behaviors bear this out as well, based on my court observations. Though case processing of adult defendants in the criminal court is bifurcated into two distinct stages, the details of these stages are likely to be different from those for adolescents. This empirical question must be answered by data on both processes and outcomes of adult defendants.

As with any case study, it is reasonable to ask the extent to which my results are generalizable or true in other states that prosecute adolescents in both juvenile and criminal courts. It is likely that the results are in fact generalizable, because the factors that shape the similarities and differences between the New Jersey juvenile court and the New York criminal court are likely to be found in other jurisdictions as well. The method of transfer to the criminal court that I examined is perhaps the most rapidly proliferating method nationally, as other states have recently enacted transfer provisions that resemble New York's 1978 Juvenile Offender Law. Greater numbers of states have recently lowered their jurisdictional boundaries between juvenile and criminal courts and also excluded greater numbers of offenders from the juvenile court by statutory exclusion.[1] In addition, the sentencing scheme in the New York criminal court —fixed sentencing with room for judicial discretion (by giving Youthful Offender status)—is similar to that of criminal courts in many other states and is increasingly common in criminal court prosecution of adolescents.[2] My results from the New Jersey juvenile court are likely to resemble results of juvenile courts in other locations as well. By retaining most adolescents rather than transferring them to the criminal court, and by maintaining a dual statutory purpose clause emphasizing both treatment and punishment, the New Jersey juvenile court has maintained a traditional juvenile justice system. This court is therefore a good example of "juvenile justice" as referred to by scholars and policy makers, and serves as an excellent comparison with the criminal court prosecution of adolescents.

Moreover, many of the similarities I find across the two court types are likely to be applicable to other jurisdictions. My results show that these similarities—especially the similar model of justice during the sentencing stage—are the result primarily of common perceptions of youth as less culpable for crime than adults, regardless of court type. Criminal court judges, prosecutors, and defense attorneys subscribe to notions about juveniles and juvenile delinquency that are similar to some of the ideas that led to the creation of the juvenile justice system. Given the resilience of the belief in the reduced culpability of adolescents, and its apparent consistency both among different court actors and over time, one might expect this culturally rooted idea to cause a strain for other criminal court communities prosecuting adolescents as well.

Court Context and Organizational Filtering

In contrast to earlier research on court communities,[3] I find very few differences between individual courts within the New Jersey juvenile court and the New York criminal court. The county-level courts within each court type are very similar to one another regarding formality of case processing, evaluation of adolescents, and sanctioning goals and punishment severity. Hence, on one level, my research fails to support the argument that local court contexts and particular modes of interaction among individual courtroom workgroups shape case processing and punishment. Instead, I find that the similarities created by a widespread conception of youthfulness outweigh any differences caused by the disparate organization of court communities.

Yet this is what one might expect, given the parameters of this study. To some extent, the extensive similarities between juvenile and criminal courts may be a product of my research site selection. As I discussed in chapter 2, I compared six counties that are adjacent to one another and comprise a single metropolitan area. The New Jersey and New York City counties in my study all have similar economic, demographic, political, and criminal justice system characteristics. This is intentional; by holding these broader factors constant, I was able to assess the impact of distinctions of a juvenile or a criminal court. As a result, I have made different types of comparisons than previous studies on court context, most of which compare jurisdictions with varying social characteristics. Sociologist Jeffery Ulmer, for example, in his book *Social Worlds of Sentencing,* compares counties he renames "Metro," "Rich," and "Southwest," which vary significantly among economic, demographic, and political dimensions.[4] If my research compared counties that varied along these dimensions, it is likely that I would have found greater county differences as well. Furthermore, it is important to note that the prior literature on local court contexts considers cases of adults, not adolescents. The distinctions between my results and those in earlier research may be a result of looking specifically at adolescent offenders' cases. It is possible, for example, that concerns of youthfulness and reduced culpability that guide case processing across courts that prosecute adolescents in both jurisdictions might mask contextual distinctions that arise during cases of older defendants.

Even though my results somewhat contradict the literature on local court contexts, the insights informing this body of literature help explain what I find when comparing juvenile and criminal courts. As I noted in chapter 5, the contextual differences between juvenile and criminal courts —particularly the familiarity of external sponsoring agencies in juvenile court—help bring about a higher punishment rate in criminal than in juvenile courts. Furthermore, as I discuss above, much of this body of research demonstrates how courtroom workgroups "filter" externally imposed policies such as sentencing guidelines by enacting these policies in ways that help them meet organizational imperatives[5] or broader structural and cultural scripts.[6] This insight explains why I find a sequential justice model in the criminal court. During the early stage of case processing, criminal court workgroups satisfy their obligation to follow legally prescribed due process rules, and to protect defendants through adversarial proceedings. Yet during sentencing, the criminal court workgroups filter case processing by implementing their conception that adolescents are less culpable than adults. Such a filtering process is not necessary in the juvenile court, because statutory goals and procedures allow courtroom workgroup members to acknowledge and follow their beliefs of reduced culpability for youth throughout each stage of case processing.

Public Perceptions and Support for Transfer Laws

If the cultural conception of adolescents as less responsible than adults is so prevalent, then why are transfer laws so popular? Despite the fact that transfer laws do not fit society's conception of youthful immaturity, nearly every state has changed its laws to transfer more youth to criminal courts. This apparent contradiction is the result of a complex interaction between race- and class-based perceptions of adolescents, and misinformation about juvenile crime.

According to the study by Daniel Mears that I discussed in chapter 1, the public overwhelmingly supports the transfer of some criminally offending youth to criminal court. In particular, Mears found that 87 percent of a survey sample supports the transfer of youth charged with violent crime to criminal court.[7] Accountability of criminal offenders, juvenile or not, is popular social policy. The popularity of juvenile transfer fits with what David Garland calls the "culture of control," a contemporary preoccupation with crime and social order that has led to increasing imprisonment.[8] Citizens' fear of crime and desire to hold offenders accountable in increasingly severe ways seem to demand harsher sanctions for youth as well as for adults.

Public support for transfer laws, however, is not only about punitiveness. It is also a rejection of the idea that immaturity should matter for delinquent youth and an acceptance of the idea that they are still criminals who must be punished. Support for transfer to criminal court assumes that youth who commit serious crimes are adultlike, or that, as the slogan goes, if they are old enough to do the crime, they are old enough to do the time. This is a form of the "hurried child" thesis, the idea that children are growing up faster now than in previous generations. Some scholars have gone so far as to suggest that the social category of childhood is disappearing because of increased accessibility to information through television and the Internet.[9] Following several high-profile murders by youth between the ages of eleven and fourteen—youth such as Lionel Tate—others have argued that these horrible murders suggest the erosion of immaturity and reduced culpability among youth.[10]

A second, very different perspective on developmental trends is offered in a recent article by sociologists Frank Furstenberg et al., who argue that a new life stage has emerged in the past several decades: early adulthood. Early adulthood involves the delay of full adulthood because young adults in their late teens and early twenties take longer than those in previous generations to prepare for adult life, as marked by education, employment, financial independence, and the ability to support a family:

> It takes much longer to make the transition to adulthood today than decades ago, and arguably longer than it has at any time in America's history. Figure 2, based on the 1960 and 2000 U.S. censuses, illustrates the large decline in the percentage of young adults who, by age 20 or 30, have completed all of the traditionally-defined major adult transitions (leaving home, finishing school, becoming financially independent, getting married and having a child).[11]

Judgments about adolescents growing up either earlier or later seem to be context dependent. As Furstenberg et al. illustrate, a detached view of trends in behaviors shows that, overall, young adults are in fact increasingly delaying adult roles and responsibilities. But this of course does not prevent nostalgic adults from lamenting the perceived adult-like behaviors of today's youth, in a way that has probably always happened and always will. The evidence offered by Furstenberg et al. pertains mainly to middle- and upper-class activities, such as going to college and delaying the onset of career and family in order to prepare for an upwardly mobile career. In contrast, in seeing acts of violence as evidence that adolescents are acting more like adults than in years past, we tend to view the actions of lower-class youth.

These generalizations about behaviors of lower-class youth versus middle-and upper-class youth are widely held and inform common perceptions of youthfulness. For example, one of the ideas commonly expressed by the court actors I interviewed was that many of the youth who appear in court have been forced to develop "street smarts." These youth are exposed to the harsh realities of life that come with poverty and living in urban blight, in contrast to the sheltered youth who live in middle-and upper-class suburbs. Court actors claim that, although these "street smart" youth are not necessarily more mature, they are wiser than other adolescents, and have been forced to grow up earlier in some ways. It is clear that poor youth living under bad conditions are exposed to a number of stimuli from which more sheltered youth are protected, but these poor youth might also be denied enriching experiences and the opportunity to grow and develop in a nurturing, protective environment. Those living in poverty may even be behind their wealthier peers developmentally. Having time to grow in a healthy, safe environment might help the wealthier youth mature, while the stresses of urban poverty might hinder the development of the poor youth. In contrast, court actors, like most other people, see poor youth as wiser, and in that way as closer to adulthood than other youth. In other words, to some extent, poverty is used as an indicator of the loss of childhood status.

Race and ethnicity might also shape views of youthfulness. In the book, *Bad Kids*, Barry Feld argues that racial prejudice is behind the growing punitiveness of the juvenile court.[12] A movement away from rehabilitation and toward punishment in the juvenile court coincided with the increasing concentration of arrests among African American youth. As a result, juvenile courts became more punitive as a means of punishing "other people's children," while diverting delinquent white youth from the court. Feld's argument is consistent with the social threat hypothesis, which argues that juvenile and criminal justice systems respond punitively to the perceived social threat of a large minority underclass. Criminologists Robert Sampson and John Laub, for example, find a significant connection between the size of minority communities and the punitiveness of juvenile courts in those areas.[13] In other words, policy and decision makers may feel threatened by African Americans or other minority groups and thus respond with greater use of formal social control.

These arguments apply directly to society's uncertainty over how to attribute youthfulness to adolescents. With these prior arguments in mind, it seems likely that youth of color are perceived differently from white youth, as if they are either more mature or less deserving of the assumption of reduced culpability. Given that racial and ethnic minority youth are far more likely than white youth to be transferred to criminal court, these youth are denied the protection of the juvenile court, at least at the policy level.

But at the individual level, the attribution of full responsibility seems more difficult. This is exactly what I find in the New York criminal court. Although policy makers have no qualms about prosecuting vast numbers of youth as adults, the court actors who prosecute and punish these individual youth still view them as youth, not as adult predators. This makes sense when one considers the contextual cues available to courtroom workgroups that are not available to policy makers. Legislatures responding to a perceived youth crime problem are dealing with very different cues than a judge who has firsthand knowledge about a particular case. Seeing an actual fourteen-year-old in criminal court and hearing about his or her childish escapades might make anyone think twice about levels of culpability.

Public support for prosecuting youth in criminal courts also seems to be based on an abstract idea that is outweighed by concerns grounded in particular problems. Though Mears has found that the public supports transfer to criminal court—results also found in other studies[14]—other research also finds that the public overwhelmingly prefers treatment and prevention for adolescent offenders over incarceration.[15] Although the public wants to get tough on juvenile offenders, it also wants to give them second chances and offer them rehabilitation rather than punishment when possible. Moreover, when survey respondents who support the abstract idea of transfer are given contextual information about juvenile defendants, such as information on the defendants' backgrounds and mental abilities, or available treatment options for dealing with these youth, support for transfer drops considerably.[16] Clearly, transfer to criminal court is a desired option when presented as an abstract idea; but when offered other, more practical potential solutions to juvenile crime, the public prefers rehabilitation and reduced punishments. Unfortunately, however, only these abstract and punitive ideas seem to be governing policy makers' decisions, as illustrated by the recent growth in transfer laws across the United States.

Misperceptions about juvenile crime might also fuel rash judgments about adolescent culpability. Despite plummeting juvenile crime rates since the early 1990s, a majority of the general public believes that juvenile crime is on the rise, at least according to a 1999 survey conducted by the Building Blocks for Youth organization.[17] A society that believes that the juvenile crime problem is rising will support more punitive policies than one that knows juvenile crime has been decreasing for ten years. And, when scared of violent and predatory young thugs—"super-predators," as some have called them[18]—the public will understandably react with a lack of empathy rather than request policies that take into account adolescents' immaturity and reduced culpability.

It is a different story, however, for the judges, prosecutors, and defense attorneys who interact with these adolescents. These courtroom workgroup members might believe that transfer policies are a good idea in principle, but then view individual youth with empathy and an understanding that they are far from fully developed, cognitively and socially. This leads to the filtering of case processing that I have described throughout this book. The proliferation of transfer policies does not necessarily mean that policy makers and the public no longer believe that adolescents are different from adults. They are motivated by race-based and class-based generalizations of youth, and by misinformation about the juvenile crime problem. They also have the luxury of dealing with this policy in principle, rather than applying it to individual adolescents with whose backgrounds they become familiar.

Race/Ethnicity, Social Class, Sex, and the Prosecution of Adolescents

As I discussed in chapter 2, an important set of topics has been underdeveloped in this book because of characteristics of the areas I study: the potential impact of race/ethnicity, sex, and social class on the prosecution and punishment of adolescents. The following sections discuss whether racial, gender, or class biases shape the processes and outcomes of prosecuting youth in juvenile and criminal courts.

Race and Ethnicity

Because there is so little variation among offenders, I am very limited in how I can address this important issue. With so few white youth, so few middle-class and upper-class youth, and so few females in court, it would be unwise to base my analyses on comparisons between the cases that appear in court. However, though my analyses do not focus directly on the impact of defendants' race, ethnicity, sex, or social class on the prosecution and punishment of adolescents, they do imply that a racial screening process occurs prior to adolescents' appearances in court. During my eighteen months of court observations, I observed only three cases of white adolescents across both court types. The small number of white youths hamper comparisons between the treatment of whites and minority adolescents, yet this lack of diversity among the populations of defendants itself suggests that race might have a significant impact during earlier decision-making junctures (arrest and case filing).

Previous research has shown that racial and ethnic minorities fare worse in courts than whites, especially when decision makers have discretion to consider blameworthiness. Consider, for example, research by sociologists George Bridges and Sara Steen on evaluation of juvenile offenders by juvenile court probation officers. Bridges and Steen found that when probation officers assess juvenile offenders and make sentencing recommendations for the court, they give very different attributions of offenses for white and African American youth. Crimes of white youth are attributed to external factors, which explain their offenses as a result of external conditions such as a negative family life or prior abuse, and mitigate the blame attributed to these youth. In contrast, crimes of African American youth are more likely to be attributed to internal factors, which explain their crimes as the result of negative personality traits.[19]

It is likely that racially unequal attribution mechanisms operate among police, prosecutors, and the probation officers who decide which cases to prosecute. The vast over-representation of minorities in both the New Jersey juvenile court and the New York criminal court suggests that a racial filtering process occurs prior to court processing, but I am unable to test this possible result with my data. Of course, it is possible that few white youth commit crimes, and that the rarity of their appearances in court is representative of their actual offending rates. Yet this would contradict previous evidence illustrating that racial screening of juveniles occurs often.[20] Moreover, though many researchers conclude that racial and ethnic minority youth do commit more offenses overall than white youth,[21] self-report studies demonstrate clear disparities between the rates of offending and the risks of arrest faced by white and non-white youth.[22]

Despite the lack of racial diversity among adolescent defendants in the courts I studied, I am able to comment on the courtroom workgroups members' ideas about racial over-representation. During my interviews, I asked all court actors why they thought there were so many more minority than white adolescents in court. To my surprise, I received only three different general responses to this question: first and most often, demographics; second, social conditions; and third, a racial filtering process by the police. Some respondents offered more than one explanation, others only one.

The demographic view of minority over-representation—the most commonly stated view—is that there are so many more minorities in court than whites because the areas presided over by the courts are home to more minorities. In truth, according to the 2000 Census, the New York counties' populations are 30.1 percent (Brady County) and 41.2 percent (Brown County) white, and the New Jersey counties' populations are 44.5 percent (Pierce County) and 55.5 percent (Maxwell County) white. These numbers illustrate that the urban counties in which the courts are situated do contain large proportions of racial and ethnic minorities, but these percentages are nowhere near the racial composition of the courts' defendants. In the data I analyzed in chapter 5, 86.7 percent of New Jersey cases are racial or ethnic minorities, and 95.0 percent of New York cases. Therefore, this demographic explanation can hardly account for the full extent of the racial and ethnic disproportionality.

The second explanation given for minority over-representation is that minorities commit more crimes than whites. When respondents offer this explanation, they do so by couching it in social-structural terms. They state that because of poverty and other negative living conditions (e.g., environmental influences, lack of employment opportunities), minorities are more likely to engage in crime than relatively more advantaged white adolescents:

> I think the social conditions are just ripe for producing criminal activity. I think that a lot of these kids don't have hope for themselves or their community for the future. They don't see how they figure in the grand scheme of things. I'm just speculating. They don't see how they can. I think that for some reason drugs seem to find their way disproportion-

ately to these communities and that in turn promotes further criminal activity. Guns seem to find their way disproportionately to these communities and that promotes further criminal activity. I don't think the images that these kids are exposed to through music, videos and movies, which they are the target audiences, help the situation at all. Much of the violence you see in these movies and videos glorify the conduct that land these kids into the youth house, the court and ultimately in [the State Training School]. (#14—prosecutor)

As I stated above, prior research comparing self-reported juvenile crime rates to arrest rates suggest that though youth of color might commit more crimes than white youth, the differences in their group crime rates are nowhere near the level of disparity among arrests seen in these jurisdictions.

The third explanation is of a racial filtering process, which is precisely what prior research would lead one to expect.[23] According to one prosecutor, this occurs on a geographic basis, with police in the suburban areas of the county (in which more white adolescents live) handling cases informally rather than through official arrest:

Interviewer: Why do you think there are more minority adolescents coming before the court than white adolescents?

Prosecutor: Because the police departments selectively enforce the laws. I've been told that by police officers. That they have been told in these certain towns to look the other way, to take the kids who are caught doing drugs home to their parents with a stern warning, to refer the kids to [diversionary program]. . . . Then I have other cops in another small town, a very nice town, that because they want New Yorkers to come and live in these suburbs and bedroom communities of New Jersey, they don't want to move into a place where the kids . . . where there are gangs. . . . There are Bloods and Crips here but they don't want to move to that. You can't sell them houses if they know they are going to move to that. You can sell them houses if they don't know about that.

Interviewer: So they divert them [away from formal arrest]?

Prosecutor: They give them a stern talking to, they send them home with a warning or they take them home. They call their parents to the police department but they never spend the night in jail. They really have to screw up to spend a night in youth house. (#15)

Among the thirty-two interviews I conducted, there are no evident divisions along professional positions or jurisdictions with respect to respondents' explanations for this over-representation. Defense attorneys, prosecutors, and judges give fairly similar answers to the question of minority over-representation, as do juvenile court and criminal court actors. These responses illustrate the courtroom workgroup members' belief that the prosecution and punishment of adolescents in juvenile and criminal courts are not influenced by race or ethnicity. Even those interview respondents who acknowledge the influence of race on the justice process attribute this influence to case screening by police before court involvement.

Gender

In addition to race, my findings have important implications for understanding the impact of gender on the processes and outcomes of prosecuting adolescents. Due to the small numbers of females prosecuted in the jurisdictions I studied (see chapter 5), it is difficult for me to make conclusions about the effect of gender. However, the fact that defendants' families participate in juvenile court hearings begs the question of whether a familial style of justice—in which paternal roles are enforced—might be exerted differently on males and females.

Criminologist Meda Chesney-Lind's work on how girls are disadvantaged in the juvenile justice process would suggest that a paternalistic style of justice would indeed have disproportionately negative consequences for girls. Chesney-Lind argues that girls are policed for acting in gender-role inappropriate ways, or to protect their purity and innocence. As a result, girls are more often arrested, prosecuted, and punished for status offenses (e.g., running away, curfew violations) than boys. Moreover, their offenses, especially running away and engaging in prostitution to support themselves, often are survival strategies used to escape domestic and sexual abuse.[24] The fact that juvenile courts mandate parental participation may result in a more paternal mode of dealing with youth, which is likely to be punitive to girls in an effort either to protect them or to correct their behaviors, which are seen as gender-inappropriate. As a result, it is possible that the sex of the defendant matters more in the juvenile court than in the criminal court.

Despite my inability to compare the actual effect of gender across the juvenile and criminal courts, I am able to comment on the courtroom workgroup members' perceptions of how a defendant's sex relates to case processing. During my interviews, I asked each respondent whether boys and girls who commit similar crimes should be dealt with similarly or differently. All respondents answered that gender should not be a factor in determining court treatment. However, many also state that although gender should not have an independent effect, it often does. Respondents suggest that girls have a potential advantage over boys with regard to court dispositions. Girls who care for children may be more likely to receive discounted sentences than either boys or girls without children. Whether or not a defendant cares for a child is a factor often discussed off the record during bench conferences and may influence the decision to incarcerate. According to one criminal court prosecutor:

> *Interviewer*: Do you think males and females who commit similar crimes should be dealt with similarly?
> *Prosecutor*: Yes, and it really annoys me that if there is an unfairness in the criminal justice system, it's not necessarily racial, it's gender. I think that girls get, particularly in front of male judges, more lenient treatment. . . . I think they tend to be more lenient. They feel sorry for them. "Look at her, my God, she's pregnant." These are the kinds of comments they make so it's very obvious. Particularly for the male judges, that they have a difficulty and it may be because they don't see enough. (#17)

According to one juvenile court defense attorney as well, "The girls will always get a better break." Thus, gender may influence decision making, with girls—especially girls who are pregnant or care for children—receiving a discount in both jurisdictions. The multivariate analyses I discussed in chapter 5 support this conclusion, as these results show that girls are significantly less likely than boys to be incarcerated (see Appendix).

In addition, in my interviews I asked respondents whether there are any significant differences between the boys and girls who appear before the court. A majority of respondents answer that the girls tend to be more violent and less compliant with court sanctions than the boys:

> Girls have a tendency to . . . and somebody said this to me when I was first down there and I thought that was sort of a sexist thing to say but it seems as though the girls tend . . . have a tendency to getting involved in more of a minimal sort of offense and then having problems dealing

with the resolution of that. That is to say, they will get picked up or have a fight or some kind of marijuana or something minimal like that but then they just won't do what they are supposed to after. They won't listen. There will be problems at home. There is a very tense relationship between mother and daughter. Daughter is going out at all hours and not listening at home and grades are bad and hanging around with the wrong people or what the parent perceives to be the wrong people. And this is what someone told me when I first came down here. Girls are the worst clients to deal with. (#26—defense attorney)

Quite honestly, I find the girls to be more . . . I don't know what the word is. I don't want to say "vicious" but the girls just take things more personally and attack one another. We have a lot of girls with the slashings. If you sit in court and you see . . . you don't have girls necessarily committing robberies or burglaries for the most part. The girls are committing assaults and they are usually on girls that they know and they're usually over boys. . . . They don't slash the boy, they slash each other, because they are both pregnant by the same guy, which is very interesting that [this] is occurring at this time in our society. So there's a viciousness there. And a vindictiveness that you don't necessarily see with the males. (#17—prosecutor)

Comments similar to these are offered by several of the respondents, both male and female, and in both court types.

It is possible that, instead of female defendants actually being more violent overall, respondents assume that the girls who are violent represent the norm rather than the exception; this could occur if they find violent girls more shocking than violent boys, making these cases more noticeable. Alternatively, the respondents may be correct and the few girls in court may actually be more violent, overall, than the boys in court. It is true that over the past ten years the proportion of female juvenile arrests has grown. Overall, this is because the number of girls arrested has decreased less than the decrease among boys. However, from 1993 to 2002, arrest rates among girls for aggravated assault increased 7 percent, and for simple assault 41 percent; for boys, aggravated assault arrest rates decreased 29 percent and simple assault rates increased only 4 percent.[25] Thus it is possible that girls are now committing a larger proportion of juvenile violence than in years past. It is also possible that court actors are correct in stating that the acts committed by girls are more vicious now than in years past, and more vicious than acts committed by boys. This conclusion does receive some support, in that some research does find that girls engage in more aggression over relationships than boys, and that serious female offenders may have more serious mental health problems than male offenders.[26] But it is still difficult to assume that court actors perceive cases in gender-neutral ways; rather than girls actually being more vicious in their crimes than boys, it seems plausible that court actors attribute more emotion to their violence than to the perceived instrumental violence of boys. Furthermore, if the cases of girls that appear in court indeed involve more violence, it could easily be the result of pretrial screening mechanisms diverting most female nonviolent cases away from court. Again, to examine this more thoroughly, one would need to observe a larger number of cases with female defendants, and a wider range of offenses.

Social Class

With regard to social class, there appears to be very little variation among the youth that come before either the juvenile or criminal courts. Almost all youth in both court types are represented by public defenders; in order to qualify for a public defender, one must submit financial documents and be classified as indigent. By my estimate, this determination is made for at least 90 to 95 percent of all defendants whose cases I observed. This is consistent with the lack of diversity among both racial/ethnic groups, and to a slightly lesser extent, with sex. It seems that in the greater New York City area, both juvenile and criminal courts are institutions that deal almost exclusively with poor youth of color.

As I discussed in chapter 4, court decision makers in both the juvenile and the criminal court have ideas of "normal" delinquents. A normal delinquent is poor, has little opportunity to achieve professional or financial success, and lives in a disadvantaged community. It is likely that this perception of the normal delinquent causes a social-class bias in both court types. Youth who deviate from this stereotype by their middle-class status (e.g., living in a relatively wealthy community, hoping to go to college, and having professional parents) will be perceived as having the potential to achieve professional and financial success. For an adolescent with high potential, court actors are likely to see delinquency as aberrational. They may also be more likely to protect such an adolescent from the harm caused by conviction or incarceration. I demonstrated throughout the book that court actors in both court types seek to protect the future welfare of all deserving youth—that is, of all youth who are below an imprisonment threshold. It is likely that middle-class youth will appear to have greater future potential than normal delinquents, and as a result they will be judged more leniently. We see this in chapter 4, with the juvenile court case of the adolescent who had plans to go to college; the judge dismisses this case in order to prevent this youth from having a criminal record.

This makes sense to court actors. Rather than perceiving this mode of decision making as being influenced by a social-class bias, court actors operationalize their behaviors as an attempt to help those who have the potential to succeed, not as punishing others for being poor. But if the marker of potential is really a sign of social class, then the courts will be biased against poor youth. Because both the juvenile court and the criminal court consider a youth's potential future welfare when deciding on appropriate sentences, a social-class bias is likely to occur in both court types.

Future Research Directions

Continued research efforts can expand on this book in a number of ways. First, to help establish the generalizability of my results, future research needs to include a greater number of jurisdictions, studying the prosecution of adolescents across criminal and juvenile courts using the dimensions I have established in this project. In particular, it is important for future research to evaluate the impact on case processing of the individual judges who preside over adolescent offenders' cases. Judges in both court types exercise a significant amount of discretion, especially during the sentencing phase of case processing—it is during this phase that the criminal court judges depart from a criminal justice model of case processing and put in motion the juvenile justice practices that correspond to their attitudes and beliefs.

Second, as I discussed above, it is important to study a greater number of courts, especially courts in varying social contexts. By adding greater variation of court context, further research could better evaluate the importance of local legal culture. Though I do not find that different court contexts bring about significant distinctions among courts within each court type, this result could be because I look specifically at cases of adolescents. Research that considers cases of both adults and adolescents could test the possibility that local legal culture matters more for cases of adults than for cases of adolescent defendants.

Third, future researchers need to speak to a greater number of courtroom decision makers. Surveys sent to large numbers of people, assessing their views of adolescents and whether adolescents are fully culpable for their criminal behaviors, would be very helpful. These surveys could be sent to non-court actors as well, to compare the attitudes of courtroom workgroup members to widely held conceptions of childhood and culpability. The results I find here—of criminal court workgroup members holding juvenile justice conceptions of adolescents' maturity and culpability—can guide further analyses into perceptions of culpability.

Fourth, it is important for researchers to study a greater number of decision-making points. Future research could compare the models of justice reflected by criminal and juvenile courts regarding level of formality and evaluation of defendants at other decision-making junctures, such as arrest or case filing. The decision to arrest and the process of screening cases for prosecution are particularly important, as they establish the pool of cases that reaches the court. As prior research notes, it is likely that racial filtering processes during these early stages of decision making are responsible for the over-representation of minority youth observed in many courts, including the ones I studied.[27] This finding of discrimination in earlier research might be due to the level of formality or method of evaluating adolescents at different decision-making points, thus my results will be helpful in guiding future research on other stages of case processing.

7

Putting the Genie Back in the Bottle

Lessons for Policy

Amazingly, over the past two-and-a-half decades, states across the United States have passed transfer laws without any comparisons of how adolescents are prosecuted across juvenile and criminal courts. Though we already have some evidence that transfer may not achieve the outcomes we wish for or are promised by policy makers—most importantly that these laws fail to deter crime—these laws were passed with an insufficient understanding of what happens when adolescents face criminal court judges. The research that led to this book lets us evaluate the worthiness of transfer policies and illustrates that this popular brand of juvenile justice policy is counterproductive, inefficient, and does not match the broadly shared cultural norms that inform court workers' actions.

The results of this research have significant implications for understanding the organization of criminal and juvenile courts, as well as the impact of prosecuting and punishing adolescents in criminal court. These results challenge an often repeated but rarely examined hypothesis that adolescents transferred to the criminal court are subjected to a criminal model of justice. I show that there are greater similarities between the two court types than previously assumed, and that the veracity of these previous assumptions depends on the stage of case processing: during the early stage of case processing, the two court types do practice distinct models of justice, but they converge somewhat during the sentencing stage. Thus, the contrasts academics and policy makers assume to exist between juvenile and criminal courts may be misleading.

This book adds to an emerging picture of contemporary punishment regimes as described by other scholars. For example, in describing the "culture of control," David Garland has shown that a new penal regime has displaced earlier ways of thinking about and punishing offenders.[1] One result is mass incarceration. Here, I showed how one particular policy (transfer to the criminal court) within a broader culture of control has an effect that is both similar and different from the punitive regime described by Garland. That is, despite the increased levels of punishment that result from jurisdictional transfer, transfer to the criminal court does not subject adolescents to a vastly different model of justice than the one experienced in the juvenile court (when considering other dimensions of juvenile and criminal justice). Hence, my results add to current research and theory by describing the effect of this punitive regime on the prosecution and punishment of a particular group of offenders: adolescents.

Furthermore, this project adds to the organizational literature on courts and court contexts. My results suggest that by examining counties in which courts are situated in very different social, political, and economic contexts, earlier studies may exaggerate the dissimilarities between most local legal cultures. When comparing courts in adjacent areas matched by their social structural characteristics, I find similarity among attitudes, patterns of interaction, and other local legal cultural factors. Thus, prior research may tend to focus too little on shared beliefs among court actors across court contexts, especially in the cases of adolescent defendants.

Perhaps most importantly, though, this study reminds us that widely shared views of youth and youthfulness determine what happens in court. The forum in which we prosecute adolescents is not only guided by practical policy considerations, but also by our cultural understandings. The original juvenile court was not created until we accepted the idea that juveniles are different from adults. Removing large numbers of cases from juvenile court does not mean that we have given up on this belief. Granted, juvenile transfer policies—which are guided by misperceptions, race-based views of solutions to juvenile crime, and political and organizational expedience[2]—discount the distinction between juveniles and adults. But transfer policies are "filtered" by the court actors who must apply these policies to individual adolescents. As a result, even transferred youth are still viewed as youth, not as small adults or criminals.

In addition to developing better understandings of how courts work and of cultural understandings of youthfulness, this book also contributes to policy debates concerning transfer of youth to criminal court. I challenge taken-for-granted assumptions of policy makers about the distinctions between juvenile and criminal courts that prosecute and punish adolescents. Challenging the conventional wisdom about the relative differences between these two jurisdictions is important for informing juvenile justice policy. As Franklin Zimring notes:

> The design of sensible provision for transfer depends on clearly understanding the functions and limits of juvenile and criminal courts, and the differences between these two institutions. Finding the appropriate methods of transfer from juvenile to criminal courts thus demands that we comprehend the entire context in which such decisions must be made.[3]

In the remainder of this concluding chapter, I discuss how this study contributes to what we know about juvenile transfer policy, and what social policy lessons we can learn.

Consequences of Transfer

A number of earlier studies have considered the consequences of transferring youth to criminal court. This literature is reviewed in chapters by criminologists Donna Bishop and Charles Frazier and sociologists M. A. Bortner et al. in *The Changing Borders of Juvenile Justice* (edited by Jeffrey Fagan and Franklin Zimring).[4] I discuss some of the points raised in these two chapters below in order to establish what we already know, and how this book contributes to our knowledge.

Transfer to criminal court can have several negative consequences, both for society and for the youths who are transferred. Some studies have asked if transfer has a general deterrent effect (whether it lowers the crime rate among the public at large) and some have considered whether transfer has a specific deterrent effect (if it lowers recidivism rates among the individuals who are transferred). No study from either of these two groups has found that transfer deters crime[5]—some of these studies have in fact found that transfer might increase crime. The most convincing part about this overall conclusion—that transfer has either no effect or causes increases in crime—is that a variety of studies, each using very different methodologies and conducted in different parts of the country, have had similar results.[6] This finding is very important, since the biggest predicted benefit of transfer, and the one that seems to earn the most support from the public, is that we can lower juvenile crime only by holding youth accountable in criminal courts. As it turns out, this claim appears to be wrong, and the policies pushed by legislators and accepted by the public might be putting our safety at even greater risk.

Another consequence of jurisdictional transfer is an increase in the number of adolescents incarcerated in adult prisons. Sentencing systems vary tremendously among states, and in very complex ways. Though not all transferred youth go to adult correctional facilities, many more transferred youth go to adult prisons than youth prosecuted in juvenile courts. Compared to juveniles in juvenile correctional facilities, the adolescents who do go to adult prisons are at greater risk of physical and sexual victimization while incarcerated, and are less likely to receive counseling and therapeutic services that may speed their rehabilitation.[7] Protecting our delinquent youth from harm and offering them treatment while incarcerated is not only humane and reasonable treatment, but is also about the public good. Most of these adolescents eventually return to society, and it makes infinitely more sense to help them improve themselves as people rather than to add to their scars and bitterness.

We also have evidence that transfer to criminal court may be an unfair process. The evidence regarding race, ethnicity, and transfer conclusively shows that youth of color are over-represented among transferred cases. Not only are the proportions of racial and ethnic minority youth who are transferred greater than their percentages in the population, but these proportions are also greater than their numbers among juvenile court cases. That is, once arrested, youth of color are more likely to be transferred to criminal court than other youth. Some quantitative studies find a direct effect of race or ethnicity on the transfer decision, though others find an indirect effect whereby cumulative decisions prior to this stage of case processing, decisions that disadvantage youth of color, shape the transfer decision. For example, if minority youth are more likely to be arrested for petty offenses than white youth, then finding a large effect of prior record on the decision to transfer may not be as racially neutral as it appears.[8]

In sum, the evidence about consequences of transfer suggests that transfer policies may be unfairly applied and counterproductive. Rather than being popular because they protect society, transfer policies are popular because they appeal to a preoccupation with punitive social control strategies, or the "culture of control."[9] And, they are organizationally and politically expedient, in that they appease the public and satisfy those who perceive the juvenile justice system as insufficiently able to punish violent youth.

Does a Sequential Model of Justice Help?

Perhaps the sequential model of justice I find in the criminal court ameliorates the dangers and inadequacies of prosecuting adolescents in this court. This supposition assumes that the dangers of transfer are inherent in the ways adolescents are prosecuted and punished, rather than in the final outcomes. It is possible that the formal court environment and the focus on characteristics of offenses rather than offenders, both of which are characterized by a criminal justice model rather than a juvenile justice model, cause the counterproductive effects of transfer that earlier research has found. Perhaps a labeling effect occurs, whereby adolescents whose individual circumstances are ignored begin to view themselves as offenders rather than wayward youth.[10] If this is true, then a more formal and offense-driven model of justice might indeed have a negative effect on the identities of adolescents prosecuted in criminal court, which could in turn lead to higher recidivism rates.

This scenario seems unlikely, however, for two reasons. One is that it assumes that in other jurisdictions, and specifically the jurisdictions in which prior research on transfer outcomes has been conducted, criminal court workgroups do not filter case processing and rely on a sequential model of justice. The ideas of youthfulness that guide this sequential model are shared by the diverse court actors in my study. They are also the same ideas that are expressed by a modern conception of childhood. As a result, it is likely that other jurisdictions also filter case processing by taking youthfulness into account. The details of how this happens will vary along with local legal culture and other organizational factors, but it seems likely that a similar filtering process occurs whenever criminal court judges, prosecutors, and defense attorneys face adolescent defendants.

The second reason this hypothesis seems unlikely is because it minimizes the potential effects of harsher punishments and the symbolism of transfer. The greater use of incarceration instead of rehabilitative services in criminal court (relative to juvenile court), and longer prison terms for those adolescents who do get incarcerated, may be responsible for much of the damage caused by transfer to criminal court. Criminal court sentences are more punitive than juvenile court sentences. They are more focused on punishment and less on treatment; therefore, adolescents may be less likely to desist their offending behavior after receiving adult punishment. Even when court actors filter case processing to reintroduce the idea of reduced culpability for youth, criminal courts still give out harsher penalties than juvenile courts.

Moreover, if higher recidivism rates are caused more by how cases are processed in criminal court and not by the final outcomes of cases, then it is just as likely (if not more) that the overall symbolism of a criminal court is to blame, not the formality of case processing and the evaluation of defendants. Transferred youth know that they are going to the adult, criminal court; this in itself might communicate to them that society has given up on rehabilitating them, regardless of how the criminal court deals with their cases. Finally, the more threatening, grander architectural and structural arrangements of the criminal court might have a substantial effect on adolescents. If adolescents are affected by transfer in ways that increase recidivism, many of these factors would still have the same effect regardless of whether courts rely on a sequential model of justice.

Though my results find that criminal courts resemble juvenile courts more than one might think, and more than policy makers' rhetoric or the prior literature would lead one to believe, I am skeptical of the idea that court actors in any jurisdiction can completely dispense with widespread cultural notions about youthfulness. The particular ways in which criminal courts resemble juvenile courts during sentencing are unlikely to ameliorate the apparent negative effects of prosecuting adolescents in criminal court. The answer to the question raised in this section, then, is: no, a sequential model of justice is unlikely to help transfer policies achieve more positive outcomes.

Choosing the Best Transfer Method

It is important to point out that opponents of jurisdictional transfer make a relative argument rather than an absolute one. Very few people, and certainly not I, would argue that *no* adolescents should be transferred to the adult court. Those rare cases that involve serious violence or chronic violent offending among adolescents probably should indeed be processed in the criminal court. If the severity of the offense, such as premeditated homicide, is so great that the public would not be best protected by the limits of a juvenile court sanction, then the offending youth should be prosecuted in criminal court. Or, if repeated sanctions through the juvenile court have proved ineffective, perhaps an adolescent should graduate to the adult system. This argument holds that the idea of penal proportionality necessitates that the most serious adolescent offenders be transferred from juvenile to criminal court. Since the juvenile court is partially defined by its commitment to spare juveniles from excessively harsh punishment in an attempt to preserve their future life chances, the juvenile court might not be the best forum for punishing the most serious juvenile offenders. As described by Franklin Zimring,

> If the unwillingness of a juvenile court to disfigure is a defining characteristic of its orientation to its subjects, the very serious crime committed by a sixteen- or seventeen-year-old is exactly the kind of hard case that the juvenile court cannot easily accommodate while preserving its nondestructive mandate . . . there are, it seems, cases where the most severe secure confinement that the normally constituted juvenile court can permit itself falls far short of the minimum punishment that the community will tolerate.[11]

But these severe cases are rare. Very few adolescents intentionally kill others, and, though recidivism levels may be problematic, most youth do not revisit juvenile court after repeated sentences. Since its inception in 1899, the juvenile court has always had the ability to transfer select youth to criminal court.[12] Changes in transfer laws over the past three decades have not been about transferring the *worst* cases to the criminal court, but about transferring *more* cases to criminal court, and about entrusting prosecutors and legislators with making this decision instead of judges. These new transfer laws do not change anything for most juvenile murderers and rapists, because they would most likely have been transferred as far back as 1899; but it does mean that more first-time property offenders now go directly to criminal court. Given what we know about the consequences of transfer, and particularly the possibility of a counterdeterrent effect, this seems very foolish. If anything, increasing the number of youth we prosecute in criminal courts might increase, not decrease, crime.

One of the increasingly common methods of transferring adolescents to criminal courts is through legislative transfer. With this method, legislators establish age and offense categories of the youth who will go directly to criminal court. This is the method used by New York—the one used in this study. The problem with legislative transfer is that it leads to the greater use of transfer than necessary, because it establishes wide categories of transferred cases rather than selecting the most severe cases within those categories. Consider the difference between a fist-fight among two fourteen-year-olds, and an adolescent using a weapon to attack an innocent victim; despite the substantial differences between these two cases, both might be classified as aggravated assault and thus be automatically excluded from juvenile court.

Excluding broad categories of offenses from juvenile court means that more cases are prosecuted in criminal court than necessary in order to ensure that penal proportionality is not violated. We have already seen evidence that this practice might put the public at an increased risk of victimization. As I have shown, the excessive transfer of youth can lead to the awkward situation in which a criminal court judge is forced to reinterpret rigid laws to accommodate ideas of youthfulness. Criminal court workgroups have no training in juvenile justice, nor do they have adequate links to social service agencies such as counseling and treatment programs. Legislative transfer mandates that these people find decent solutions to their adolescent caseloads, despite having neither sufficient training nor resources. They do a good job of filtering case processing to reintroduce ideas of juvenile justice. But this process appears to be a very inefficient and unproductive use of the court's time. Because juvenile courts in the two counties I studied disposed of nine thousand cases in 2002, compared to about two hundred in the two criminal court youth parts I studied, it seems that juvenile courts make more efficient use of taxpayer money. For many of these youth, rather than transfer them, it would make more sense to prosecute them in juvenile courts, where personnel have the necessary training and resources to deal with them. Thus, the results of this study suggest that legislative transfer is not a productive system.

A second method by which youth are transferred is through direct file. Direct file laws allow prosecutors to select the youth that should be prosecuted in criminal court, and directly file them there. Like legislative exclusion, direct file laws allow prosecutors to forgo any hearing in front of a juvenile court judge. One problem with direct file is that it is a conceptual violation (though not a legal violation) of the Supreme Court's *Kent v. U.S.* decision (see chapter 1). Rather than mandating a fair hearing before any adolescent can be transferred to criminal court, direct file statutes allow prosecutors to make this decision without judicial over-sight or opportunity for the defense to make a case against it.

Furthermore, direct file decisions are made by prosecutors, who have a biased agenda and do not usually have access to all the information one might want to consider before making such a decision. This observation is not meant as an insult or an accusation of unfairness, but rather as a description of how a good prosecutor must act. Prosecutors are only one part of the judge-defense-prosecution triad, and in an adversarial system they are responsible for protecting the community via a rigorous and one-sided argument. They have a duty to the citizens to proceed in a way that aggressively, though fairly, pursues punishment for criminal offenders. This, at least, is the prosecutor I want in office in my jurisdiction. Of course, prosecutors seek to "do justice" and to prosecute only those who are guilty and blameworthy; but within that mandate they have a duty to pursue conviction and punishment as strongly as possible, rather than to seek balanced resolutions that take into consideration the needs and future welfare of the offenders. Prosecutors typically only have access to information about offenses, and not about offenders. A prosecutor might not know, for example, that a fourteen-year-old is behind his or her peers developmentally, which might be relevant to a decision about prosecuting in juvenile or criminal court. I find it to be shocking that several of the prosecutors I spoke to had given absolutely no thought to what it means when we prosecute youth as adults, or why we should do so. Instead, they focus on offense severity, and on punishments that fit these crimes.

Direct file thus seems to result in large numbers of youth being prosecuted in criminal courts. There are no reliable national counts of transferred youth, so it is hard to state the following unequivocally, but some evidence suggests that prosecutors take advantage of direct file laws by applying them liberally.[13] This leads to the same problem with regard to legislative exclusion: more youth are transferred than necessary. Practically speaking, does it make sense to transfer adolescents to the criminal court, only to have its workgroups invent ways to deal with these youth that take into account their youthfulness and reintroduce elements of juvenile justice? I would think not.

Judicial transfer is the third broad transfer mechanism. It is the traditional method of transfer, whereby a judge selects the cases that are beyond the reach of the juvenile court and transfers them to criminal court. This method has fallen out of favor recently as legislative transfer and direct file policies have proliferated and removed much of the power over transfer decision making from the hands of judges. Despite the fading popularity of judicial transfer, and unlike legislative transfer and direct file, judicial transfer can lead to a more efficient allocation of limited resources. Judges are in a good position to decide which cases are beyond the capacities of the juvenile court and need to be sent to the criminal court. Unlike legislative transfer, it does not exclude broad categories of offenders, but instead chooses from among them. And unlike direct file, it does not rest the decision in the hands of a party with a biased agenda; in contrast to prosecutors, a judge's role is to decide between competing claims brought forward in an adversarial style.

Judicial transfer is therefore the best way to select the youth who are beyond the juvenile court's capacity. If only the most serious youth are selected for transfer on a case-by-case basis, then criminal court workgroups can avoid the predicament of having to filter case processing to reintroduce elements of juvenile justice. This allows "child saving" to be carried out only by those in juvenile court, a group that is better trained and more experienced in dealing with juvenile offenders and has more resources for helping these youth. This system would put only those youth who are already "last resort" cases in the criminal court, or those who do not receive much benefit from a sequential model of justice.

Unfortunately, though, judicial transfer has its problems, too. Judges might not be very good at making the case-by-case decisions about who should be transferred. This discretionary stage is a primary avenue through which racial and ethnic biases can cause disproportionate minority representation among transfer cases. Judicial discretion also can lead to poor selection of transferworthy cases based on the offenses in question. Judges who see few serious crimes may transfer many property offenses, and as a result the juvenile court might transfer an abundance of property offenders rather than the serious violent offenders who are beyond the capacity of the juvenile court. Judicial discretion is an advantage of judicial transfer, because it allows a judge to make decisions and limit the overreach of transfer policies; but discretion is also the drawback of judicial transfer, since it opens the door to biases and unequal treatment.

Despite this substantial problem, judicial transfer seems like the best option for selecting the most severe juvenile offenders for criminal court. There is no reason to think that a judge's use of discretion is any worse than a prosecutor's, or that judicial transfer rules are less fair than direct file. Even with its faults, judicial transfer certainly seems to be a lesser evil than the broad reach of legislative transfer. Additionally, judicial transfer can still provide necessary political and organizational functions. When serious cases arise and cause the public to challenge the juvenile court for being too lenient, these cases can be considered for transfer. Of course, public opinion should not be the criterion for transfer; the point is that one does not need to implement the more extreme direct file and legislative exclusion policies to maintain the perceived legitimacy of the juvenile court.[14]

Alternative Models

Blended Sentencing

In response to some of the problems with current methods of transferring youth to criminal court, a number of alternative strategies have been proposed. One of these alternatives, blended sentencing, is more a collection of different types of policies than a single, coherent policy. Blended sentencing refers to a legislatively prescribed combination of both juvenile and criminal justice for adolescents. Ironically, it is the reverse of what I find actually happens in the criminal court. Instead of adolescents being prosecuted in criminal courts where juvenile justice is reintroduced, blended sentencing usually involves adolescents being prosecuted in juvenile courts where criminal justice is introduced. Blended sentencing usually means that youth are convicted and sentenced by a juvenile court judge, but that this judge can give out criminal court sentences. Sometimes these youth are given two-part sentences; they may serve a relatively short juvenile sentence, and then get reevaluated. If they are later evaluated as needing more punishment, they will serve an adult correctional sentence. This gives an intermediate option between juvenile and adult sentences and depends on a juvenile's initial behavior.[15] The goal of blended sentencing is to offer a "middle ground" option between juvenile justice and criminal justice. This way, juvenile courts can retain jurisdiction over more youth yet still have the capacity to prescribe appropriate punishment for serious juvenile offenders. It is a compromise between the conflicting realizations that serious juvenile offenders require serious punishments, and that adolescents are not fully culpable for their offenses. This compromise is an affirmation of the tension between criminal justice and juvenile justice that I have illustrated.

Blended sentencing is certainly an improvement over direct file and legislation exclusion, policies that lead to greater numbers of youth in criminal court. Although blended sentencing makes sense as a middle ground solution to two competing paradigms, it carries substantial risks. The most significant potential problem with blended sentencing is the likelihood of net widening. Blended sentencing is intended to reduce the number of youth who are transferred to criminal court. Thus, the pool of cases that would be transferred without a blended sentencing policy should be lower once the policy is enacted, while the pool of cases retained in the juvenile court and given juvenile sentences should remain intact. However, early evidence about this fairly new policy type suggests that this is not what actually happens. Instead, blended sentencing provisions add to the overall number of adolescents who receive adult punishments; rather than being used as an *alternative* to transfer, blended sentencing is used *in addition to* transfer.[16] In the end, the net of criminal court punishments widens to include more youth. Since we have some evidence that these punishments contribute to the juvenile crime problem, this system seems like a bad idea. If blended sentencing were indeed used as intended, however, and applied as an alternative to transfer, then this practical concern would be moot.

Blended sentencing is a risky proposition also because it dilutes a coherent system with an incoherent one. We still believe that adolescents are different from adults and should be judged and punished as if they are less blameworthy for their offenses than adults. This is why criminal court workgroups filter case processing for adolescents and reintroduce elements of juvenile justice. For most youth, the juvenile justice model makes sense; it takes into account the diminished capacity of adolescents, and still subjects them to punishment when appropriate. The problem with blended sentencing is that it works in the opposite direction. If a juvenile justice model is more appropriate for adolescents than a criminal justice model, then why would we introduce elements of a criminal justice model to the juvenile court? Granted, it makes good sense to dole out increased punishment rather than request transfer to criminal court for the most serious juvenile court cases. But trying to accomplish this through a blended sentencing policy risks introducing elements of a criminal justice model to the juvenile court as well. If juvenile courts have the ability to prescribe full adult punishments, then they should also offer the procedural rights and protections of criminal courts. This means that the rigid formality and offense-based evaluative criteria of a criminal justice model would pervade the juvenile court and might change how the juvenile court operates beyond what punishments are offered. Such changes could undermine the juvenile court's rehabilitative mission.[17] Whether this happens remains to be seen.

Abolishing the Juvenile Court

A second proposed alternative to our current transfer policies is more extreme: abolishing the juvenile court. Occasionally, critics of the juvenile court suggest abolishing it altogether in order to give all youth more severe punishment. Such suggestions, however, are infrequent, completely at odds with the culturally rooted ideas of youthfulness, and are rarely taken seriously. On the other hand, a couple of legal scholars have offered sincere proposals to abolish the court, and they have been taken seriously. Although no legislative bodies are currently considering their proposals, they warrant discussion here.

Barry Feld, the most prominent scholar in favor of abolition, has contended that the juvenile court should be abolished because it punishes youth like adults without providing the procedural protections offered in criminal court. He has argued that despite the euphemisms used in juvenile court, juvenile courts have a punitive bite to them—perhaps as much as criminal courts. And yet many juveniles go without attorneys, they have no right to a trial by jury, and rules concerning evidence are less rigidly enforced.[18] The remnants of a Progressive-era style of justice fail to help youth, yet they render a procedural laxness that hurts them. Furthermore, the high levels of subjectivity and discretion in juvenile court lead to greater racial and ethnic biases than in the criminal courts. According to Feld:

> In the three decades since *Gault*, judicial decisions, legislative amendments, and administrative changes have transformed the juvenile court from a nominally rehabilitative welfare agency into a scaled-down, second-class criminal court for young people. These revisions have converted the historical ideal of the juvenile court as a social welfare institution into a penal system that provides young offenders with neither therapy nor justice.[19]

Feld has offered a clear and compelling case for abolishing the court. His solution is to prosecute all youth in criminal courts, but with a sliding punishment scale. Though he has not offered precise calibrations of sentences, he has suggested that offenders who are fourteen might receive one-quarter to one-third of the penalty for an adult who commits the same crime, with one-half to two-thirds of an adult sentence for a sixteen-year-old, and a full sentence for an eighteen-year-old.[20] A scheme like this would afford youth the full legal protections given to adults, but would spare them full punishments.

Based on my research, however, there appear to be weaknesses with this proposal to abolish the juvenile court. One is the lack of fit between adolescents and a criminal justice model. Throughout this book I have illustrated how criminal court actors go out of their way to filter laws so as to take youthfulness into consideration. Adolescents are a poor fit in the criminal court, and criminal court workgroups reinterpret legal norms and statutes to try to improve this fit by reintroducing a juvenile justice model. Abolishing the juvenile court would make this lack of congruence much worse and complicate the problem severely. As I have already suggested, it seems inefficient to prosecute adolescents in criminal court, only to have decision makers adopt principles of juvenile justice as they prosecute and punish these youth.

Moreover, the idea of abolishing the juvenile court negates the importance that criminal court actors place on several strategies adopted for adolescents during sentencing: importing external sponsoring agencies, involving defendants in hearings, and basing decisions on more than just the adolescents' offenses. These are elements of the sentencing phase that Feld has tried to avoid by suggesting abolition, since they have the potential to lead to harmful paternalistic judgments. Yet my results suggest that, to some extent, these practices might be inevitable. Court actors who view adolescents as different from adults might always introduce these elements of case processing to make court practices better fit their conceptions of youthfulness.

Another problem with the proposal to abolish the juvenile court is that it would limit the number and suitability of noncustodial options for adolescents. Although criminal court workgroups approach adolescents' cases with the goal of "child saving," they still prescribe more severe punishments than meted out by juvenile courts. An important reason for this is the limitations of their noncustodial punishment options. Criminal court judges frequently complained to me about the lack of intermediate punishments that fall short of incarceration but offer more than probation. Without the tight connections to treatment agencies that are found in the juvenile court, criminal court actors have fewer options to use programs that might help defendants while still keeping them under surveillance. Appropriate sentences for youth cannot be achieved by limiting the legislatively prescribed custodial sentence lengths to a fraction of an adult's. This is what the New York criminal courts currently do, but their judges still want options that are unavailable in the criminal court but available in the juvenile court. Thus, I again argue that for most adolescents, the juvenile court seems to be the most appropriate legal forum for prosecution.

Each of these responses to Feld's proposal uses my research to suggest that the cultural construction of youthfulness would impede the criminal court prosecution of all youth. But so far, I have not addressed Feld's motive for this proposal: eliminating the unfairness engendered by the procedural laxness in the juvenile court. The pursuit of individualized justice through a juvenile justice model necessitates less standardization and greater discretion and subjectivity than when following a criminal justice model. There is no question that juvenile courts—at least prior to sentencing—follow a less rigid set of procedures than criminal courts. As Feld has argued, these conditions lead to unfair disparities among cases and between geographic areas, and they deny juveniles the ability to fully defend themselves in a legally adversarial system, yet these youth still face severe punishments.

Feld is correct in pointing out that juvenile courts can fail to provide young defendants with necessary legal protections, and that prosecution in the juvenile court can lead to unfair punishments. The juvenile court's goal of therapeutic intervention and its less formal style of case processing certainly have the potential to introduce these problems, or at least to fail to prevent them. But as I find by studying the New Jersey juvenile court, a juvenile justice model does not *necessarily* lead to a lack of legal protections and unfair punishments. The contextual and organizational features of individual court communities can prevent these problems. In the juvenile courts I study, the aggressive and well-trained public defenders who work in the juvenile court assert their strong influence over case processing and ensure that defendants receive adequate legal representation. Furthermore, because prosecutors have significant autonomy and there is little public scrutiny of what happens in juvenile court, courtroom workgroups face very little external pressure to react in any particular way for specific cases. As a result, youth in the New Jersey juvenile court seem to get the best of both worlds, not the worst—they avoid the stigma and harsh punishments of criminal courts, and they receive legal protections in a balanced legal forum. This court can and does prescribe harsh punishment for those who deserve it, and it transfers to the criminal court the few adolescent cases deemed too severe for the juvenile court; yet it also spares the vast majority of youth from prosecution in criminal court while still providing legal due process protections.

These contextual and organizational factors can also protect the juvenile court from having a greater propensity for racial and ethnic bias than in criminal court, as Feld has argued. Granted, an individualized decision-making process with a legacy of a social welfare orientation has the potential to be less fair across groups of defendants than a more rigid and formal style of case processing. But this is not an inevitable outcome. As I have pointed out, both juvenile and criminal courts in the New York City area appear to be reserved for people of color, suggesting that how one gets to court is not a fair process distributed evenly across groups. But once in court, I do not find that youth of color are better served by a procedurally more formal criminal court than by a juvenile court.

Together with Feld's arguments, these results offer a very important policy lesson. Feld teaches us that there are significant potential hazards to juvenile court prosecution that we must avoid if we are to deal with juvenile delinquency in a fair way. But we can do this by improving, rather than abolishing, the juvenile court. A goal of therapeutic intervention, when coupled with strong legal defense and little external pressure to punish, does not necessarily mean that youth receive the worst of both worlds. It can also mean that youths' crimes are dealt with in ways that respect their due process rights, while providing punishments that take into account their future welfare by not permanently damaging their lives as criminal court punishments have been found to do.

Concluding Remarks

Prosecuting adolescents in criminal court does not fit cultural conceptions of youthfulness. As I demonstrate throughout this book, criminal court actors who process cases of adolescents filter case processing to reintroduce aspects of a juvenile justice model during sentencing. This practice runs contrary to what policy makers promise with transfer laws and what scholars assume about the differences between juvenile court and criminal court.

In this final chapter, I considered what we can learn about juvenile justice policy from this research. Given the mismatch between adolescents and the criminal court—a mismatch seen even in a case as serious as that of Lionel Tate—it makes little sense to prosecute large numbers of youth in criminal court. My argument adds another piece to a very strong argument against widespread jurisdictional transfer. We already know that transfer exacerbates the racial and ethnic disparities in juvenile punishments, that it runs contrary to what we know about adolescents' cognitive and emotional development, and that it might actually increase crime rates and put the public in greater danger.

This does not mean that no adolescents should be prosecuted in criminal courts, but that the number of youth for whom we reserve this practice should be limited. Adolescents who commit severe violence, who chronically offend, or who are beyond the capacity of the juvenile court should be transferred to criminal court. Not to do so would subject the juvenile court to unnecessary public criticism and the general public to an increased risk of victimization. But recent expansions of and changes to transfer laws have led to growing numbers of youth charged with less serious offenses being transferred to criminal courts, which seems both counterintuitive and counterproductive. Furthermore, placing this decision in the hands of prosecutors and legislatures, an increasingly common phenomenon, seems to be a less practical or efficient method than judicial transfer. As a result of these recent changes in transfer laws, we see growing numbers of less serious offenders in criminal court. If this trend continues, it seems very likely that criminal court decision makers will increasingly rely on filtering mechanisms like those I have described in this book.

Appendix
Research Methods

The preceding chapters have focused on how juvenile and criminal courts vary, with little attention given to research methods or the results of quantitative data analyses. In this appendix, I add these details. With regard to site selection, appendix table 1.1 illustrates the overall similarity among populations in the six adjacent counties I studied in 2000. Despite some distinctions among them—each is part of the New York City Metropolitan Statistical Area—they are overall very similar. The New Jersey (juvenile court) counties contain slightly greater proportions of whites and of people living above the poverty line. This is probably because these counties consist of both inner cities and suburbs, while the New York (criminal court) counties consist only of urban areas. As a result, there is more diversity in New Jersey at the county level, yet the urban areas within these counties closely mirror the New York counties.

Quantitative Data

To quantitatively analyze case processing and punishments across New York's criminal court and New Jersey's juvenile court, I sampled cases of fifteen- and sixteen-year-old defendants who were charged with aggravated assault (1st and 2nd degree), robbery (1st and 2nd degree), or burglary (1st degree) in 1992 or 1993 in three counties of New York City and three counties of northeastern New Jersey.[1] As I stated in chapter 2, I use these three offense types because all are serious felony charges and they are among the most common offenses from the list of "JO eligible" offenses (thus providing a large sample).

Precautions helped ensure that the cases in both states were of equal severity: (1) I sampled after an initial screening process in each system. In New York, cases were sampled at arraignment, after screening by prose-

APPENDIX TABLE 1.1 *Demographic Comparison of Six Studied Counties, 2000*
(% of County Populations)

	Criminal Courts (NY)			Juvenile Courts (NJ)		
County	1	2	3	County 1	2	3
Racial composition						
White	30.1	44.1	41.2	55.5	44.5	62.3
Black	35.8	19.8	36.2	13.3	41.0	13.0
American Indian and Alaska Native	0.8	0.4	0.3	0.3	0.2	0.3
Asian	3.0	17.7	7.5	9.4	3.7	3.8
Native Hawaiian and other Pacific Islander	0.1	0.1	0.1	0.1	0.1	0.0
Other race	25.1	11.7	10.2	15.5	6.8	16.7
Two or more races	5.9	6.2	4.4	5.9	3.7	3.9
Below poverty line	29.9	14.4	24.8	15.3	15.1	12.1
Population under age 18	29.9	22.8	26.7	22.5	26.0	26.0
High school graduate or higher	37.4	50.3	43.3	47.3	48.9	47.4

SOURCE: 2000 U.S. Census; data downloaded from http://factfinder.census.gov.

cutors for legal sufficiency and appropriate charging. In New Jersey, they were sampled at court filing, after having passed an initial screening by a prosecutor. As a result of the screening, one can be fairly confident that most of the sampled offenses are appropriately charged. (2) The sample includes only the most serious subcharges within each offense type.

I use this age range because in New York it includes both adolescents excluded from the juvenile court by the JO Law (fifteen-year-olds) and individuals who are above the state's general age of criminal majority (sixteen-year-olds). Thus, the New York data are able to show how adolescents fare in the criminal court regardless through which legal method they arrive there (both exclusion from the juvenile court and surpassing the general age of majority).

I should note that both states have transfer provisions that have the potential to introduce dissimilarities between the two state-level subsamples; this would occur if the more serious cases from New Jersey were transferred (to the criminal court) and thus not included here, as with less serious cases from New York (transferred to the juvenile court). Yet this does not seem to be the case. New Jersey courts have the option to transfer adolescents up to the criminal court, though prior research in the same counties with a similar sample shows that this option is used extremely rarely.[2] In New York, fifteen-year-olds may be transferred down to the juvenile court. However, descriptive comparisons of the fifteen- and sixteen-year-olds in the New York sample here show that they are subjected to nearly identical outcomes. As a result of the infrequent use of transfer in New Jersey, and the similarity of court handling of transfer eligible and ineligible cases in New York, the opportunity for transfer in these jurisdictions should not introduce a sample selection bias.

The quantitative data I use are a subset of data collected under the supervision of Professor Jeffrey Fagan at Columbia University. Professor Fagan gathered these data to compare recidivism rates across adolescents prosecuted in New Jersey's juvenile court and New York's criminal court. I assisted in the data collection as a research assistant early in the project, and then supervised the later stages of data collection as the project director working under Professor Fagan.

We assembled the data from a variety of sources. The New Jersey Administrative Office of Courts provided data for one of the three New Jersey juvenile courts in automated format. For the other two New Jersey courts, other researchers and I manually collected data at the county courthouses from case files of sampled individuals. This involved a painstaking process of reading through sampled individuals' entire case files—held in manila folders, some of which were well over two inches thick—and collecting information on the particular sampled cases. The data collection process for these two New Jersey courts took over two years to complete. The New York City Criminal Justice Agency, the city's pretrial services agency, which collects and stores data on all New York City criminal defendants, provided the New York criminal court data. The New York data were supplemented by data from the New York Department of Criminal Justice Services.

Qualitative Data and Methods

To compare the models of justice that guide case processing in both court types, I used qualitative data on the formality of case processing and the evaluation of adolescents. I observed court proceedings and interviewed courtroom actors in two county-level courts in the New Jersey juvenile court system (Brady and Brown counties) and two county-level courts in the New York criminal court system (Pierce and Maxwell counties).[3]

The most influential previous studies of juvenile courts, especially those by sociologists Aaron Cicourel and Robert Emerson, both note that qualitative research is necessary for understanding how juvenile courts function.[4] I would add that when comparing different types of courts—including those that may not record or maintain data in similar fashion, or that may have different official categories of dispositions and reasons for dispositions—qualitative research becomes even more crucial. For this reason I use both quantitative and qualitative methods to compare juvenile and criminal courts.

Interviews

I conducted interviews with judges, prosecutors, and defense attorneys who work in the two sampled counties within the New York criminal court system and two counties in the New Jersey juvenile court system.[5] Between December 2000 and April 2002 I undertook thirty-two interviews across both jurisdictions. The interviews consisted of both open-ended questions followed by probes to explore themes, and closed-ended questions asking respondents to give answers to questions using scaled response sheets. The interviews were semistructured, with several guided questions and room for exploring topics in an open-ended fashion, and ranged from fifty minutes to two hours in length. The subjects discussed include the criteria used by court actors to make decisions, the manner in which these individuals interact with one another, the practical difficulties court actors face and strategies for dealing with these difficulties, and both formal and informal procedures for prosecuting adolescents. The interviews assessed strategies used for interacting with other courtroom workgroup actors, as well as the frames of relevance[6] and ideas of adolescent culpability on which actors rely when dealing with adolescent defendants. They are designed to address my research question by inquiring about the formality of case processing, the evaluation procedures of adolescent defendants, and the punishments. All interviews were tape-recorded and transcribed by a professional transcriber. Appendix table 1.2 lists the number of interview respondents by their positions in each court type, as well as by sex and race. The number of interviews conducted (N = 32) would certainly be insufficient for tests of statistical significance, but enabled me to reach a qualitative understanding of how court actors process cases. This is especially true given the consistency among responses from court actors, as noted throughout this book. Although I attempted to recruit a sample of respondents that is representative of the populations of court actors in these positions, this sample is nonrandom.

APPENDIX TABLE 1.2 *Number of Interview Respondents by Court Type, Race/Ethnicity, Sex, and Professional Role*

	White		African American		Latino/a or Other		
	Male	Female	Male	Female	Male	Female	Total
Juvenile Court							
Judges	2	0	0	0	0	0	2
Prosecutors	2	2	2	1	0	0	7
Defense attorneys	5	1	1	0	0	1	8
Criminal Court							
Judges	1	0	0	0	1	0	2
Prosecutors	1	4	0	0	0	0	5
Defense attorneys	4	4	0	0	0	0	8

In addition to asking respondents open-ended questions and closed-ended scaled questions, I gave each interview respondent a brief survey to complete and return. This survey asks respondents to evaluate how important several goals or ideas should be, as well as how important they are in practice, on a scale of one to four, for the prosecution and punishment of adolescents.[7] Of the thirty-two respondents, twenty-six returned the surveys.

Court Observations

In addition to interviews, my qualitative data consist of field notes from observing case processing of adolescents in two county-level courts in both the New York criminal court system and in the New Jersey juvenile court system. I visited these courts over the course of eighteen months (October 2000 to April 2002), and observed a total of 978 hearings. Rather than following individual cases (which occasionally take years to complete), I attended court on days for which a large number of cases were scheduled to be heard. In the New York criminal court, I attended all court "calendar" days, when all active cases not on trial are scheduled for whatever action or hearing type is required. This procedure ensured that I observed the full array of each court's caseload, because all cases appear on calendar days at some time. The New Jersey juvenile court has no specific calendar day, so I attended court on the days with the most cases scheduled each week. I also observed at least one trial in each court.

In the two criminal courts, the judges allowed me to sit up front with the court clerk rather than in the audience. This was of enormous benefit, since it allowed me to observe the off-the-record posturing and negotiation that frequently occur at each judge's bench. This is not necessary in the juvenile courts I observed; because juvenile court hearings are confidential and closed to the public, court actors hold almost all conversations in the open (usually between cases, with no defendants present and no formal records being taken) rather than approaching the judge's bench during hearings. No participants ever acknowledged my presence during hearings (either verbally or through physical gestures), and I remained silent during all hearings; thus it is unlikely that my presence had any effect on the content or interaction of these hearings.[8]

In three of the four courts I was able to develop a rapport with the judges and court staff, and was seen to some extent as a "regular."[9] In one of the New York criminal courts, in Brady County, the court clerk occasionally deputized me to help the judge find defendants' files in his filing system when the court clerk had to step away from her desk. This was of course very helpful; court staff were not afraid to speak freely in front of me, they allowed me to observe all court activity, and they were generous with their time in answering my questions and offering their opinions of each day's activities.

Despite my good rapport with court staff in three of the four courts, I was treated as an "outsider" in Maxwell County.[10] According to the few attorneys with whom I was able to form a friendship here, the local legal culture includes careful oversight of judges by county administrators, which makes judges feel very vulnerable to any negative evaluation. According to these attorneys and my observations, much more so than in the other three courts, judges in Maxwell County are afraid of "getting caught" doing anything inappropriate, and therefore are wary of visitors to the court (especially those armed with notebooks). For example, one of the two judges in this court read the following script before every hearing I observed, directly after each attorney stated his or her appearance for the court record:

Also in the courtroom is Mr. Aaron Kupchik of the Center for Violence Research and Prevention at Columbia University.[11] He has been granted permission by the Supreme Court to observe proceedings given the following criteria: one, that he obtain consent from the judge presiding over this matter, which he has; two, that no names of juveniles be recorded; and three, that no party objects to his presence. Do either of you object to Mr. Kupchik's presence for this matter?

No attorney ever objected to my presence, but this script labeled me as an outsider and made acceptance into the court community more difficult in this one county.

In addition to court observations, I observed meetings and peripheral court actions as well. I attended several meetings held by the Brown County judge with members of the probation office, correctional facilities, the district attorney's office, and representatives from treatment programs working with the court. I also observed a meeting between the lead juvenile court judge in Pierce County and heads of various treatment program agencies. And, though less directly relevant (but more exciting), I accompanied probation officers and police in Pierce County, New Jersey, on surprise nighttime curfew checks and drug monitoring in the homes of juveniles on probation.

When observing court I noted all participants (judge, prosecutor, defense attorney, defendant, and any other participant), including their sex, race, and manner of dress (for defendants); the content and nature of discussions in court; the content and nature of off-the-record conversations; the requests made to the judge by different parties; and the reasons and explanations given for these requests or for any decisions that court actors made. I was able to note accurately this dialogue due to the typical nature and repetition of most interactions. The frequency of identical or very similar exchanges between court actors allowed me to use brief notations for many of these exchanges and focus my note-taking efforts on any unusual interaction. I transcribed these field notes daily in order to translate my notes into nearly complete records of all court activities. Though exact transcriptions of hearings would be preferable to much of the data used,[12] the field notes I recorded are quite adequate and are consistent with data used by others for similar research.[13]

I analyzed the field notes and interviews using both traditional qualitative methods and the qualitative data analysis software, NU-DIST. The traditional methods involved reading through each transcript, coding the data into themes, and manually searching for patterns in the data.[14] I selected the transcripts and field notes presented in the preceding chapters because they best characterize the repeated patterns that emerge from my analyses.[15] These patterns were clear in both data sources and were identified by both methods of analysis, thus adding confidence to the reliability and validity of the findings.

Results of Multivariate Analyses

In appendix table 1.3, I display the mean, standard deviation, and range of each offender- and offense-level variable included in my multivariate analyses. Variation Inflation Factors reveal that no independent variables are sufficiently correlated to one another to risk multicollinearity in the following multivariate models.[16]

In figure 5.2 I showed that adolescents in the criminal court are more likely to be convicted (to receive any court action), and if they are, less likely to receive probation and more likely to be incarcerated than adolescents in the juvenile court. In figure 5.3, I displayed the far greater average custodial sentence length in the criminal court than the juvenile court. Appendix table 1.4 continues these observations by illustrating that each of these relationships holds true within each offense category as well. Overall, and within each offense category, the criminal court offers more severe punishment than the juvenile court. Yet these results do vary somewhat as a function of offense type. The most significant departure from this pattern is a nearly equal likelihood of incarceration for aggravated assault cases in both court types. Because of the possible influence of offense type on case outcomes, I include offense type as a series of dummy control variables in the following multivariate analyses.

Next, to determine the impact of court type on sentence severity while controlling for characteristics of offenders and offenses, I estimated multivariate equations predicting a dependent variable of incarceration. The offender-relevant independent variables in the multivariate models include age, sex (coded 1 = male, 0 = female), and race/ethnicity (dummy variables indicating white, Latino/a, African American, and all other ethnicities). The offense-relevant independent variables are number of prior arrests, number of arrests during the time the sampled case was being processed, if the defendant was previously incarcerated (coded 1 = yes, 0 = no), presence of an associated weapon charge (coded 1 = yes, 0 = no), most serious offense type (dummy variables indicating robbery, aggravated assault, and burglary), if the defendant was detained by the court pending adjudication (coded 1 = yes, 0 = no), whether a warrant for the

APPENDIX TABLE 1.3 *Summary Measures of Offender and Offense Characteristics in Sentencing Severity Models*

	Mean	Std. Deviation	Range
Offender Characteristics			
Age (years)	16.20	0.55	15.0–17.0
Race/ethnicity			
White	0.09	0.28	0–1
African American	0.56	0.50	0–1
Latino/a	0.30	0.46	0–1
Other Race / Ethnicity	0.05	0.22	0–1
Sex (Male)	0.86	0.35	0–1
Offense Characteristics			
# Prior arrests	2.40	4.17	0–26
# Arrests during case	0.45	0.96	0–9
Previously incarcerated	0.10	0.30	0–1
Associated weapons charge	0.38	0.49	0–1
Offense type			
Robbery	0.54	0.50	0–1
Aggravated assault	0.29	0.46	0-1
Burglary	0.17	0.38	0-1
Detained preadjudication	0.46	0.50	0–1
Arrest warrant	0.13	0.34	0–1
Dependent Variable			
Incarcerated	0.15	0.36	0–1

defendant's arrest was executed during case processing (coded 1 = yes, 0 = no), and court type (coded 2 = criminal, 1 = juvenile).[17]

I used Heckman two-stage models to predict incarceration. I did so because any model predicting sentencing practices includes a censored sample, in that only convicted cases are included in models with sentencing as the dependent variable.[18] The Heckman two-stage model produces parameter estimates that take censoring into account—a censoring parameter is estimated and then incorporated into the probit analysis of the dependent variable.[19] I use probit analyses because the dependent variable is dichotomous; probit models take into consideration that the dependent variable varies only between 0 and 1 and are thus better suited for a dichotomous dependent variable than OLS regression, which assumes the dependent variable to be continuous.[20] Conviction in the original court is the censorship value included in each model, meaning that cases remain in the censored sample only if they result in conviction.[21] I

APPENDIX TABLE 1.4A *Percentage of Cases Acted On, and Percentage Receiving Each Sentence Category, by Court Type and Offense Type at Case Filing*

	Juvenile Court (New Jersey)				Criminal Court (New York)			
	Robbery (n = 261) %	Agg. Assault (n = 460) %	Burglary (n = 327) %	All Juvenile Court (n = 1048) %	Robbery (n = 930) %	Agg. Assault (n = 190) %	Burglary (n = 55) %	All Crim. Court (n = 1175) %
Any Court Action	55.6	51.3	66.7	57.2	68.2	58.2	72.7	66.8
If any court action:								
Adjourned disposition/ adjourned in contemplation of dismissal	26.2	27.1	22.5	25.2	24.1	57.3	35.0	29.4
Fine/alternative to incarceration	6.9	3.4	4.2	4.5	0.6	3.6	0.0	1.0
Probation or suspended sentence	52.4	54.3	67.9	58.8	37.2	23.6	30.0	34.9
Incarceration	14.5	15.3	5.5	11.5	38.0	15.5	35.0	34.7

APPENDIX TABLE 1.4B *Average Custodial Sentence Length for Incarcerated Cases, in Months, by Court Type and Offense Type at Case Filing*

	Juvenile Court				Criminal Court			
	Robbery	Agg. Assault	Burglary	All Juvenile Court	Robbery	Agg. Assault	Burglary	All Crim. Court
Average sentence length	12.2	8.0	9.4	9.5	28.1	15.1	26.2	27.2

estimate the models using a robust cluster by county-level court, which adjusts the standard error of each coefficient to account for any systematic differences among cases from each of the six included courts. The robust cluster procedure is a form of estimation that allows for nonindependence of observations within a given group, in this case within each court.

I estimated two separate models to examine the effect of court type on the likelihood of incarceration, controlling for other factors, with the results displayed in appendix table 1.5. The first model estimates the probability of incarceration among all convicted cases, using the independent variables. The second model restricts the analysis to robbery cases only. I did this to test whether the results from the first model are the result of the greater proportion of robbery cases in New York. Though the results regarding the coefficient for court type were reported in figure 5.4 (after being converted to odds ratios), appendix table 1.5 displays the regression results for all other independent variables.

I should note that in these models I did not estimate the likelihood of conviction or custodial sentence lengths. I did not predict conviction (other than being included as the censorship parameter in the Heckman two-stage procedure) for two reasons: (1) The data contain no information about quality of evidence against the defendant, which is perhaps the most important factor in determining conviction within an adversarial system.[22] Without data concerning quality of evidence against defendants, models of conviction would suffer from omitted variable biases. (2) Because the dispositional categories and court procedures for reaching conviction vary across the two court types, it would be misleading to compare them using multivariate procedures.[23]

Additionally, I did not estimate length of custodial sentences because the data are not comparable across court type. In New York, sentence length is estimated as two-thirds of the maximum sentence given by the judge.[24] In contrast, because New Jersey juvenile court judges prescribe

APPENDIX TABLE 1.5 *Heckman Two-Stage Probit Regression of Incarceration, Total Sample and Robbery Cases Only*

	Model 1: Total Sample			Model 2: Robbery Cases		
	B	Std. Error	Z	B	Std. Error	Z
Age	−0.053	0.072	−0.73	−0.112	0.089	−1.26
Sex (0 = female; 1 = male)	0.413	0.156	2.62 **	0.487	0.279	1.75
Race/ethnicity (contrast = African American)						
White	−0.114	0.157	−0.73	0.230	0.366	0.63
Latino/a	0.071	0.124	0.57	−0.023	0.202	−0.11
Other race/ethnicity	−0.151	0.139	−1.09	-0.196	0.128	−1.53
Offense Type (contrast = robbery)						
Burglary	−0.365	0.199	−1.84			
Aggravated assault	−0.149	0.096	−1.55			
Associated weapon charge	0.270	0.112	2.42 *	0.268	0.136	1.96 *
Detained preadjudication	0.873	0.239	3.66 ***	1.296	0.185	7.01 ***
Number of prior arrests	0.064	0.006	10.72 ***	0.037	0.013	2.75 **
Number of arrests during case processing	0.101	0.052	1.95	0.147	0.067	2.20 *
Previously incarcerated	0.928	0.125	7.43 ***	1.097	0.149	7.36 ***
Arrest warrant	0.312	0.149	2.10 *	0.487	0.297	1.64
Court type (1 = juvenile; 2 = criminal)	1.200	0.103	11.62 ***	1.163	0.143	8.16 ***
Constant	−2.814			−2.584		
Log likelihood	−1803.608			−1047.983		

* p < .05; ** p < .01; *** p < .001

indeterminate prison sentences, there is great variation in the actual amount of time served, and it would not be feasible to make this kind of estimate of time served. Instead, I obtained the custodial release dates for each sampled individual and calculated the length of custodial sentence actually served. Furthermore, the data set contains no information on custodial facility bed space or parole board decision making, both of which would be crucial for predicting the length of sentences that are served. By restricting the analyses to whether or not courts prescribe prison sentences, I was able to analyze relatively accurate and complete data bearing upon a crucial sentencing decision (i.e., incarceration).

As we already know from figure 5.4, the coefficient for court type is positive and statistically significant in model 1 of appendix table 1.5. In fact, as measured by its coefficient size (B) and its z-score, court type tells us more about the likelihood of incarceration than any other variable in model 1. This result supports the distinction between a juvenile justice model and criminal justice model by demonstrating that sentencing is more punitive in the criminal court than in the juvenile court. This suggests that, with regard to punishment severity, criminal courts do indeed follow a criminal justice model and juvenile courts do indeed follow a juvenile justice model.

Additionally, overall, model 1 suggests that more serious cases are more likely to end in incarceration. A number of variables relating to offense severity are significant: number of prior arrests, being detained during case processing, having an associated weapons charge, having an arrest warrant filed during case processing, and a history of incarceration. Preadjudication detention may be significant either because it acts as a proxy for offense severity (assuming more serious offenses are more likely to be detained), or because judges' decision making at previous stages of case processing informs subsequent sentencing decisions. The significance of prior arrest records and histories of incarceration may indicate either the importance of an offending background, that decision makers are less willing to offer second chances to more persistent offenders due to considering the risk of reoffending (and thereby jeopardizing public safety), or that defendants with prior justice system experience are labeled as having a bad character and are punished more severely due to the personal degradation. Having an associated weapons charge is a decent measure of offense severity, as it indicates whether the defendant committed one of the sampled offenses (robbery, burglary, or assault) with a weapon. Finally, an arrest warrant indicates that the defendant either failed to appear before the court or was suspected of a crime while the case was progressing; this variable might be used as an indicator by court decision makers of untrustworthiness or continued offending behavior.

The only significant variable in the model (other than court type) that is not at least indirectly related to offense severity or severity of the defendant's offending history is sex. The coefficient for the variable for sex indicates that male defendants are more likely to be incarcerated when controlling for other factors. It comes as no surprise to find that males stand a greater risk of incarceration than females, though a more thorough test of gender differences in sentencing would need to add cases of less serious and status offenses to the sample, and test whether females are punished more severely for status offenses. Status offenses would allow for a better test of gender differences among adolescents because prior research focuses on juvenile courts' efforts to police girls' morality through punishment for status offenses.[25]

Race is not a significant predictor of incarceration in this model. As I discuss in chapter 6, however, there are very few white youths in this sample; according to a citywide report on minority overrepresentation among JO defendants in New York, only 4 percent of JO cases filed in New York City's criminal court—and 2 percent of cases convicted there—involved white defendants.[26] The under-representation of white youth makes statistical comparisons difficult and suggests that a racial filtering process occurs before court at earlier decision-making junctures such as the decision to arrest or to formally prosecute (see chapter 6).

Model 2 in appendix table 1.5 presents the results of the analysis using only robbery cases. If the results of model 2 are vastly different than model 1, this would suggest that the sentencing process for robbery cases varies from the sentencing process for assault and burglary cases, which would complicate the comparisons between the two court types (given their disparate distributions of offense types). However, this is not the case. Most of the statistically significant coefficients in model 1 also are significant in model 2 (despite some differences: coefficients for sex and arrest warrants are not significant in model 2, but the variable for arrests during case processing is significant),[27] and all significant coefficients are of the same sign. Overall, one can conclude that the sentencing process for robbery cases empirically is very similar to the sentencing process for the entire sample.[28] Hence, regardless of the distribution of offense types, the criminal court reflects a criminal justice model and the juvenile court reflects a juvenile justice model regarding punishment severity, as measured by likelihood of incarceration.

Supplemental Data Analysis

Given the gap in time between the quantitative data I analyze in chapter 5 (cases from arrests in 1992–1993) and the qualitative data I analyze in chapters 3, 4, and 5 (collected from 2000 to 2002), I perform further analyses with more recent data. The second data set also includes fifteen- and sixteen-year-olds charged with aggravated assault (1st and 2nd degree), robbery (1st and 2nd degree), or burglary (1st degree) in the same six counties. Yet these data are more recent than the data in the first data set I analyze in chapter 5 and above: they are from cases disposed of in 1998. In addition, these data are the populations of all eligible cases rather than samples across two years. This more recent data set contains fewer variables than the 1992–1993 data set, thus, my analyses using this more recent data are not as rigorous as those using the older data. Their importance is that they permit me to verify that the courts I study produced similar outcomes in the years following 1993, closer to the time during which I collected qualitative data in these courts.

In appendix table 1.6 I display a comparison of the juvenile court and criminal court cases in the second data set. Though it misses several variables included in the first data set, this second data set is very similar in composition to the first with regard to both offender and offense characteristics. The two state samples here show age, sex, and race distributions similar to the first data set. Again, the criminal court sample contains more sixteen-year-olds, more males, and more robbery defendants than the juvenile court sample. And, again, the juvenile court cases are more likely to have prior arrest records than the criminal court cases. Unfortunately, this second data set does not contain information on preadjudication detention, arrests during case processing, previous incarceration, and arrest warrants.

The New York Department of Criminal Justice Services and the New Jersey Administrative Office of Courts provided these more recent data.[29] During the time elapsed between the two data collection efforts, each statewide criminal justice system improved its automated data collection

APPENDIX TABLE 1.6 *Offense and Offender Characteristics of Cases in Each Court Type, 1998 Data*

		Juvenile Court/ New Jersey (n = 864) %	Criminal Court/ New York (n = 1577) %
Offender Characteristics			
Age:	15	44.3	17.9
	16	55.7	82.1
Sex:	Male	82.2	87.9
	Female	17.8	12.1
Race/ethnicity:	White	13.3	5.0
	African American	60.4	65.8
	Latino/a	23.7	25.5
	Other and unknown	2.7	3.7
Offense Characteristics			
Offense Type:	Robbery	23.4	81.8
	Aggravated assault	49.2	7.2
	Burglary	27.4	11.0
Associated weapon charge		28.1	32.8
Presence of prior arrests		64.6	41.0

system. As a result, one agency provided each statewide data set without the need for any manual data collection.

The primary importance of this second data set is to verify that no significant changes in court outcomes occurred across the time period separating my quantitative cases (1992–1993) and my qualitative data (2000–2002). Therefore, I use these data to compare adjudication and sentencing rates across the two quantitative data sets. Appendix table 1.7a displays the punishment outcomes in the second data set. A comparison of this table and appendix table 1.4a verifies that the courts I studied did indeed produce very similar outcomes in 1998 and in 1992–1993. The frequency of court action in each court type in 1998 is lower than in the first data set, though the disparity between the two court types is consistent with the older data. A larger percentage of cases are acted on in the criminal court than in the juvenile court. The percentages of adolescents incarcerated are slightly higher in the more recent data set than in the first data set, but again the discrepancy between the two court types is almost identical in both data sets.

APPENDIX TABLE I.7A *Percentage of Cases Acted On, and Percentage Receiving Each Sentence Type, by Court Type and Offense Type at Case Filing, 1998 Data*

	Juvenile Court (New Jersey)				Criminal Court (New York)			
	Robbery %	Agg. Assault %	Burglary %	All Juvenile Court %	Robbery %	Agg. Assault %	Burglary %	All Crim. Court %
Any Court Action	44.1	40.2	44.7	42.4	58.8	65.5	63.2	59.7
If any court action:								
Adjourned disposition/ adjourned in contemplation of dismissal	6.0	15.2	11.4	11.9	20.4	11.0	27.8	20.5
Fine/ATD	6.0	9.0	13.4	9.6	0.0	0.0	0.9	0.1
Probation or suspended sentence	63.9	58.4	61.0	60.5	37.0	32.9	39.8	37.0
Incarceration	24.1	17.5	14.3	18.1	42.6	56.2	31.5	42.4

APPENDIX TABLE I.7B *Average Custodial Sentence Length for Incarcerated Cases, in Months, by Court Type and Offense Type at Case Filing*

	Juvenile Court				Criminal Court			
	Robbery	Agg. Assault	Burglary	All Juvenile Court	Robbery	Agg. Assault	Burglary	All Crim. Court
If incarcerated:								
Average sentence length (months)	18.5	13.1	9.1	13.9	27.7	27.0	14.8	26.5

As appendix table 1.7b illustrates, the custodial sentence lengths among cases incarcerated in the juvenile court in the second data set are higher than in the first, though once again the disparity between the two court types remains. Adolescents incarcerated in the New York criminal court receive sentences that are an average twice as long in time served than adolescents sentenced in the New Jersey juvenile court.

Thus, the newer data demonstrate that the relative court outcomes across court types did not change markedly from 1992–1993 to 1998. Despite some shifts among the distribution of punishments in the two court types, the changes maintain a consistent distinction between them; the base punishment rates may have changed, but if so, they seemed to have changed consistently in both court types.

Notes

NOTES TO CHAPTER I

1. See Phillip Aries (1967) *Centuries of Childhood: A Social History of Family Life*. NY: Vintage Books; Barry C. Feld (1999) *Bad Kids: Race and the Transformation of the Juvenile Court*. NY: Oxford University Press; Viviana A. Zelizer (1987) *Pricing the Priceless Child: The Changing Social Value of Children*. Princeton: Princeton University Press.

2. Howard Snyder and Melissa Sickmund (1999) *Juvenile Offenders and Victims: A National Report*. National Center for Juvenile Justice.

3. According to Charles Gibson's report on *Good Morning America*, 1/26/04.

4. Quoted in Sam Handlin, "Fourteen-year-old Lionel Tate Sentenced to Life in Prison." Court TV.com, 3/9/02.

5. In Appeal Court Opinion, *Tate v. State of Florida*, 12/10/03.

6. Court TV.com, "Where It All Began: 14-Year-Old Gets Life." 11/7/00.

7. Quoted in Handlin (2002).

8. Quoted in *Lionel Tate v. State of Florida*, 864 So. 2d 44, 2003.

9. See AAMR.org for definition of mental retardation.

10. See Laurie Schaffner (2002) "An Age of Reason: Paradoxes in the U.S. Legal Construction of Adulthood." *The International Journal of Children's Rights* 10:201–232.

11. Under *Stanford v. Kentucky* (1989, 492 U.S. 361), the U.S. Supreme Court upheld execution of offenders who commit crimes at age sixteen or older. This decision governed capital punishment at the time of Malvo's prosecution. However, in *Roper v. Simmons* (2005, 03-633), the Supreme Court later invalidated execution for anyone who commits an offense while younger than eighteen.

12. Dahlia Lithwick (2003) "The Pied Sniper: Was Lee Boyd Malvo Brainwashed into a Killing Machine?" *Slate*, 9/25/03.

13. Of course, in cases with two defendants, a leader of the offenses will often receive a harsher penalty than a follower. But this does not seem to be what is driving the differences in sentences between Malvo and Muhammad. One might think that the severity of the offenses would eliminate a sentencing "dis-

count" for the follower. More importantly, by his own admission, Malvo was the triggerman in the murders, not just an accomplice along for the ride; being the one who actually perpetrated the lethal violence would also mitigate any potential sentencing discount for being a follower rather than a leader. Finally, the defense's argument was about Malvo's devotion to Muhammad as a father-figure, not about Muhammad's leadership among two equals involved in crime.

14. Sociologists studying courts have used this term to describe the prosecutors, judges, defense attorneys, and any other professionals who work together to process defendants, e.g., James Eisenstein and Herbert Jacob (1977) *Felony Justice: An Organizational Analysis of Criminal Courts*. Boston: Little Brown. James Eisenstein, Roy Flemming, and Peter Nardulli (1988) *The Contours of Justice: Communities and Their Courts*. Boston: Little, Brown.

15. E.g., Abraham S. Blumberg (1967) *Criminal Justice*. Chicago: Quadrangle Books; Malcolm Feeley (1973) "Two Models of the Criminal Justice System: An Organizational Perspective." *Law and Society Review* 7:407–425; Malcolm Feely (1979) *The Process Is the Punishment*. New York: Russell Sage Foundation; Mike McConville and Chester Mirsky (1995) "Guilty Plea Courts: A Social Disciplinary Model of Justice." *Social Problems* 42:216–234; Herbert L. Packer (1964) "Two Models of the Criminal Process." *University of Pennsylvania Law Review* 113:1–68; Herbert L. Packer (1968) *The Limits of the Criminal Sanction*. Stanford, CA: Stanford University Press; Jerome Skolnick (1967) "Social Control in the Adversary System." *Journal of Conflict Resolution* 11:53–70.

16. Packer (1964, 1968).

17. Packer (1964 p. 11).

18. Even though most defendants plead guilty rather than face a jury, the possibility by law of a jury trial is central to both a crime control model and a due process model (Packer 1964), and is an important factor in the difference in formality between juvenile and criminal courts.

19. Feld (1999); see also Barry C. Feld (1989) "The Right to Counsel in Juvenile Court: An Empirical Study of When Lawyers Appear and the Difference They Make." *Journal of Criminal Law and Criminology* 79:1185–1346; Barry C. Feld (1998) "Juvenile and Criminal Justice Systems' Responses to Youth Violence." In *Crime and Justice: An Annual Review*, ed. Michael Tonry and Mark H. Moore, 24:189–261; M. A. Bortner (1982) *Inside a Juvenile Court: The Tarnished Ideal of Individualized Justice*. New York: New York University Press.

20. Though several studies find significant effects of race and gender on case outcomes, many interpret them as indicating systematic categorization and discrimination rather than as evidence of individualized justice. See Celesta A. Albonetti (1997) "Sentencing under the Federal Sentencing Guidelines: Effects of Defendant Characteristics, Guilty Pleas, and Departures on Sentence Outcomes for Drug Offenses, 1991–1992." *Law and Society Review* 31:789–822; Cassia

Spohn, John Gruhl, and Susan Welch (1982) "The Effect of Race on Sentencing: A Re-examination of an Unsettled Question." *Law and Society Review* 16:72–88; Jeffery T. Ulmer and John H. Kramer (1996) "Court Communities under Sentencing Guidelines: Dilemmas of Formal Rationality and Sentencing Disparity." *Criminology* 34:383–407; Marjorie S. Zatz (1985) "Pleas, Priors and Prison: Racial/Ethnic Differences in Sentencing." *Social Science Research* 14:169–193; for a review, see Marjorie S. Zatz (2000) "The Convergence of Race, Ethnicity, Gender and Class on Court Decisionmaking: Looking Toward the 21st Century." *Criminal Justice* 3:503–552.

21. See David Garland (2001) *The Culture of Control*. New York: Oxford University Press.

22. Francis A. Allen (1981) *The Decline of the Rehabilitative Ideal: Penal Policy and Social Purpose*. New Haven: Yale University Press.

23. Malcolm Feeley and Jonathan Simon (1992) "The New Penology: Notes on the Emerging Strategy of Corrections and Its Implications." *Criminology* 30:449–474; Jonathan Simon and Malcolm Feeley (1995) "True Crime: The New Penology and the Public Discourse on Crime." In *Punishment and Social Control*, ed. Thomas G. Blomberg and Stanley Cohen. New York: Aldine de Gruyter.

24. E.g., David Garland (1995) "Penal Modernism and Post-Modernism." In *Punishment and Social Control*, ed. Thomas G. Blomberg and Stanley Cohen. New York: Aldine De Gruyter; Karol Lucken (1998) "Contemporary Penal Trends: Modern or Postmodern?" *British Journal of Criminology* 38:106–123.

25. E.g., Bill McCollum (Senator) (1999) *Putting Consequences Back into Juvenile Justice: Federal, State and Local Levels: Hearing before the Subcommittee on Crime of the House Committee on the Judiciary*, 106th Cong. 10, 1999.

26. Donald T. DiFrancesco (1980) "Juvenile Crime Must be Handled With Maturity." *New York Times*, November 16, 1980; National District Attorneys Association (2000) *Resource Manual and Policy Positions on Juvenile Crime Issues*; see also Eric K. Klein (1998) "Dennis the Menace or Billy the Kid: An Analysis of the Role of Transfer to Criminal Court in Juvenile Justice." *American Criminal Law Review* 35:371–412.

27. Quoted in its Resource Manual and Policy Positions on Juvenile Crime Issues (2000).

28. See also DiFrancesco (1980); Michael D. Rushford (1994) *Taking Crime Seriously: An Agenda for the Governor's Crime Summit*. Sacramento, CA: Criminal Justice Legal Foundation; Pete Wilson (2000) "How Is Juvenile Justice Served? Outmoded System Was Designed to Deal with Less Serious Crimes." *San Francisco Chronicle*, February 27, 2000.

29. Thomas J. Bernard (1992) *The Cycle of Juvenile Justice*. New York: Oxford University Press; Donna M. Bishop and Charles E. Frazier (1991) "Transfer

of Juveniles to Criminal Court: A Case Study and Analysis of Prosecutorial Waiver." *Notre Dame Journal of Law, Ethics, and Public Policy* 5:281–302; Feld (1999); Edwin Lemert (1970) *Social Action and Legal Change: Revolution within the Juvenile Court*. Chicago: Aldine; Anthony Platt (1977) *The Child Savers: The Invention of Delinquency* (2nd ed.) Chicago: University of Chicago Press; David J. Rothman (1980) *Conscience and Convenience: The Asylum and Its Alternative in Progressive America*. Boston: Little, Brown; Ellen Ryerson (1978) *The Best Laid Plans: America's Juvenile Court Experiment*. New York: Hill and Wang.

30. See Bernard (1992); Rothman (1980); Steven Schlossman (1977) *Love and the American Delinquent: The Theory and Practice of Progressive Juvenile Justice, 1825–1920*. Chicago: University of Chicago Press; John Sutton (1988) *Stubborn Children: Controlling Delinquency in the United States*. Berkeley: University of California Press.

31. Platt (1977); see also Jacques Donzelot (1979) *The Policing of Families*, trans. Robert Hurley. Baltimore, MD: Johns Hopkins University Press.

32. In Franklin E. Zimring (2000) "The Punitive Necessity of Waiver." In *The Changing Borders of Juvenile Justice*, ed. Jeffrey Fagan and Franklin E. Zimring. Chicago: University of Chicago Press, p. 210. See also Bortner (1982); Gray Cavender and Paul Knepper (1992) "Strange Interlude: An Analysis of Juvenile Parole Revocation Decision Making." *Social Problems* 39:387–399; Francis T. Cullen, Kathryn M. Golden, and John B. Cullen (1983) "Is Child Saving Dead? Attitudes toward Juvenile Rehabilitation in Illinois." *Journal of Criminal Justice* 11:1–13; Robert M. Emerson (1969) *Judging Delinquents: Context and Process in Juvenile Court*. Chicago: Aldine; Linda F. Giardino (1997) "Statutory Rhetoric: The Reality behind Juvenile Justice Policies in America." *Journal of Law and Policy* 5:223–276; Don M. Gottfredson (1999) *Effects of Judges' Sentencing Decisions on Criminal Careers*. Washington, DC: U.S. Department of Justice, Office of Justice Programs; Thomas Grisso, Alan Tomkins, and Pamela Casey (1988) "Psychosocial Concepts in Juvenile Law." *Law and Human Behavior* 12:403–437; Gordon A. Martin (1992) "The Delinquent and the Juvenile Court: Is There Still a Place for Rehabilitation?" *Connecticut Law Review* 25:57–93; Howard Parker, Maggie Casbarn, and David Turnbull (1981) *Receiving Juvenile Justice: Adolescents and State Care and Control*. Oxford: Basil Blackwell. For evidence of a juvenile justice model operating in juvenile court, see Joseph B. Sanborn, Jr. (1994) "Remnants of *Parens Patriae* in the Adjudicatory Hearing: Is a Fair Trial Possible in Juvenile Court?" *Crime and Delinquency* 40:599–614.

33. Donzelot (1979, p. 110).

34. Eisenstein et al. (1988); see also Jo Dixon (1995) "The Organizational Context of Criminal Sentencing." *American Journal of Sociology* 100:1157–

1198; Jeffery T. Ulmer (1997) *Social Worlds of Sentencing: Court Communities under Sentencing Guidelines.* New York: SUNY Press; Ulmer and Kramer (1996); Jeffery T. Ulmer and John H. Kramer (1998) "The Use and Transformation of Formal Decision-Making Criteria: Sentencing Guidelines, Organizational Contexts, and Case Processing Strategies." *Social Problems* 45:248–267.

35. Aaron V. Cicourel (1968) *The Social Organization of Juvenile Justice.* New York: Wiley; Emerson (1969).

36. E.g., DiFrancesco (1980); National District Attorneys Association (2000); Rushford (1994); Wilson (2000).

37. Stewart Asquith (1983) *Children and Justice: Decision-making in Children's Hearings and Juvenile Courts.* Edinburgh: University of Edinburgh Press.

38. See also Blumberg (1967); Dixon (1995); Ulmer (1997); Ulmer and Kramer (1996, 1998).

39. Joachim Savelsberg (1992) "Law That Does Not Fit Society: Sentencing Guidelines as a Neoclassical Reaction to the Dilemmas of Substantivized Law." *American Journal of Sociology* 97:1346–1381.

40. David Tanenhaus (2004) *Juvenile Justice in the Making.* New York: Oxford University Press.

41. Snyder and Sickmund (1999).

42. Patrick Griffin (2003) *Trying and Sentencing Juveniles as Adults: An Analysis of State Transfer and Blended Sentencing Laws.* Pittsburgh, PA: National Center for Juvenile Justice.

43. Other states have used presumptory transfer, a close alternative to legislative transfer. With presumptory transfer, youth in defined age and offense categories are presumed to be transferred unless they can successfully petition against it.

44. See Sara Raymond (2000) "From Playpens to Prisons: What the Gang Violence and Juvenile Crime Prevention Act of 1998 Does to California's Juvenile Justice System and Reasons to Repeal It." *Golden Gate University Law Review* 30:258–289.

45. Not only are these youth (e.g., sixteen- and seventeen-year-olds in New York) not counted for any transfer research, but they are excluded from estimates of how many youth get prosecuted as adults; e.g., Steven D. Levitt (1998) "Juvenile Crime and Punishment." *Journal of Political Economy* 106:1156–1185; Gerard A. Rainville and Steven K. Smith (2003) *Juvenile Felony Defendants in Criminal Courts.* Washington, DC: Office of Justice Programs.

46. Linda J. Collier (1998) "Juvenile Crime and Punishment." *Journal of Political Economy* 106:1156–1185; National District Attorneys Association (2000); Wilson (2000).

47. Donald P. Mears (2001) "Getting Tough with Juvenile Offenders: Explaining Support for Sanctioning Youths as Adults." *Criminal Justice and Behavior* 28:206–226.

48. See Feld (1999).

49. Loretta J. Stalans and Gary T. Henry (1994) "Societal Views of Justice for Adolescents Accused of Murder." *Law and Human Behavior* 18:675–696.

50. Garland (2001).

51. See Allen (1981).

52. See Barry Feld's (1999) *Bad Kids*, which offers a comprehensive view of the rise of transfer policies and other punitive juvenile justice legislation. Feld's work is particularly helpful in understanding the potential role of racial politics in the creation of punitive juvenile justice policies; he argues that the rise of transfer laws corresponds to the increasingly disproportionate representation of African American youth in juvenile arrests, and that transfer laws are a way to punish "other people's children."

53. Eric L. Jensen and Linda K. Metsger (1994) "A Test of the Deterrent Effect of Legislative Waiver on Violent Juvenile Crime." *Crime and Delinquency* 40:96–104; Edwin A. Risler, Tim Sweatman, and Larry Nackerud (1998) "Evaluating the Georgia Legislative Waiver's Effectiveness in Deterring Juvenile Crime." *Research on Social Work Practice* 8:657–667; Simon Singer and David MacDowall (1988) "Criminalizing Delinquency: The Deterrent Effects of the Juvenile Offender Law." *Law and Society Review* 22:521–535.

54. Donna M. Bishop, Charles E. Frazier, Lonn Lanza-Kaduce, and Lawrence Winner (1996) "The Transfer of Juveniles to Criminal Court: Does It Make a Difference?" *Crime and Delinquency* 42:171–191; Jeffrey Fagan (1996) "The Comparative Advantage of Juvenile versus Criminal Court Sanctions on Recidivism among Adolescent Felony Offenders." *Law and Policy* 18:79–113; Lonn Lanza-Kaduce, Charles E. Frazier, Jodi Lane, and Donna M. Bishop (2002) *Juvenile Transfer to Criminal Court Study: Final Report*. Report to Florida Department of Juvenile Justice; David L. Myers (2001) *Excluding Violent Youths from Juvenile Court: The Effectiveness of Legislative Waiver*. New York: LFB Scholarly Press; Marcy R. Podkopacz and Barry Feld (1996) "The End of the Line: An Empirical Study of Judicial Waiver." *Journal of Criminal Law and Criminology* 86:449–492; Lawrence Winner, Lonn Lanza-Kaduce, Donna M. Bishop, and Charles E. Frazier (1997) "The Transfer of Juveniles to Criminal Court: Reexamining Recidivism over the Long Term." *Crime and Delinquency* 43:548–563.

55. Emile Durkheim (trans. W. D. Halls, 1984 [1893]) *The Division of Labor in Society*. New York: Free Press.

56. Carrie S. Fried and N. Dickon Repucci (2001) "Criminal Decision Making: The Development of Adolescent Judgment, Criminal Responsibility, and Culpability." *Law and Human Behavior* 25:45–61; Thomas Grisso and Robert Schwartz, eds. (2000) *Youth on Trial: A Developmental Perspective on Juvenile Justice*. Chicago: University of Chicago Press; Thomas Grisso, Laurence Steinberg, and Jennifer Woolard (2003) "Juveniles' Competence to Stand Trial: A

Comparison of Adolescents' and Adults' Capacities as Trial Defendants." *Law and Human Behavior* 27:333–363; Elizabeth S. Scott, N. Dickon Repucci, and Jennifer L. Woolard (1995) "Evaluating Adolescent Decision Making in Legal Contexts." *Law and Human Behavior* 19:221–244; Laurence Steinberg and Elizabeth Cauffman (1996) "Maturity of Judgment in Adolescence: Psychosocial Factors in Adolescent Decision Making." *Law and Human Behavior* 20:249–272.

57. For a review, see M. A. Bortner, Marjorie S. Zatz, and Darnell F. Hawkins (2000) "Race and Transfer: Empirical Research and Social Context," in Fagan and Zimring (2000).

58. See Zimring (2000).

59. Scholars have discussed adolescents' level of maturity and cognitive functioning, and whether it is good policy to prosecute them in criminal courts; see Grisso and Schwartz (2000). Recently, this debate has been reenergized by academics using the reduced maturity and culpability of youth to argue against executing adolescents; see Barry C. Feld (2003) "Competence, Culpability and Punishment: Implications of *Atkins* for Executing and Sentencing Adolescents." *Hofstra Law Review* 32:463–552. Yet no prior research compares case processing of adolescents in criminal court to examine if anything changes with transfer to criminal court, or how ideas of reduced culpability among youth shape the criminal court prosecution of adolescents.

NOTES TO CHAPTER 2

1. E.g., Bishop et al. (1996); Daniel P. Mears and Samuel H. Field (2000) "Theorizing Sanctioning in a Criminalized Juvenile Court." *Criminology* 38:983–1020; Podkopacz and Feld (1996); Winner et al. (1997).

2. See Lanza-Kaduce et al. (2002).

3. An alternative strategy would be to compare cases of adolescents in criminal court to cases of adults in criminal court. This has the advantage of holding court context constant, while considering the effect of defendants' youthfulness. Though this strategy has its advantages, it does not allow us to consider whether or how transfer laws shape case processing so that criminal and juvenile courts prosecute youth in substantially different ways. These comparisons have not been made empirically by any previous research, despite great speculation in the literature about the similarity and differences between these two forums.

4. See Jeffrey A. Fagan (1991) *The Comparative Impacts of Juvenile and Criminal Court Sanctions on Adolescent Felony Offenders.* Report to National Institute of Justice; Jeffrey A. Fagan (1995) "Separating the Men from the Boys: The Comparative Advantage of Juvenile versus Criminal Court Sanctions on Recidivism among Adolescent Felony Offenders." In *Serious, Violent and Chronic Juvenile Offenders: A Sourcebook,* ed. James C. Howell, Barry Kris-

berg, J. David Hawkins, and John J. Wilson. Thousand Oaks, CA: Sage; Fagan (1996).

5. Eisenstein et al. (1988).

6. In New York, the court system designated for juveniles is formally called "family court." I use the more common term, "juvenile court," as a synonym here.

7. According to the FBI Uniform Crime Report, New York and New Jersey arrest rates show overall similarities as well. For example, in 2000, the arrest rate per 100,000 population for all index offenses in New Jersey was 658.2, and 737.0 in New York; see Kathleen Maguire and Ann L. Pastore, eds. (2002) *Sourcebook of Criminal Justice Statistics*. Washington, DC: Bureau of Justice Statistics: calculated from table 4.5.

8. In the Appendix, I provide a table comparing demographic and social characteristics across the six counties I studied.

9. This list was initially set at twelve but has since expanded to seventeen through legislative amendments; see Eric Warner (2000) *The Juvenile Offender Handbook*. New York: Looseleaf Law Publications, Inc.

10. Quoted in Simon I. Singer (1996) *Recriminalizing Delinquency: Violent Juvenile Crime and Juvenile Justice Reform*. New York: Cambridge University Press, p. 52.

11. Quoted in Singer (1996, p. 53).

12. Criminal Justice Agency (2001) *Annual Report on the Adult Court Case Processing of Juvenile Offenders in New York City, January through December 2000*. New York: Criminal Justice Agency.

13. Warner (2000).

14. In New York, individual courtrooms are called "court parts." Each court part is referred to by a number and is presided over by a single judge.

15. Akiva Liberman, William Raleigh, and Freda Solomon (2000) *Specialized Court Parts for Juvenile Offenders in New York City's Adult Felony Courts: Case Processing in 1994–1995 and 1995–1996*. New York: New York City Criminal Justice Agency.

16. NJ Stat. Ann. §2A:4-2 (1952).

17. 109 NJ Super. (1970).

18. Senate Judiciary Committee Statement No. 641-L, 1982; see also Aaron Kupchik, Jeffrey Fagan, and Akiva Liberman (2003) "Punishment, Proportionality and Jurisdictional Transfer of Adolescent Offenders: A Test of the Leniency Gap Hypothesis." *Stanford Law and Policy Review* 14:57–83.

19. It is unclear why the New Jersey legislature chose to enhance sentencing in the juvenile court rather than exclude large numbers of adolescents from the court, as the New York legislature did just four years earlier. Simon Singer (1996) explains New York's adoption of the Juvenile Offender Law as an organizationally expedient reclassification of delinquents that was shaped by the insti-

tutional history of legislation in New York. A similar sociological analysis of the factors preventing similar legislation in New Jersey has not been conducted. The fact that these two similar states chose different paths within five years of each other would be an interesting subject for future research on the passage of juvenile justice legislation.

20. Defendants convicted of murder in juvenile court can be sentenced to up to twenty years in prison.

21. Fagan (1991). Analyzing a larger data set from which the quantitative data analyzed in the following chapters were taken, Kupchik et al. (2003) found that only 1.2 percent of cases with the same sampling criteria here are transferred from New Jersey's juvenile court to the criminal court. It is important to note that after most of the research for this book took place, New Jersey did slightly amend its transfer laws to give prosecutors greater power in moving cases forward for transfer. Yet judges still oversee this process by judging whether the evidence against the juvenile meets a "probable cause" standard; more importantly, my observations of the initial months of this law's use demonstrate that still very few youth are transferred. Long-term effects of this shift are the subject of future studies.

22. New Jersey Code of Criminal Justice 2002 §2A:4A-21.

23. See David Garland (1985) *Punishment and Welfare: A History of Penal Strategies*. Brookfield, VT: Ashgate.

24. New Jersey Code of Criminal Justice, 2002 §2A:4A-43.

25. In the Appendix, I analyze more recent (though less complete) data, taken from the same time period as the qualitative data.

26. I use the term "court" to refer to a county's assemblage of courts, rather than each individual courtroom. For example, four adjacent courtrooms on one floor of a government building comprise the juvenile court in Pierce County.

27. Note that throughout the book I indicate when quotations are based on field notes rather than verbatim transcripts.

28. Ulmer (1997).

29. Eisenstein and Jacob (1977); Eisenstein et al. (1988); Emerson (1969); David Sudnow (1965) "Normal Crime: Sociological Features of the Penal Code in a Public Defender's Office." *Social Problems* 12:255–270; Ulmer (1997).

30. See the Appendix for a discussion of court observations and "calendar" days.

31. In New York, misdemeanor cases are prosecuted in the "Criminal Court" and felonies in the "Supreme Court" (after an initial arraignment in the lower Criminal Court).

32. This wage was increased in 2004 to $60–$75.

33. Jane Fritsch, and David Rohde (2001a) "Lawyers Often Fail New York's Poor." *New York Times*, April 8, 2001, p. 1; Jane Fritsch and David Rohde (2001b) "For the Poor, a Lawyer with 1,600 Clients." *New York Times*, April 9,

2001, p. 1; Jane Fritsch and David Rohde (2001c) "For Poor, Appeals Are Luck of the Draw." *New York Times,* April 10, 2001, p. 1; see also John Baldwin and Michael McConville (1977) *Negotiated Justice: Pressures to Plead Guilty.* London: Martin Robertson.

34. Defense attorneys may announce their status as a private or court-appointed attorney when they state their organizational affiliation while reading their appearance into the record at the start of each hearing. Or, it may be expressed when the court actors discuss monetary bail, a discussion that often includes the topic of the defendant's financial status and inability to pay a high bail amount.

35. Harold Garfinkel (1956) "Conditions of Successful Degradation Ceremonies" *American Journal of Sociology* 61:420–424.

36. Feeley (1979).

NOTES TO CHAPTER 3

1. Sudnow (1965).

2. Blumberg (1967).

3. See also Packer (1964, 1968).

4. Platt (1977); Rothman (1980); Ryerson (1978).

5. Feld (1987, 1998, 1999).

6. Donzelot (1979, pp. 107–108).

7. Bernard (1992); Feld (1999); Christopher P. Manfredi (1998) *The Supreme Court and Juvenile Justice.* Lawrence: University Press of Kansas.

8. E.g., Bortner (1982); Feld (1999); Mark D. Jacobs (1990) *Screwing the System and Making It Work: Juvenile Justice in the No-Fault Society.* Chicago: University of Chicago Press.

9. Emerson (1969).

10. I refer to the sentencing phase not as a formally declared hearing following official conviction, but as discussions that involve a consideration of a sentence assuming conviction. These discussions often precede formal conviction, but do not occur until all workgroup members have implicitly agreed that the case will soon lead to conviction, at which point they begin to negotiate a sentence in exchange for a guilty plea.

11. In this chapter I focus on a comparison of court types (New York criminal court and New Jersey juvenile court) rather than a comparison of the two courts within the juvenile court system and the two courts within the criminal court system. I restrict my analysis to court type because the formality of case processing is extremely similar across courts within each court type, with only small county-level differences. Instead, significant differences between court types account for most of the variation I find between adolescent cases processed in the New Jersey juvenile courts and in the New York criminal courts. Thus, I

find no support for prior arguments that the distinctions between local legal cultures will result in different levels of procedural formality across courts within jurisdictions; see Dixon (1995); Eisenstein et al. (1988); Roy Flemming, Peter Nardulli, and James Eisenstein (1992) *The Craft of Justice: Work and Politics in Criminal Court Communities.* Philadelphia: University of Pennsylvania Press; Peter Nardulli, James Eisenstein, and Roy Flemming (1988) *The Tenor of Justice: Criminal Courts and the Guilty Plea Process.* Chicago: University of Illinois Press; Ulmer (1997).

12. See David Matza (1964) *Delinquency and Drift.* New York: Wiley.

13. The involvement of parents in case processing might raise the question of whether male and female defendants receive different treatment in court. As I demonstrate in chapter 5 by way of the quantitative data I analyze, a small proportion of defendants in the courts I studied were females (about 14 percent of my sample). As a result of the small numbers of female defendants overall, I was able to observe relatively few cases involving girls, which makes qualitative comparisons difficult. Thus, my research did not focus on comparing the treatment of male and female adolescent defendants, though I will return briefly to this topic in the conclusion (chapter 6) and suggest avenues for further inquiry.

14. Of course, "treatment" programs—even rehabilitative ones—are considered by some writers to be subtle versions of social control; see Donzelot (1979); Michel Foucault (1977) *Discipline and Punish: The Birth of the Prison.* London: Allen Lane; Platt (1977). The distinction I suggest here is between rehabilitative treatment directed at reforming a defendant's behavior through education and counseling, and a more coercive regime that focuses on supervision and threats of punishment.

15. Emerson (1969).

16. See Aaron Kupchik (2004) "Youthfulness, Responsibility and Punishment: Admonishing Adolescents in Criminal Court." *Punishment and Society: The International Journal of Penology* 6(2):149–173 (reprinted by permission of Sage Publications Ltd.; © SAGE Publications. London, Thousand Oaks, and New Delhi, 2004). In this article I expand on this admonishment and demonstrate its utility in resolving the tension of prosecuting youth in criminal courts.

17. See Lynn M. Mather (1979) *Plea Bargaining or Trial? The Process of Criminal-Case Disposition.* Lexington, MA: Lexington Books.

18. Emile Durkheim (1958 [1895]) *The Rules of Sociological Method,* trans. S. A. Solvay and J. H. Mueller. Glencoe, IL: Free Press; Durkheim (1984). One of the best illustrations of this principle is sociologist Kai T. Erikson's classic book, *Wayward Puritans* (1966) New York: John Wiley & Sons. Erikson uses the early Puritan settlers as a case study in how members of society seek punishment as a way to reaffirm a collective consciousness in times of struggle or doubt. By banishing Anne Hutchinson, torturing Quakers, and eventually hanging witches, early Massachusetts colonists reaffirmed their social rules and norms, and

strengthened bonds with one another by directing communal wrath at common enemies.

19. Robert E. Shepherd, Jr. (1999) "Film at Eleven: The News Media and Juvenile Crime." *Quinnipiac Law Review* 18:687–700.

20. Donna Bishop and Charles Frazier (2000) "Consequences of Transfer." In Fagan and Zimring (2000); M. A. Bortner (1986) "Traditional Rhetoric, Organizational Realities: Remand of Juveniles to Adult Court." *Crime and Delinquency* 32:53–73.

21. Singer (1996).

22. Donna M. Bishop and Charles E. Frazier (1988) "The Influence of Race in Juvenile Justice Processing." *Journal of Research in Crime and Delinquency* 25:242–263; Dale Dannefer and Russell K. Schutt (1982) "Race and Juvenile Justice Processing in Court and Police Agencies." *American Journal of Sociology* 87:1113–1132; Miriam D. Sealock and Sally S. Simpson (1998) "Unraveling Bias in Arrest Decisions: The Role of Juvenile Offender Type-scripts." *Justice Quarterly* 15:417–457.

23. See generally, Grisso and Schwartz (2000); Thomas Grisso (2000) "What We Know about Youths' Capacities as Trial Defendants." In Grisso and Schwartz (2000).

24. Richard E. Redding and Elizabeth J. Fuller (2004) "What Do Juvenile Offenders Know about Being Tried as Adults? Implications for Deterrence." *Juvenile and Family Court Journal* 55:35–45.

NOTES TO CHAPTER 4

1. See James C. Howell (1996) "Juvenile Transfers to the Criminal Justice System: State of the Art." *Law and Policy Review* 18:17–60; Mears and Field (2000); Zimring (1998, 2000).

2. Sudnow (1965).

3. Celesta A. Albonetti (1991) "An Integration of Theories to Explain Judicial Discretion." *Social Problems* 38:247–266; Cicourel (1968); Emerson (1969); Milton Heumann (1978) *Plea Bargaining: The Experiences of Prosecutors, Judges and Defense Attorneys.* Chicago: University of Chicago Press; Sudnow (1965).

4. Eisenstein et al. (1988); Emerson (1969); Heumann (1978).

5. James Holstein (1988) "Court Ordered Incompetence: Conversational Organization in Involuntary Commitment Hearings." *Social Problems* 35:458–473.

6. In an analysis of court-ordered parenting classes taught by juvenile probation officers, Laurie Schaffner (1997), in "Families on Probation: Court-Ordered Parenting Skills Classes for Parents of Juvenile Offenders." *Crime and Delinquency* 43:412–437, shows that some parents accused of lacking parenting skills

react by agreeing with probation officers that their children deserve to be punished for their misbehavior. Her illustration of how probation officers focus exclusively on discipline as a parenting technique resembles the reactions of juvenile court judges illustrated in the following transcripts.

7. Sudnow (1965); Emerson (1969).

8. Emerson (1969).

9. See Franklin E. Zimring (1981) *The Changing Legal World of Adolescence.* New York: Free Press.

10. This contradiction could have emerged because I received generalized "party-line" responses to general questions about adolescents' maturity, yet more nuanced and thoughtful responses to detailed questions about specific capacities of maturity.

11. See also Lemert (1970); Parker et al. (1981) have found similar results.

12. See Robert M. Emerson (1981) "On Last Resorts." *American Journal of Sociology* 87:1–22.

13. By law in New York, bail conditions only reflect the likelihood of the defendant's return to court. Appearance in court by a family member is one of the conditions factoring into a recommendation for pretrial release by the New York City Criminal Justice Agency, the city's pretrial services agency. Thus the defense attorney mentions the father in this hearing not to discuss the defendant's family background or behavior at home, but to demonstrate community ties and a greater likelihood of returning to court for subsequent appearances.

14. Sudnow (1965); Emerson (1969).

15. Emerson (1981).

16. Criminal Justice Agency (2001); Criminal Justice Agency (2000) *Annual Report on the Adult Court Case Processing of Juvenile Offenders in New York City, January through December 1999.* New York: Criminal Justice Agency.

17. See Eisenstein et al. (1988).

18. The judge stated this on November 12, 2000, at a meeting he held with all agencies who work in the court.

19. It is important to note that, unlike prosecutors and judges, defense attorneys do not have a conflict between juvenile and criminal models of justice regarding strategies for defending their clients. Their role in both models is to attack the state's case and to humanize the defendants (make them appear more deserving of compassion) by presenting mitigating evidence.

20. Singer (1996).

NOTES TO CHAPTER 5

1. Peter Greenwood, Allan Abrahamese, and Franklin Zimring (1984) *Factors Affecting Sentence Severity for Young Adult Offenders.* Santa Monica, CA: RAND Corp.; see also Kristine Kinder, Carol Veneziano, Michael Fichter, and

Henry Azuma (1995) "A Comparison of the Dispositions of Juvenile Offenders Certified as Adults with Juvenile Offenders Not Certified." *Juvenile and Family Court Journal* 46:37–42; Inger Sagatun, L. L. McCollum, and L. P. Edwards (1985) "The Effect of Transfers from Juvenile to Criminal Court: A Loglinear Analysis." *Crime and Justice* 8:65–92.

2. Bishop et al. (1996); Joel Eigen (1981) "Punishing Youth Homicide Offenders In Philadelphia." *Journal of Criminal Law and Criminology* 72:1072–1093; Fagan (1996); Eric J. Fritsch, Tory Caeti, and Craig Hemmens (1996) "Spare the Needle but Not the Punishment: The Incarceration of Waived Youth in Texas Prison." *Crime and Delinquency* 42:593–609; Marilyn Houghtalin and G. Larry Mays (1991) "Criminal Dispositions of New Mexico Juveniles Transferred to Adult Court." *Crime and Delinquency* 37:393–407; Lanza-Kaduce et al. (2002); David L. Myers (2003) "Adult Crime, Adult Time: Punishing Violent Youth in the Adult Criminal Justice System." *Youth Violence and Juvenile Justice* 1:173–197; Podkopacz and Feld (1996); Cary Rudman, Eliot Hartstone, Jeffrey Fagan, and Melinda Moore (1986) "Violent Youth in Adult Court: Process and Punishment." *Crime and Delinquency* 32:75–96; Kevin Strom, Steven Smith, and Howard Snyder (1998) *Juvenile Felony Defendants in Criminal Courts.* Washington, DC: Bureau of Justice Statistics, U.S. Department of Justice; Winner et al. (1997); for a review, see Kupchik et al. (2003).

3. Feld (1999); Zimring (1998).

4. See Mears and Field (2000).

5. Adolescents arrested for homicide or sexual assault are excluded because, although their cases receive great attention by policy makers and the media, they are rare and potentially atypical. Rather, robbery, assault, and burglary represent prototypical serious felonies committed by adolescents; see Zimring (1998).

6. It is important to note that statutorily, the decisions to detain at pretrial hearings are guided by different factors in the two court types. In the New York criminal court, the detention result is shaped by a defendant's economic status, because most defendants are offered some monetary bail. According to statute, the bail should be set at a level that will ensure the defendant's reappearance in court, with no other factor being considered. In contrast, New Jersey juvenile court judges have greater discretion in this area, and no monetary bail is allowed. As a result, juvenile court judges are allowed to consider a wide array of offense and offender-oriented factors in deciding simply whether the defendant should be detained or released.

7. I perform this analysis for robbery but not for the other two arrest charges included—aggravated assault and burglary—because of the small number of New York burglary and assault cases.

8. For the entire sample model, I first transform the probit model regression coefficient, 1.200, into a logit coefficient, using the conversion formula Logit = Probit*1.813, and then take the exponentiated coefficient of this value to obtain

an odds ratio; see John H. Aldrich and Forrest D. Nelson (1984) *Linear Probability, Logit, and Probit Models.* Newbury Park, CA: Sage.

9. See Emerson (1981).

10. In a separate work, I describe how juvenile court actors achieve a balance between goals of punishment and rehabilitation through a negotiated order. See Aaron Kupchik (2005) "Punishing to Protect? Balancing Punishment and Future Welfare in Juvenile Court." In *Ethnographies of Law and Social Control: Sociology of Crime, Law and Deviance,* Vol. 6, ed. Stacy Burns. New York: Elsevier.

11. Rothman (1980).

12. For a discussion of the cyclic nature of juvenile justice policies, see Bernard (1992).

13. See Kupchik (2004).

14. Darrell Steffensmeier and Steven Demuth (2000) "Ethnicity and Sentencing Outcomes in U.S. Federal Courts: Who Is Punished More Harshly?" *American Sociological Review* 65:705–729; see also Darrell Steffensmeier, Jeffery Ulmer, and John Kramer (1998) "The Interaction of Race, Gender, and Age in Criminal Sentencing: The Punishment Cost of Being Young, Black, and Male." *Criminology* 36:763–798.

15. Megan C. Kurlychek and Brian D. Johnson (2004) "The Juvenile Penalty: A Comparison of Juvenile and Young Adult Sentencing Outcomes in Criminal Court." *Criminology* 42:485–517.

16. See Steffensmeier et al. (1998); Darrell Steffensmeier and Steven Deumth (2001) "Ethnicity and Judge's Sentencing Decisions: Hispanic-Black-White Comparisons." *Criminology* 39:145–178.

17. It is not clear from their study how many of the youth in their data set are judicially transferred to criminal court, and how many arrive there via statutory exclusion.

18. DiFrancesco (1980); Alfred E. Regnery (1986) "A Federal Perspective on Juvenile Justice Reform." *Crime and Delinquency* 32:39–51; Wilson (2000).

19. This pattern resembles what science and technology studies scholar Torin Monahan has called "fragmented centralization": the centralization of decision making and decentralization of accountability and inflexibility brought about by contemporary public policy making. In this case, sentencing decisions are somewhat fixed by policy makers, yet the accountability and inflexibility is distributed to judges, defendants, and courtroom workgroups; see Torin Monahan (2005) *Globalization, Technological Change, and Public Education.* New York: Routledge.

20. These contextual features are consistent with the types of local organizational variables that scholars such as Eisenstein et al. (1988) find to be important predictors of courts' actions.

NOTES TO CHAPTER 6

1. Feld (1998, 2000).
2. Feld (1998).
3. E.g., Eisenstein et al. (1988); Flemming et al. (1992); Nardulli et al. (1988); Ulmer (1997).
4. Ulmer (1997).
5. E.g., Dixon (1995); Rodney L. Engen and Sara Steen (2000) "The Power to Punish: Discretion and Sentencing Reform in the War on Drugs." *American Journal of Sociology* 105:1357–95; Ulmer and Kramer (1996, 1998).
6. Savelsberg (1992).
7. Mears (2001).
8. Garland (2001).
9. Neil Postman (1982) *The Disappearance of Childhood.* New York: Vintage Books. See also Peter Applebome (1998) "No Room for Children in a World of Little Adults." *New York Times,* May 10, 1998, sec. 4, p. 1; David Elkind (1981) *The Hurried Child.* Reading, MA: Addison-Wesley.
10. Allison James and Chris Jencks (1996), in "Public Perceptions of Childhood Criminality," *British Journal of Sociology* 47:315–331, consider a similar offense in Britain, the murder of Jamie Bulger in 1993, and how it led to similar shifts in popular conceptions of childhood. See also Jeffrey A. Butts and Adele V. Harrell (1998) *Delinquents or Criminals: Policy Options for Young Offenders.* Washington, DC: Urban Institute; Dana Canedy (2002) "Boys' Case Is Used in Bid to Limit Trials of Minors as Adults." *New York Times,* October 6, 2002; Simona Ghetti and Allison D. Redlich (2001) "Reactions to Youth Crime: Perceptions of Accountability and Competence." *Behavioral Sciences and the Law* 19:33–52; Ann Patchett (2002) "The Age of Innocence." *New York Times Magazine,* September 29, 2002, p. 17.
11. Frank F. Furstenberg, Jr., Sheela Kennedy, Vonnie C. McLoyd, Ruben G. Rumbaut, and Richard A. Settersten, Jr. (2004) "Growing Up Is Harder to Do." *Contexts* 3:33–41, p. 37. See also Patricia Passuth Lynott and Barbara J. Logue (1993) "The 'Hurried Child': The Myth of Lost Childhood in Contemporary American Society." *Sociological Forum* 8:471–491.
12. Feld (1999).
13. Robert J. Sampson and John H. Laub (1993) "Structural Variations in Juvenile Court Processing: Inequality, the Underclass, and Social Control." *Law and Society Review* 21:285–311.
14. Mark Soler (2001) *Public Opinion on Youth, Crime and Race: A Guide for Advocates.* Washington, DC: Youth Law Center.
15. Soler (2001); see also Melissa M. Moon, Jody L. Sundt, Francis T. Cullen, and John Paul Wright (2000) "Is Child Saving Dead? Public Support for Juvenile Rehabilitation." *Crime and Delinquency* 46:38–60.

16. Stalans and Henry (1994).

17. Soler (2001).

18. Political scientist John J. DiIulio, who was later tapped by George W. Bush to direct his faith-based initiative effort, coined this term in the mid-1990s; see John DiIulio (1996) *How to Stop the Coming Crime Wave*. New York: Manhattan Institute. Ironically, DiIulio made his bleak prediction of a coming wave of juvenile crime two years into a historic decrease in juvenile crime and violence.

19. George Bridges and Sara Steen (1998) "Racial Disparities in Official Assessments of Juvenile Offenders: Attributional Stereotypes as Mediating Mechanisms." *American Sociological Review* 63:554–570.

20. Bishop and Frazier (1988); Michael J. Leiber and Katherine M. Jamieson (1995) "Race and Decision Making within Juvenile Justice: The Importance of Context." *Journal of Quantitative Criminology* 11:363–388; Michael J. Leiber and Jayne M. Stairs (1999) "Race, Contexts, and the Use of Intake Diversion." *Journal of Research in Crime and Delinquency* 36:56–86; Sealock and Simpson (1998).

21. Richard E. Redding and Bruce Arrigo (2005) "Multicultural Perspectives on Delinquency among African-American Youth: Etiology and Intervention." In Craig L. Frisby and Cecil R. Reynolds (eds.), *Comprehensive Handbook of Multicultural School Psychology*. Hoboken, NJ: John Wiley & Sons.

22. David Huizinga and Delbert S. Elliott (1987) "Juvenile Offenders: Prevalence, Offender Incidence, and Arrest Rates by Race." *Crime and Delinquency* 33:206–223.

23. See Bishop and Frazier (1988); Dannefer and Schutt (1982).

24. See Meda Chesney-Lind (1977) "Judicial Paternalism and the Female Status Offender: Training Women to Know Their Place." *Crime and Delinquency* 23:121–130; Meda Chesney-Lind and Randall G. Shelden (1998) *Girls, Delinquency, and Juvenile Justice*, 2nd ed. Pacific Grove, CA: Brooks and Cole.

25. Howard N. Snyder (2004) *Juvenile Arrests 2002*. Washington, DC: Office of Juvenile Justice and Delinquency Prevention.

26. See Marlene M. Moretti, Candice L. Odgers, and Margaret A. Jackson (eds.) (2004) *Girls and Aggression: Contributing Factors and Intervention* Principles. New York: Kluwer Academic/Plenum.

27. Bishop and Frazier (1988).

NOTES TO CHAPTER 7

1. Garland (2001).

2. See Singer (1996).

3. Zimring (2000, p. 208).

4. Fagan and Zimring (2000).

5. One study, conducted by economist Steven Levitt (1998), is occasionally cited as evidence of a general deterrent effect; see Richard E. Redding (in press—2006) "Adult Punishments for Juvenile Offenders." In R. Dowd, D. Singer, and N. Dowd (eds.) *Handbook on Children, Culture and Violence*. However, though Levitt's analysis shows that relative punitiveness does deter crime, the analysis does not demonstrate that transfer to criminal court can have a general deterrent effect. In fact, in table 5 (p. 1177) of Levitt's manuscript, each regression coefficient indicating the effect of aging into a state's criminal court on percentage changes in crime rates is positive, indicating a potential counterdeterrent effect of transfer.

6. See Bishop et al. (1996); Fagan (1996); Jeffrey Fagan, Aaron Kupchik, and Akiva Liberman (2003) "Be Careful What You Wish For: The Comparative Impacts of Juvenile versus Criminal Court Sanctions on Recidivism among Adolescent Felony Offenders." Final Grant Report to Office of Juvenile Justice and Delinquency Prevention; Jensen and Metsger (1994); Myers (2001); Podkopacz and Feld (1996); Risler (1998); Singer (1996); Singer and MacDowall (1988); Winner et al. (1997).

7. Martin Forst, Jeffrey Fagan, and T. Scott Vivona (1989) "Youth in Prison and Training Schools: Perceptions and Consequences of the Treatment Custody Dichotomy." *Juvenile and Family Court Journal* 40:1–14; Jodi Lane, Lonn Lanza-Kaduce, Charles E. Frazier, and Donna M. Bishop (2002) "Adult versus Juvenile Sanctions: Voices of Incarcerated Youths." *Crime and Delinquency* 48:431–455.

8. Bortner et al. (2000).

9. See Garland (2001).

10. Labeling theory argues that delinquency is often exacerbated by crime control initiatives, as juveniles self-identify with the label of delinquent they receive upon arrest; see Edwin Schur (1971) *Labeling Deviant Behavior: Its Sociological Implications*. New York: Harper & Row.

11. Zimring (2000, p. 210).

12. Tanenhaus (2004).

13. See Donna M. Bishop, Charles E. Frazier, and John C. Henretta (1989) "Prosecutorial Waiver: Case Study of a Questionable Reform." *Crime and Delinquency* 35:179–201; Bishop and Frazier (1991); Barry C. Feld (2000) "Legislative Exclusion of Offenses from Juvenile Court Jurisdiction: A History and Critique." In Fagan and Zimring (2000).

14. Singer (1996).

15. Richard E. Redding and James C. Howell (2000) "Blended Sentencing in American Juvenile Courts." In Fagan and Zimring (2000).

16. See Marcy R. Podcopacz (1998) "A First Look at Blended Sentencing: Extended Juvenile Jurisdiction in Hennepin County, Minnesota." Paper pre-

sented at the American Society of Criminology annual meeting, November 1998, Washington, DC; Redding and Howell (2000).

17. Zimring (2000).

18. Feld (1999); see also Janet E. Ainsworth (1991) "Re-imagining Childhood and Re-constructing the Legal Order: The Case for Abolishing the Juvenile Court." *North Carolina Law Review* 69:1083–1133.

19. Feld (1999, p. 287).

20. Feld (1999).

NOTES TO THE APPENDIX

1. See Aaron Kupchik (in press) "The Decision to Incarcerate in Juvenile and Criminal Courts." *Criminal Justice Review*, copyright 2006 by Sage Publications.

2. In Jeffrey Fagan's previous work—of which the quantitative data used here is a replication and extension—only 1.4 percent of all cases were transferred from the New Jersey juvenile court to the New Jersey criminal court; see Fagan (1991, 1996). Among cases in his most recent sample, from which the data I analyze in chapter 6 are taken, only 1.2 percent are transferred; see Kupchik et al. (2003).

3. See Aaron Kupchik (2003) "Prosecuting Adolescents in Criminal Courts: Criminal or Juvenile Justice?" *Social Problems* 50: 439–460 (© 2003 by Society for the Study of Social Problems, Inc.); Kupchik (2004).

4. Cicourel (1968); Emerson (1969); see also Bortner (1982).

5. Given that the goal of the study was to understand institutional decision making, I did not attempt to interview defendants.

6. Stewart Asquith (1983) uses this term to describe the institutionalized goals and normative frameworks adopted by court actors in England's juvenile courts and Scotland's children's hearings.

7. Values of the scale were as follows: 1 = not important at all; 2 = somewhat important; 3 = important; 4 = very important.

8. Many judges conduct hearings with a legal or administrative clerk by their sides, thus attorneys are accustomed to a person sitting next to a judge.

9. See Mather (1979).

10. Mather (1979).

11. At the time, I was working at a research center at Columbia University. Because of this center's previous research and affiliation with the courts I was studying, this position allowed me access to courts that might have been unavailable to a graduate student working alone.

12. I was able to purchase transcripts for a few of the criminal court hearings. These transcripts, which are only available from the criminal court, are

publicly available but expensive; rather than obtaining them from the court, one must pay the individual transcriber his or her requested rate per page. Like the verbatim transcripts of interviews, these hearings (for which I have official transcripts) are not identified as field notes.

13. Holstein (1988); see also J. Maxwell Atkinson and Paul Drew (1979) *Order in Court: The Organization of Verbal Interaction in Judicial Settings*. Atlantic Highlands, NJ: Humanities Press.

14. John Lofland and Lyn H. Lofland (1984) *Analyzing Social Settings: A Guide to Qualitative Observation and Analysis*. Belmont, CA: Wadsworth.

15. See Robert M. Emerson, Rachel I. Fretz, and Linda L. Shaw (1995) *Writing Ethnographic Fieldnotes*. Chicago: University of Chicago Press.

16. All Variation Inflation Factors are less than 2.0.

17. When a weapon charge is present, it is a secondary, less serious, offense. For all sampled cases, the sampled arrest charge (robbery, aggravated assault, or burglary) was the most legally severe charge. Other indicators of offense severity —level of injury and defendant's role in the offense (primary vs. secondary) were collected but not used in the final data set. These data, which were taken from police reports, were discarded because they were unreliable, often contradictory (depending on which reports were used to gather the information), and not available for all counties. For the variables used, tolerance statistics indicate that multicollinearity is not a problem.

18. Richard A. Berk (1983) "An Introduction to Sample Selection Bias in Sociological Data." *American Sociological Review* 48:386–398.

19. After much experimentation, I included the following predictors of the first-stage analysis, the selection stage: age, sex, white, bench warrant, detained, number of prior arrests, associated weapon charge, the total number of charges, and dummy variables for each individual court other than the contrast.

20. All multivariate analyses are performed in the STATA 7 statistical package.

21. Consistent with the above descriptive analysis, I consider "conviction" to mean any court action other than diversion from court, acquittal, or dismissal.

22. Kenneth Adams (1983) "The Effect of Evidentiary Factors on Charge Reduction." *Journal of Criminal Justice* 11:525–537; David Rauma (1984) "Going for the Gold: Prosecutorial Decision-Making in Cases of Wife Assault." *Social Science Research* 13:321–351; Vera Institute of Justice (1977) *Felony Arrests: Their Prosecution and Disposition in New York City's Courts*. New York: Vera Institute of Justice.

23. See the above discussion of the "adjourned in contemplation of dismissal" disposition in New York and "adjourned disposition" in New Jersey.

24. This estimate was used after consulting with the New York City Criminal

Justice Agency, which provided the data and have tested this ratio and found it to be the best available estimate.

25. Chesney-Lind (1977); Chesney-Lind and Shelden (1998).

26. Akiva Liberman, Laura Winterfield, and Jerome McElroy (1996) *Minority Over-Representation among Juveniles in New York City's Adult and Juvenile Court Systems during Fiscal Year 1992*. New York: New York City Criminal Justice Agency.

27. Although these coefficients vary between the two models, the differences are not large. The coefficients for sex and arrest warrants are close to statistical significance in model 2, as is the coefficient for arrests during case processing in model 1.

28. I repeat this analysis by excluding burglary offenses from the full sample. Using only the aggravated assault and robbery cases, the results mirrored those of both previous models.

29. I owe special thanks to Sharon Lansing of the New York Department of Criminal Justice Services, and to John Shutack of the New Jersey Juvenile Justice Commission for their patience and assistance.

Index

About the Author

Aaron Kupchik is an assistant professor in the Department of Sociology and Criminal Justice at the University of Delaware.